D0891402

ROMAN SATIRISTS AND THEIR SATIRE

ROMAN SATIRISTS
AND THEIR SATIRE

THE FINE ART OF CRITICISM IN ANCIENT ROME

Edwin S. Ramage
David L. Sigsbee
Sigmund C. Fredericks

NOYES PRESS
Park Ridge, New Jersey

Published in the United States by
NOYES PRESS
Noyes Building
Park Ridge, New Jersey 07656

To Our Wives

PREFACE

No general and all-inclusive treatment of Classical Roman satire has yet appeared in English. The books by Duff, Van Rooy, and Witke, that are listed in the bibliography, come closest to serving the purpose, but in each case the writer's intentions preclude a thorough literary study of the genre. What follows is meant to fill this gap, and it is written for the general reader who is interested in the history of literature as well as for the student and scholar of the classics.

The task of describing the various satirists and their works has been divided as much as possible according to the interests and competencies of the authors, as the Table of Contents shows. Although we have criticized each other's efforts freely, we believe that each writer's approach must be respected. Any unevenness of style or treatment that may be felt is the result of this division of labor and will hopefully be excused. It should also be pointed out that the translations which appear from time to time are the work of the person writing the particular chapter.

The texts which have been used are the standard ones and are listed in the bibliography. The fragments of Livius Andronicus, Naevius, Ennius, and Lucilius are conveniently gathered together and translated in E. H. Warmington, *Remains of Old Latin* (London: 1935-1938), vols. 1-3 [*LCL*]. The two fragments of Andronicus mentioned on page 8 appear in Warmington, vol. 2, p. 22 (frags. 5 and 6); those of Naevius discussed on page 9 appear in the same volume on pp. 110 (frag. 107), 144 (frag. 20), 80 (frag. 22-26), and 154 (frag. 2).

Since the scanty remains of Ennius' *Satires* are easily accessible in Warmington (vol. 1, pp. 382-95), line numbers have been omitted in the discussion in Chapter 1. The numbering of Warmington (vol. 3 [repr. 1961], pp. 2-423) has been used for Lucilius' fragments throughout.

The remains of Varro's *Menippean Satires* are gathered together under the title *Varronis menippearum reliquiae* which is published as an appendix to F. Buecheler (rev. W. Heraeus), *Petronii saturae*[6] (Berlin: 1922). The fragment numbers from this edition are used throughout Chapter 3. The italics at the bottom of p. 59 and the top of p. 60 designate Greek words in Varro's original.

In Chapter 2 comments of later Classical writers are mentioned a number of times. The ancient references discussed on p. 41 follow in the order in which they appear: Cicero, *Ad familiares* 12.16.3. Quintilian, *Institutio oratoria* 10.1.94. Horace, *Satires* 2.1.62-65; 2.1.68-69. Persius, *Satires* 1.114-15. Juvenal, *Satires* 1.151-53; 1.165-67. Those on p. 49 in order are: Cicero, *Ad fam.* 9.15.2; *De oratore* 1.72. Quintilian, *Inst. orat.* 10.1.94. Horace, *Sat.* 1.4.7; 1.10.3-4; 1.10.64-65. The references in the paragraph which bridges pp. 51-52 are: Horace, *Sat.* 1.10.20-30; 1.4.8-13; 1.10.1-10; 1.10.50-75.

For explanation of the many Classical people, places, and things that appear in the text, the reader is referred to the *Oxford Classical Dictionary*,[2] while for matters of verse and meter he should consult Rosenmeyer, Ostwald, and Halporn, *The Meters of Greek and Latin Poetry*.

A number of people have helped. We appreciate the assistance of Paul Stecher of Noyes Press for suggesting changes and modifications in the manuscript. Martha Gillies of the Press has been a most considerate, helpful, and efficient editor.

We also wish to express our thanks to Lynne L. Merritt, Jr., Vice-President and Dean for Research and Advanced Studies at Indiana University and his Research Committee for providing funds which supported part of the research and preparation of the manuscript.

Edwin S. Ramage
David L. Sigsbee
Sigmund C. Fredericks

Bloomington, Indiana
May, 1974

TABLE OF CONTENTS

INTRODUCTION

Before we look at Roman satire in detail, something must be said in a general way about the Roman concept of satire and the satirist's view of his relationship to his poetry and to the society about which he was writing. Nowadays we use the word "satire" quite loosely, usually in a collective, abstract sense, to describe social and personal criticism of one kind or another. We have no preconceptions about the form in which it should appear; it may crop up in a stage play, newspaper column, television program, poem, essay, or novel, to name only a few possibilities. Because there is no one form, literary or otherwise, that belongs exclusively to satire, we seldom say that something is "a probing satire," though it is perfectly normal to speak of a play or a novel as being "probing satire."

The Romans used their word for satire, *satura,* in a much more restricted way. At no time did it have any abstract connotations, but always signified a specific genre of literature which took its place beside epic, lyric, drama, and the like as a separate, identifiable form of poetic literary expression. Quintilian, writing in the first century after Christ, makes this clear when he lists it after epic and elegy (10.1.93) and goes on to insist that "satire, at any rate, is all ours." There can be no doubt that he is thinking quite specifically of Roman verse satire, for he immediately turns to discuss Lucilius, Horace, and Persius as its writers.

The Roman was careful to differentiate between this kind of satire written completely in verse and the Menippean satire which was a mixture of prose and verse. For him the latter was distinctly different and not to be called satire without added qualification. Quintilian, for instance, in the passage referred to above, separates it out as "that other even earlier kind of satire." Indeed, what is left of the Latin Menippeans suggests that there was little literary connection between these and the writings of Lucilius, Horace, Persius, and Juvenal.

In spite of the fact that the Romans clearly thought of satire as a separate literary genre, it is difficult to generalize about it. This is to some extent true of any form of literature. Epic poetry, for example, showed quite different characteristics in the hands of Ennius, Vergil, and Lucan, while the historical writings of Livy and Tacitus suggest as many contrasts as comparisons. But in the case of Roman satire there seem to be fewer generic common denominators. The German scholar Wilamowitz went to the extreme of suggesting that "There really is no Latin satire; there is only Lucilius, Horace, Persius, Juvenal." The skepticism here is perhaps exaggerated, and the writer probably would not want his statement to be interpreted too literally, but what he says does underline the problem. The differences between the writings of the four major satirists are so striking that some justification for speaking generically of satire and not of four different literary creations is necessary.

There are two main reasons for the impression of heterogeneity that Roman satire leaves. Put simply, these are the personality of the poet and the basically miscellaneous nature of this kind of poetry. It is impossible to miss or to ignore the role of the poet in Roman satire, for he is constantly visible directing thought and action. And, as might be expected, the poetic personality differs widely from one satirist to the other. Lucilius is a confident, extroverted, outspoken critic who rambles freely about Rome pointing a finger at whomever and whatever he chooses. Horace is a quieter, more disciplined critic of the world around him, who strives to leave the impression of being a sophisticated, contemplative soul. While he too walks among men and points his finger, he does so with less abandon and even retreats at times to contemplate humanity and its failings from the peace and quiet of the countryside.

Persius, on the other hand, has removed himself to a safe, philosophic distance from the society he is criticizing. His Stoicism has insulated him against humanity. Finally, there is Juvenal who is essentially an angry man, completely intolerant of the vice that he feels surrounds and envelops him. In view of the wide differences between the personalities generating the poetry, it is no wonder that there are also wide differences between their satiric products.

The point will be made later that when Roman satire began it was basically a medley of poems showing a variety of subject matter in which criticism did not yet have a leading part to play. It will also become clear that each satirist in his turn exploited the miscellaneous nature of satire for his own purposes. This was perfectly natural and even necessary, for it gave the poet free rein to move about in subject matter that could include every personality and every institution in Roman society. The resulting differences between writers were reinforced by the fact that each poet's times had their own peculiar influence on his style and subject matter.

The question remains, then: In view of the seeming dissimilarities that exist between satirists, are we justified in thinking of Roman satire as a separate, unified genre of literature? Perhaps it is enough to say that because the Romans had no trouble viewing it as a distinct literary creation, we who study it from such a distance should not question its existence. But it is necessary to try to ascertain what those elements were that enabled a Roman to view writers as widely different as Horace and Juvenal as being in the same literary tradition.

These common denominators do exist. Paradoxically enough, two of them are the poetic personality and the idea of variety that have just been mentioned as factors of disunity. More will be said about these in the chapters which follow, but it should be pointed out here that each satirist stands in essentially the same relationship to his poetry and makes this obvious through the poetic personality that he creates for himself. Moreover, each satirist maintains and develops the miscellaneous aspects of satire, extending them from subject matter to mood and form.

Another unifying element is the meter. Except for that which was written very early, the verse of Roman satire is the dactylic hexameter. Although this was the verse form of epic poetry, the satirists, beginning with Lucilius, gradually molded it into the proper blend of formality and informality that suited the everyday subject matter and at the same time met the demands of a formal literary genre.

Finally, there is the satiric or critical element which permeates Roman satire. Elaboration here is perhaps unnecessary, but it should be pointed out that criticism represented the common purpose of all the satirists. Its intensity and direction might vary from poet to poet or even within the poems of a single satirist, but it remained perhaps the most obvious common bond between him and his fellow satirists.

These four characteristics, then—the personality of the poet, the miscellaneous element, criticism, and the informal hexameter—together set Roman satire off as a separate genre of literature. If any one of these is missing, the poetry has a tendency to blend with other genres. It was an awareness of these characteristics that made it possible for Quintilian to speak of satire as one branch of Latin literature and for Horace, Persius, and Juvenal to consider themselves as writing poetry that was in a direct line from Lucilius.

Something must be said about the relationship between the satirist and the society about which he is writing, for this is another factor conditioning his poetry. Each of these poets reflects his own times. Ennius' satires are perhaps too fragmentary to use with any confidence, but the point will be made in the next chapter that as a new literary creation they reflect a formative period in the literary, political, and social life of the city. Lucilius' freewheeling approach was both possible and natural for a number of reasons. The age in which he lived was an age of criticism, with reformers like the Gracchi setting the mood. At the same time, Lucilius' senatorial rank and his close friendships with the leading men in the state not only gave him access to a wide range of material, but also offered him a certain amount of protection. Moreover, literary standards were such that they promoted a freer style. Add to these conditions the natural genius of Lucilius, and it is easy to see how the frank, outspoken criticism of Lucilian invective came about.

Horace clearly states that the undisciplined Lucilian satire could have no place in the Augustan period. This was a time when peace had finally been established and attempts were being made to develop a social and political discipline that had been badly needed for a long time. The order of Augustan empire had followed Republican chaos, and in this atmosphere criticism such as Lucilius promoted was not only dangerous, but was even out-of-date. What is more, his style was archaic. Horatian satire reflects the restraint and self-control that was so much a part of Augustan policy. Horace wrote much less than his predecessor; he avoided the extravagances of Lucilian style; he did not allow unrestrained invective to play any large part in his satires.

Persius lived at a time when individual freedom had been all but lost and philosophy offered consolation and retreat for many. And so he withdrew into his Stoicism to criticize moral faults and vices that he saw around him. His satire moved from the streets into the drawing room with the other poetry and oratory of the times and became about as detached from real life as satire ever could be.

Juvenal, on the other hand, produced his poems when a limited freedom of speech had been restored. Much of the bitterness in his criticism comes from the fact that he wrote in reaction to a period of oppression and vice that had immediately preceded. By his time, too, the search for striking ways to say things had been going on for a long time. All of this is reflected in his angry approach to satire and in the colorful and at times disjointed way in which he expresses himself. But the times make Juvenal careful, and he names only names from the past. He uses them in great numbers, however, and speaks of them in such a way as to leave the impression that the satire applies directly to his own times and not to any earlier period.

The Roman satirist of every era was in a unique relationship to the society in which he lived. While he had to conform to the current literary demands in order to communicate, most of what he had to say ran against the grain of the times. He was out to criticize and to "name names," and, as he did so, he tended to alienate members of his society and isolate himself from them. This isolation is reflected in the intensely personal nature of satire that has already been discussed. The poet does not speak for a group, but for himself alone.

But this conflict and tendency towards isolation presents another problem for the satirist. He is himself a member of the society he is criticizing, and so he must decide whether he wants to remain part of it or not. It might be argued that he criticized the world around him out of a genuine concern for people and institutions, and that this is indication enough of a desire to participate as a member of society. Moreover, the poems of defense and purpose that each poet wrote show a concern that the satire be understood and taken as it is meant.

However this may be, each of the satirists solves the problem of his relationship to society in his own way. Horace joins the world that he is finding fault with by insisting that he himself has at least moderately serious shortcomings. Persius has little use for society as he finds it, but he at least suggests the common ground of Stoicism as a means of drawing people to his side. Juvenal leaves a vague impression that he is a member of that part of society that has suffered most at the hands of those who indulge in vice and depravity. He does not, however, speak for a group, but only for himself, and he remains a commentator who stands at a distance from what he is criticizing. In many respects, this is the simplest and easiest stance to take, and this is at least one reason for Juvenal's setting the mood for satire when later generations revived the study and writing of it.

There remains the question of why the Roman satirists wrote. Did they have as their purpose the improvement of Roman society, or were they simply pointing to the shortcomings of contemporary life without further implication? It might be argued that any writer who sets pen to paper to criticize the world around him must have a moral purpose, whether he admits it or not. But it is significant that none of the Roman satirists says that he is out to improve society. If such a purpose lay behind the criticism, it must remain implicit.

Actually, it seems that the Romans considered it outside the province of verse satire to suggest changes that might make the world a better place in which to live. This was the task of philosophy. Here we are fortunate in having Horace's *Epistles,* which are in essence the philosophic extension of the *Satires.* There is some overlap between the two works, and it is clear from references that Horace makes in the *Epistles* that this was intentional. Generally speaking, this repetition appears as a recognition of the need for moral improvement. But there is a difference. In the *Satires* this need is the message or point, while in the *Epistles* it serves as a reason for and justification of the positive philosophical recommendations that Horace wishes to present.

The balance between the *Epistles* and *Satires* of Horace is a reflection of the more general relationship between philosophy and satire. Each looks in the direction of the other, inasmuch as the satirist at least implies that some kind of moral reform is necessary, while the philosopher must recognize valid criticisms before he can make his suggestions for moral improvement. The satires of Persius help to make this clear, for here the overlap between satire and philosophy is quite apparent. An impartial reading of his six poems, however, proves Persius to be a satirist and not a philosopher, simply because his overriding purpose is to point out the ills of men and the society in which they live. He is criticizing, not preaching and philosophizing. This is not to say, however, that moral and philosophical advice never appears in Roman satire. It does appear from time to time, but it never dominates and it is never developed with any consistency.

Perhaps now it can be seen why there was no Greek predecessor for the genre satire. For the Greeks the exposition of the problems of people and society was not something to be pursued for its own sake, but was always at best part of a broader purpose. Homer, Thucydides, Plato, the Greek orators all used it to good effect. It also had a part to play in the personal poetry of a Theognis or a

Callimachus. But none of these were satirists in the strict sense of the term. Aristophanes is a little different. One of his primary purposes is to ridicule the shortcomings of the society in which he lives, and he shares this purpose with the Roman satirists. It is significant that Horace, Persius, and Juvenal all express a feeling of literary kinship with Aristophanes and the other writers of the so-called Old Greek Comedy. This is perhaps the closest the Greeks came to writing satire, but no one would mistake the genre comedy for the genre satire.

I

ENNIUS AND THE ORIGINS OF ROMAN SATIRE

Roman satire as a literary genre began with Ennius early in the second century B.C. But there is evidence that informal satire—perhaps it should be called a satirical spirit—existed in Rome at a much earlier time. It evidently had an important part to play in the mysterious and elusive Fescennine verses which were sung at weddings and on other festive occasions well before formal literary activity began. Though little is known about them, what Horace says is significant. For he describes these performances as being free and unrestrained and says that the impromptu poetry thus produced took the form of rustic insults or lampoons. This is not much to go on, of course, but it is enough to indicate that the seeds of satire existed in Rome in the fourth and perhaps as early as the fifth century B.C.

The fragments of the poems of Livius Andronicus and Gnaeus Naevius show that this element had a place in Latin literature almost from its beginnings in 240 B.C. In spite of the poor condition of the remains, two instances have been preserved from Livius. At one point in an unidentified comedy, the poet or one of his characters seems to have described someone as "a foolish evil-minded blockhead." In another fragment, probably from a different play, a speaker has a note of incredulity or even contempt in his voice as he addresses a protagonist: "You are really a hare and yet you're hunting fresh meat!" The criticism implied in both of these observations cannot be missed.

A glance at the fragments of Naevius, who wrote a little later than Livius, provides additional evidence of an awareness of satire in this early period. In one of his comedies reference is made to a new group of orators which is made up mainly of "stupid young men." There is no context, but the sarcasm that is evident here makes the complaint sound surprisingly modern.

In another unassigned comic fragment Naevius uses invective to make a point against a rival when he describes him as "the worst of the worst, an unbridled degenerate, a good-for-nothing, a gambler." This foreshadows the concentrated abuse that was such an important part of satire as Lucilius and Juvenal wrote it.

Naevius also follows the satiric practice of naming names as he offers criticism. In a fragment from his play, *The Soothsayer,* he pokes fun at the people from the Latin towns of Praeneste and Lanuvium:

> Speaker A: Who was at your house yesterday?
> Speaker B: I had some guests from Praeneste and Lanuvium.
> Speaker A: You should have welcomed them each with their own food. The Lanuvians should have been given a little plain sow's belly you'd boiled up and nuts should have been poured out for the Praenestines in heaps.

Presumably the speaker is an urbanite who feels that good Roman cooking is wasted on such boors.

But more striking than this is Naevius' well-known comment on the Metelli: "It is by fate that the Metelli are made consuls at Rome." The ancient commentator who quotes this line calls the remark both clever and insulting. The point that Naevius is trying to make is that the Metelli, in spite of their position, have to rely on fate and not on honesty and family prestige to attain high office. As with the invective mentioned earlier, this kind of remark anticipates the outspoken commentary that is found in Lucilius, Horace, Persius, and Juvenal, where personalities are singled out in much the same way.

But the writer who provides the clearest picture of the satiric spirit that was at work in this early period is the comic writer Plautus (c. 250-184 B.C.). Actually, he was an older contemporary of Ennius, and so for our purposes his plays are useful as indicators of the literary atmosphere in which the genre satire began its development.

Some of the connections between the comedies of Plautus and the writings of the satirists are perfectly obvious. Both adopted the banquet as a recurring theme, for example, and both made full use of the mock-heroic, mock-tragic, and ironic elements to produce much the same kind of humorous effect. There is also a moral sententiousness that comes from the mouth of the satirist and from certain of Plautus' characters. That Lucilius and Horace recognized this relationship between comedy and verse satire is clear from the fact that they took scenes or part-scenes directly from comedy. Moreover, Horace is indebted to the language of comedy for an important part of his satiric diction.

But a closer examination of Plautine comedy and verse satire shows that they have much more in common—too much to cover in any detail here. The comic playwright, for example, indulges in irreverence, burlesque, and caricature much as Lucilius, Horace, and, to some extent, Persius and Juvenal do. The irreverent attitude that Plautus displays in the *Amphitryon* where he treats Jupiter and Mercury like conniving human beings is found again in Lucilius' mock-epic account of the gods and their Senate-like assembly in the first book of his *Satires*. Again, as a character, Plautus' Mercury is much like Horace's Priapus (*Sat.* 1.8), for both have a similarly healthy, outspoken, and completely ungodlike attitude to life.

There is burlesque in the *Amphitryon,* of course, and there is more of it in the classic banquet scenes created by Plautus, Lucilius, Horace, and Juvenal. The meal attended by Sangarinus, Stichus, and eventually Stephanium at the end of the *Stichus* (683-775) is a delightful parody in miniature of a full-fledged banquet, containing as it does all the necessary ingredients—wine, woman, song, and food. Although it is better developed, there is much the same kind of parody in Lucilius' description of Troginus' banquet in his final book. It is everything a banquet should not be. The same is true of the frightful and farcical feast given by Nasidienus which caps Horace's collection in much the same way as the banquet scene concludes the *Stichus*. Again, though the humor has been replaced by a bitterness and an irony, Juvenal's account of Virro's insulting entertainment of a guest in his fifth satire also falls into the category of burlesque.

Plautus was also a master of caricature and used it to heighten the humorous and satiric effect of his comedy. Parasitic characters like Ergasilus in *The Captives* and Gelasimus in the *Stichus* were open to the same kind of criticism as Ennius brings against a parasite in a fragment preserved from his *Satires*. And there is Plautus' striking parody of the proud and overbearing military man Pyrgopolynices in *The Braggart Warrior* which anticipates Lucilius' mock-heroic treat-

ment of the gladiators and their contest in his third book and foreshadows the satirist's description of the epic encounter between
Aeserninus and Pacideianus that appears in the next book. The pompous soldier turns up again later in the satires of Persius and Juvenal.

Periplectomenus' lengthy characterization of himself in *The
Braggart Warrior* (635-68) as an agreeable, tactful, mannerly, versatile
Greek is delightful Plautine satire and immediately calls to mind
Juvenal's ironic criticism of these people who have flocked to Rome
with their foreign habits and a willingness to do any job and play any
part (3.58-125).

Finally, there is Plautus' caricature of the greedy man in the person of Euclio in *The Pot of Gold*. Although he is without any clear
parallel in Roman satire, his presence is felt in the anonymous miser
whom Horace sets up as a straw man in the first poem of his collection and in the numerous avaricious characters that appear in Lucilius
and Juvenal.

But even more striking than the methods and moods that
Plautus and the satirists have in common are the subjects that come
up for criticism. There is a wide spectrum of satiric comment in the
comedies involving most of the foibles and faults of society. Among
those habits and shortcomings which are criticized in one way or
another are irreligion, greed, pride, ingratitude, dishonesty, superstition, love and its effects, immorality, hypocrisy, backbiting, and
sententious moralizing. The abuses of wealth, luxury of all kinds, the
patron-client relationship, the excesses of the urban and rustic ways
of life, and even a man's less than perfect diction and accent all come
in for criticism at one time or another. Some of the people whom
Plautus satirizes have already been noticed. Others that should be
mentioned include women of all kinds (especially wives), city dandies,
pimps, bankers, rustics, and lawyers. Greeks and other foreigners as
well as Italians living in the small towns near Rome are also the butts
of his joking.

Although it is not a habit with him, Plautus every now and then
follows the satiric practice of naming names as Naevius had before
him. In *The Rope* (86), for example, Sceparnio refers with a smile to
Euripides' play, the *Alcmena,* while in *The Captives* (880-85) Hegio
and Ergasilus together laugh at Italian towns like Cora, Praeneste,
Signia, Frusino, and Alatrium, calling them rough, wild, and barbarian.
The Praenestines' propensity for boasting is also alluded to with
sarcasm in a fragment of *The Two Bacchises.* Finally, in *The Braggart*

Warrior (211-12), there is the well-known reference to the "barbarian poet" who is usually taken to be Naevius.

Even a brief survey of the earliest Latin literature, then, reveals the presence of what might be called a satiric spirit. As yet it has no exclusive literary form, but appears in drama and perhaps in other forms of literature as part of the subject matter and methods that the poet uses. It remained for Ennius to take the next step and begin the process of making these elements of parody, burlesque, caricature, invective, and ironic criticism part of a formal literary genre called satire.

Quintus Ennius (239-169 B.C.) was born just one year after Livius Andronicus brought formal literary activity to the city by translating and adapting Greek drama and Greek epic. In this formative period in her history Rome was making her first significant steps towards domination of the eastern Mediterranean through new alliances in Greece and wars with Illyria and Macedonia. In the west she was pursuing a policy of military expansion, more or less forced on her by the intense rivalry with Carthage. Ennius took part in the Second Punic War while still in his 20's and saw Rome become supreme in the west after the defeat of her rival. Like most Romans, he was deeply impressed by personalities like the Carthaginian Hannibal and the victorious Scipio Africanus.

All of this expansion brought greater luxury and wealth to Rome than ever before. Capitalistic interests flourished, and wealthy middle-class businessmen made their appearance. Rome was well on the way to becoming the dominant economic power in the Mediterranean.

This was a formative period for Latin literature, too. Livius Andronicus and Naevius had drawn the Romans' attention to Greek drama and epic and had interpreted these to their audience by using the unimproved native diction, idiom, and verse forms. Ennius' achievement consisted in taking this nascent Latin literature and applying to it the conventions, techniques, and forms of Greek literature. He was so successful, that he almost singlehandedly began the development of a truly literary Latin.

Although he seems not to have begun writing until he was thirty-five years old, Ennius was so prolific and his influence on the literary tradition was so profound, that he was known to subsequent genera-tions as the father of Latin literature. His genius manifested itself in a number of striking ways in his writings. The fragments that survive indicate a wide spectrum of interests and a bold versatility, and they leave the impression of a poetic personality interested in creative experimentation and striking innovation.

Ennius' versatility is especially evident in the number of different forms in which he wrote—dramatic, epic, philosophic, didactic, with even an excursion into literary prose. The scope of his interests may be seen in the many various sources of inspiration, both Greek and Roman, that lay behind his writings. Greek writers of all times from Homer through near contemporaries in the Hellenistic period provided form and subject matter, while Roman history and Roman life, as well as the literary tradition established at Rome by his predecessors Andronicus and Naevius, were the base on which he was able to build.

In synthesizing Greek and Roman elements for his Roman audience Ennius showed a striking originality. It was a daring experiment to present works like the *Epicharmus* with its exposition of the Pythagorean philosophy and the *Hedyphagetica,* or gourmet's guide to good eating, to Romans who had little experience with such writing, though it is only fair to admit that no one can know how much Ennius achieved with these. His efforts within the established forms can be more easily judged, and here everything points to his being successful. To choose only one example, his adaptation of Homeric techniques to the Roman epic tradition took the form of a unique epic history of the city, the *Annals,* which was to profoundly influence Roman poetry in most periods of its development. Ennius also brought new forms to Latin that were to become an important part of Roman literature—the dactylic hexameter for epic, literary prose, and the elegiac couplet.

It is not surprising, then, that this writer should be the originator of a new genre of Latin literature—Roman verse satire. When his *Satires* were written cannot be known with any certainty. For that matter, only a vague chronology has been worked out for Ennius' work as a whole. But in spite of the difficulties, these poems are generally thought to be a late work, and the fragments present no evidence to the contrary. It is also possible that the *Satires* were written individually over a long period of time and put together fairly late in Ennius' life.

There were apparently four books of satires of which very little has survived. In all, there are only thirty-three lines or part lines, most of them coming as random quotations from late writers, although classical writers like Cicero, Varro, and Quintilian provide the odd line. The corpus is dangerously small, then, and the problems

thus presented are compounded by the fact that seven of the lines
have been attributed to the *Satires* by modern authorities without
any ancient evidence.

Characteristics of Ennius' Satires

Though no satire has survived in its entirety, the subject matter
of two of them is described by ancient writers. In one of these
Ennius apparently depicted life and death as arguing with each
other in much the same way as pleasure and virtue do in the extant
Choice of Heracles written much earlier in Greek by the sophist
Prodicus.

More is known about the second poem, the fable of the crested
lark, for Aulus Gellius, writing about A.D. 150, has provided a prose
paraphrase followed by two lines in trochaic verse quoted directly
from the poem. In this tale, which was well known in antiquity, a
lark has a nest of chicks in a field that will soon be harvested. She
reveals her knowledge of human nature by refusing to evacuate her
family when the owner of the field and his son first ask friends to
help and then seek the assistance of relatives. But when the chicks
report that the two farmers are planning to harvest the grain themselves the next day, the mother lark quickly decides it is time to move
her brood. The moral of the story appears in the two verses that
follow: "Always keep this lesson in mind: do not wait for friends
to do what you can do yourself."

Although this poem of Ennius cannot be reconstructed in its
details, Gellius' paraphrase indicates a number of general characteristics. It seems clear, for instance, that there was a fair amount of
dialogue, with the mother lark speaking to her children and the
owner of the field addressing his son. The fable is found again in the
collection put together by Babrius in the second century after Christ,
and if this represents a standard form, then it is possible that Ennius
increased the amount of dialogue for his own purposes. Moreover,
the two lines which Gellius quotes suggest that the whole poem was
written in trochaic septenarii. This too hints at dialogue, since this
meter is one of those most commonly used for conversation in
Roman comedy. It is entirely possible that the use of septenarii for
fable is unique with Ennius, for the fabulists who wrote in verse
generally used iambic meters. But, no matter what the innovations
of Ennius may have been, the story of the crested lark remains a

fable with the formulae, repetitions, development of plot, and statement of moral that one would expect. The form had long been used
for comment on people's habits, and this was what, at least in part,
attracted Ennius to it.

It is almost impossible to recognize the themes of other individual
satires from the fragments. One poem may have dealt with the
achievements of Scipio Africanus in the Second Punic War and
another almost certainly treated parasites and their habits. Such
impressions, however, are largely subjective and must not be pressed.

From what has already been said about content and form it might
be concluded that Ennius' *Satires* were basically a collection that was
miscellaneous in nature. Indeed, a glance at the remaining fragments
tends to confirm this impression. For the lines of autobiographical
content, mention of the one-eyed Arimaspeans who live at the end
of the world, and the description of a bothersome crowd, to name
only a few examples, suggest a number of different approaches and
themes.

Not only did the various poems differ widely in subject matter,
but they were also written in a number of meters. Besides the trochaic
septenarii of the fable of the lark, there are also iambic senarii. Both
of these recall Roman comedy with which they had been closely
identified by Ennius' time. It should also be remembered, however,
that Archilochus and Callimachus had written satiric poetry in Greek
in which iambics and trochaics predominated. The dactylic hexameter
which also appears in the *Satires* had by now become associated with
narrative-epic poetry. The sotadeans are a special case, since they are
a direct imitation of the form used earlier in Greek by Sotades for
his poetry of criticism and parody. The simple fact that Ennius used
a variety of meters is important, then, but the associations that these
meters had for the Roman poet confirm the impression of a miscellaneous subject matter that has already been noticed.

In view of what has been said, it is perhaps not surprising to find
that moods vary from fragment to fragment. Indeed, both serious and
humorous elements are present with the serious ranging in turn from
eulogy through moral and didactic comment to sarcastic criticism
and attack. Serious praise of Scipio may be presumed to lie behind
Ennius' mention of Africa, out of context though it may be: "The
witnesses are the broad fields which Africa keeps neatly cultivated."
Again, there is a serious moral and didactic purpose in the two lines
from the lark fable. This appears again in Ennius' warning against the
false accuser and his observation that some people, presumably those

who are excessively critical, are the kind who look for knots in a
bullrush. In these examples it is also possible to see a touch of
criticism, though sarcasm and attack are much more evident in the
poet's curse on a gourmand, his description of a "pushy" crowd, and
his frank appraisal of a parasite. More will be said about this aspect
of Ennius' *Satires* a little later.

The satirist's attempts at humor show a similar range. A light
humor, for example, runs through the narrative portion of the fable
of the crested lark, while elsewhere the poet smiles good-naturedly at
himself for being able to get down to writing only when he is im-
mobilized by the gout. There is a similarly humorous touch in his
address to himself: "Hail, poet Ennius, you who hand on to men
flaming verses from your very marrow." It should be noticed that
Ennius here begins the tradition of employing the mock-heroic in
satire. This must have played an important part in other satires, for it
appears again when the poet calls sheep "the wool-bearing breed"
and when he describes the Arimaspeans as "one-eyes" digging their
silver "on the Ripaean mountaintops."

The fragments leave the clear impression, then, that Ennius'
Satires was a collection of poems on a variety of subjects written in a
number of meters and moods. The ancients appreciated this characteristic of these poems, for Diomedes the grammarian, who was writing in the late fourth century after Christ but was using classical
writers as his sources, made a careful differentiation between Ennius
and Pacuvius on the one hand who composed "poetry which consisted of a variety of poems" and the later satirists on the other whose
writings were primarily critical. This quality of Ennius' *Satires* cannot
be overemphasized, since it remains a part of Roman satire throughout its development.

At this point someone may object that the *Satires* as they have
been described seem to be simply a number of poems which fall
together without any cohesion. And yet the fact that Ennius collected
them and gave them a common title suggests that he had some concept of unity. The common denominator between all of these poems
is apparently the personality of the poet himself, for he appears in
enough of the fragments to suggest that he took a strong personal
part. Although at times it is impossible to know whether an "I" or a
"we" refers to Ennius, in other fragments there can be no doubt. "I
never poetize unless I am laid up with the gout," he says in the well-
known line mentioned earlier, as he laughs good-naturedly at him-

self. Not only is he minimizing his ailment, but he is also twitting himself for not being able to settle down to writing. Somewhat the same atmosphere prevails in his pompous greeting to himself, and there may also be a trace of his genial personality in another line as the poet offers a defense: "It is not my way as if a dog has bitten me." Gout, drinking, and dog-bites also suggest the level at which the poet's interests lie; these subjects are hardly the stuff of elegy, tragedy, lyric, and epic.

When he is addressing a second person, Ennius becomes a teacher, a moralist, a helpful friend, or a critic. The teacher-moralist-critic combination appears in the warning against the false accuser mentioned earlier, for not only is the poet telling his listener to beware, but he is also passing judgment on the action of a third person. The same may be said of the moral appended to the fable of the lark. In Ennius' address to the parasite there is a positive personality offering clear judgment on a situation of which he does not approve.

Although it is impossible to find any direct participation of the poet in the other fragments, some of them may be seen as coming from the temperament described above. The poem in honor of Scipio was probably generated by Ennius' personal convictions, while the clever play upon *frustra* ("in vain") and its cognates comes from an outlook that is half playful and half serious.

While this personal involvement of the poet is important as a unifying influence in the *Satires,* we must not ignore the fact that it is another original aspect of these poems. For the first time in Latin literature the poet addresses himself directly to the reader on a wide variety of subjects in many different moods. But even though the writer's personality controls the content, form, and atmosphere, this is not to say that the poet appears as a first person singular in each poem. He is present in many cases by implication with his presence in one poem carrying over to another in which he does not explicitly participate. This function of personality is very important for Roman satire, for it is perhaps the most important factor conditioning the nature of the genre in any particular instance.

Something has already been said about the critical component of the *Satires,* and it is now time to look at it a little more closely. Although it is not possible to find more than a hint of criticism in most instances, there appears to have been a wide spectrum of satire in these poems. Human foibles, among other things, come in for their fair share of censure. In the moral of the lark fable Ennius gently chides the dependent man; when he smiles at himself for putting off writing, he is smiling at procrastinators in general.

In another fragment there is the hint that he took the self-styled gourmet to task for avoiding the harsher and more mundane foods like mustard and onion. Here the metaphoric use of the adjectives describing the mustard as harsh and the onion as tearful carries over-tones of irony. Much clearer is the writer's rebuke of a gourmand which takes the form of a one-line curse: "By heaven, may he go on eating without stopping, and may he suffer badly for it." When describing a milling crowd he piles up verbs for effect: "They stop, they run up, they get in the way, they interfere, they are an aggrava-tion." In still another satire Ennius makes a pointed comparison between humans and apes, where not only what is said but also the alliterative *s*'s of the Latin suggest strong satire. The warning against the man who gives false testimony was mentioned earlier.

Finally, there is Ennius' attack on the parasite which is important enough to quote in its entirety:

> Why, when you arrive well-washed and happy without a
> worry in the world, your cheeks unstuffed, your arm
> ready for action, quickly tippy-toeing along, waiting
> to attack like a wolf—when soon you are lapping up
> the groceries of another man, what feeling do you think
> the master has? My god, he's deep in despair as he
> presides over the food, and you devour it with a laugh.

These six lines provide interesting insights into Ennius' satiric tech-nique. The ironic *quippe* ("Why!"), the accumulation of pointed modifiers, the loose progression of thought, the feeling of indignation that causes the satirist to ask and answer his question in almost the same breath, and the bald statement of rebuke that concludes the passage may remind the reader of Roman comedy, but they suggest as well the informality, the anger, and the epigrammatic bite that characterize later satire.

The tenor of the satire varies from context to context. Ennius mounts a determined, deadly serious, almost bitter attack against the gourmand and the parasite. When he deals with the dependent man or the man who gives false testimony, his criticism takes the form of a warning. On the other hand, he uses a light touch in criticizing his own procrastination.

It is not surprising that criticism and satire should play a part in poetry that was in essence the informal expression of a perceptive Roman poet's personality, for the tradition of raillery had been strong among the Romans, as performances like the Fescennines show. It was another manifestation of Ennius' achievement, however, to discipline this propensity and channel it into a form with literary potential. At the same time it must be put in the proper perspective, for though it played an important part in a number of satires, there is no reason to believe that the critical element dominated the collection. Roman satire as Ennius wrote it was primarily a miscellany held together by the personality of the poet in which the critical was but one of a variety of moods and approaches. It was Ennius' successors in the genre that made Roman satire primarily a vehicle of criticism.

Influences and Origins

As a literary genre and as a title *saturae* are new with Ennius. But since it is difficult to imagine them as springing from the poet's mind without any inspiration from another source, much scholarly attention has been directed toward discovering the antecedents and origins of Roman satire. The problem has proved to be a vexing one, but by now attempts to resolve it have taken two tracks: (1) description of the relationship between Roman satire and earlier satiric writing and (2) explanation of how the word *satura* came to be applied to this kind of poetry.

As far as antecedents are concerned, various Greek writings have been championed as the prototype of Roman satire. Among the most commonly suggested have been Old Comedy, the mime, iambic poetry, epigram, and the Stoic-Cynic diatribe. Contributing to the confusion is the fact that no history of Greek satirical literature has yet been written.

The existence of the satiric element in earliest Greek poetry is evidenced by passages of the *Iliad* and *Odyssey,* and it is also found in early epics of parody such as the *Margites* and the *Batrachomyomachia.* A little later came Archilochus, Semonides of Amorgos, and Hipponax with their critical iambic poetry. Greek comedy of the fifth century was laced with commentary on contemporary affairs, and Horace insists that Lucilius found inspiration in comic writers like Eupolis, Cratinus, and Aristophanes. Roughly contemporaneous with the later plays of Old Comedy are some of

the dialogues of Plato which are pervaded with the subtle satire of
the Socratic irony.

In the Hellenistic period there were many writings in which the
satiric element had a place, and as early as Ennius the Romans must
have been familiar with most of these. Rhinthon produced phlyax-
plays that were burlesques of tragic themes, while Herodas, the
writer of mimes, professed to be following Hipponax as he parodied
people and their habits. Callimachus revived the iambic poetry of
Archilochus and wrote on various themes, often in a satiric tone.

Finally, there was the diatribe, the weapon of the Cynics and
Stoics, which was written in prose and was a mixture, as most preaching is, of philosophy, oratory, and dialogue. It was characterized by a
wide range of moods, and the preacher made full use of rhetorical
example, especially myth and fable. The diatribist's purpose was a
serious one, since he was determined to improve society by lashing
out at human foibles, faults, habits, and institutions.

An attempt to equate Roman satire as Ennius wrote it with any
one of these types can be only partially successful, for it is only too
obvious that the extant lines have affinities with many Greek sources.
The debate between life and death has been compared to the debate
between virtue and pleasure in Prodicus' *Choice of Heracles* and to
similar debates between abstracts in Aristophanes' comedies, *Clouds*
and *Wealth*. When we remember the part that debate has to play in
Thucydides' *History* and Plato's dialogues, as well as in the law
courts of Athens, it becomes almost impossible to imagine any one
source as providing the necessary inspiration.

The situation is the same with the fable of the crested lark. While
it could have been drawn from a particular writer, the fact that it had
appeared earlier in works of writers as widely different as Aesop,
Callimachus, and the diatribists makes a specific attribution dangerous. The fragment describing the fluteplayer standing beside the sea
has been related with more confidence to a story in the first book of
Herodotus' *History* (1.141), while the two lines in which Ennius
hails himself in mock-heroic tones are reminiscent of a passage quoted
by Athenaeus (15.669e) from Dionysius Chalcus, a writer of sympotic
elegies in the fifth century B.C. When the possibilities are considered,
then, it seems a reasonable assumption that if the *Satires* were extant
a Greek prototype could be found for each poem. Apparently, there
was in Greek literature no parallel to the *Satires* as a collection.

The Romans themselves had no problem with the origins of verse
satire. For them it was a Roman creation, pure and simple. In a

passage to which we shall return in a later chapter, Horace refers to the originator of satire as "the author of poetry that was rough and untouched by the Greeks." Whether he means Ennius or some other early writer it is difficult to tell, for what he says is vague, perhaps designedly so. But he does make it clear that in his mind the Greeks did not write the satiric poetry that he is discussing.

Quintilian puts it a little differently, when, as he lists the various kinds of Roman writers and writings with their Greek counterparts, he comes at last to satire and says, almost with a sigh, that it is exclusively Roman (10.1.93). There is only one way to interpret these statements: verse satire originated as a genre in Rome. Since efforts to find a single Greek source have thus far proved unsuccessful and because no sound rebuttal can be offered to what Horace and Quintilian say, it is perhaps safest and simplest to accept their point of view.

The question of how the word *satura* came to be applied to this kind of poetry has also been the subject of much serious investigation. By pursuing the derivation and meaning of the word, scholars have hoped to shed light on the nature of Roman satire in general and Ennius' satire in particular. Unfortunately, neither Ennius nor any of the other satirists whose works are extant helps with matters of definition, and the sources that do offer information are for the most part from much later times and are not all reliable. There are two passages, however, that must be taken into account by anyone attempting this kind of study.

The earlier of these is Livy's discussion of the development of drama in Rome in which *satura* plays a part. When describing the events of the year 364 B.C. in his *History of Rome* (7.2), Livy insists that nothing of importance happened beyond the fact that a plague came upon the city. After trying all the usual religious remedies without success, the Romans finally resorted to something new by importing actors from Etruria. At this point the historian undertakes a brief account of the growth of dramatic performances at Rome which he describes as passing through five stages. The first presentations, those brought by the Etruscans, are described as dances accompanied by the flute, in which, Livy is careful to point out, there was no singing. The second stage was a burlesque of these by the Roman youth who added rough jests in verse and danced to the words. There was apparently some passage of time between this step and the next during which these burlesques maintained a popularity, but how long this

interval was it is impossible to tell. At the third stage native professional actors performed what Livy calls *saturae*. These were full of
various rhythms or meters and included both singing, which was
written down for the flute, and dancing, or at any rate gesticulation,
that was suited to the music. Some years later a fourth stage was
reached when Livius Andronicus deserted the *saturae* to produce the
first plays with a plot. Finally, something called *exodia* made their
appearance along with the Atellan farces which, according to Livy,
represented a reversion to the earlier less formal kind of dramatic
performance.

Though these five divisions are generally accepted nowadays,
Livy's account does present problems. In the first place, it is not
entirely clear that the historian meant the *saturae* to be a separate
stage, since he is careful to articulate the other steps in his Latin, but
omits any transition between the burlesques and the *saturae*. Secondly, the date of the *saturae* is not clear. There is no indication whether
they developed closer to 364 or to 240 when Andronicus translated
his first play from the Greek. Finally, Andronicus himself is a problem, since, in all likelihood, there was no connection between his
literary translations and the Italian folk tradition represented by the
other forms that Livy mentions.

In favor of Livy's account, it may be said that the progression,
so long as one does not press Andronicus' part, is a logical one. Moreover, this historian's insistence on Etruscan influence in the early
stages of dramatic activity at Rome is recognition of the true state
of affairs. The Etruscans did influence Roman performances in many
respects, and their effect might have been felt quite early in the way
Livy suggests.

Those who accept what the historian says have used it in two
different ways. Starting from the information he provides, some have
attempted to establish a derivation for the word, taking the origins of
satura back to Etruria, Anatolia, and Illyria by complicated processes
of reasoning that must remain theory until collateral evidence is
found. Others have tried to find a logical connection between the
semidramatic performance and Roman satire. But the dialogue and
other dramatic features that mark both are hardly strong links, for
the other forms on which Ennius and his successors drew—the fable
and philosophical dispute, for instance—also contained these elements.

The second passage that is important for the derivation of *satura*
is to be found in the rhetorical treatise of the grammarian Diomedes,

who was mentioned earlier. This brief historical description of satire
is worth quoting at length:

> Satire is the name given to poetry amongst the
> Romans which is nowadays abusive and put together in
> the manner of Old Comedy to condemn people's faults.
> This is the kind of thing that Lucilius, Horace, and
> Persius wrote. At an earlier time, however, poetry that
> was made up of a variety of poems was called satire.
> This was what Pacuvius and Ennius wrote.
>
> Now *satura* or satire received its name either from
> the satyrs, because in this kind of poetry humorous or
> off-color things are discussed which are just like the
> things brought up or acted out by satyrs in plays, or
> else it took its name from the plate which was filled with
> many different first offerings and presented to the gods
> at a religious festival by the early Romans. The plate
> received the name *satura* from its abundant and over-
> flowing contents .... Or else *satura* comes from a certain
> kind of stuffing which Varro says had this name applied
> to it because it was filled with many ingredients. There
> is also this observation in the second book of his *Plautine
> Inquiries*: "*Satura* is raisins, barley, and pinenuts sprin-
> kled with winehoney." Others add pomegranate seeds to
> these ingredients.
>
> Still others say that satire received its name from a
> law called *satura,* which includes many proposals to-
> gether in one enactment, apparently because many
> poems are brought together in the poetic version of
> *satura.*

How far we can go in accepting what Diomedes says is debatable.
He is a late writer, and, like so many scholars of his time, he seems to
have been of a less than original genius, relying upon earlier gram-
marians and commentators for his discussion of the classical Roman
writers. The present passage illustrates both his strengths and his
weaknesses. His omission of Juvenal from the canon of Roman satirists
is clear commentary on his thoroughness. On the other hand, his
account takes a certain authority from the fact that in a number of
important respects it goes back to Varro who lived much closer to

the events which are being described and was himself enough of an expert to warrant a hearing.

Of the four derivations that Diomedes offers, the first can be rejected out of hand. In spite of its being perhaps the most popular explanation at the time the grammarian wrote, it is impossible to see any relationship between Roman satire and Greek satyrs. It is more than a little ironic that our form "satire" has come from this confusion in spelling (*satura* > *satyra* > *satira* > satire). The other three definitions all have fullness and variety in common. The platter is described as being "filled with many various first offerings," and Diomedes says that it received the name *satura* from the idea of abundance and fullness that is associated with it. The stuffing was "filled with many ingredients," while the law going under the name *satura* "embraced many measures in one form of legislation." As evidence of the original meaning of *satura* this legal definition can be only confirmatory, since it originated in 150 B.C. at the earliest. On the other hand, the use of *satura* as a platter of mixed offerings and a stuffing made of a mixture of ingredients could easily go well back into the preliterary period of Roman history.

It would appear, then, that the Latin word *satura* with its connotations of fullness and variety is closely related to the adjective *satur* meaning "full" or "rich." The stem in this case would be *sat-*, which appears in words like *satis* ("enough"), *satietas* ("a sufficiency," "abundance"), and *satio* ("to satisfy," "to fill"). But in the description of the contents of the platter there is an emphasis on variety as well, and the ingredients that make up the stuffing are similarly quite miscellaneous. It is not difficult to imagine how the meaning "full of many things" developed into "full of many different things."

There is no good reason to dispute the reliability of either of these two definitions, and if one is accepted, both must be accepted. At the same time, it is impossible to know which represents the earlier application of the word, for both uses of *satura* probably go well back into the dim, dark past of the preliterary period. But it does not really matter which came first. It is more important to recognize the fact that in the colloquial idiom of early Rome *satura* had come to stand for a plate of offerings which was part of a harvest ceremony and that it was also used to designate a kind of stuffing that appeared from time to time on the dinner table. The possibility exists that there were other uses of the word which have not survived. We may well wonder whether Livy's dramatic *satura* does not represent another earlier application of the noun, this time to a performance presented in a variety of rhythms and meters.

Now perhaps it is easier to see why Ennius chose *Saturae* as a title for his collection of poetry and why later satirists continued the tradition. This application of the noun is parallel to the religious, culinary, dramatic, and legal uses just mentioned. Because of its connotations of variety and miscellany, the word was an appropriate designation of poetry which was basically miscellaneous. This, of course, is what Diomedes is referring to early in his discussion of satire, and Quintilian offers confirmation, when he speaks of this kind of satire as "an assortment of poems" (10.1.95). By using *saturae,* then, Ennius was in essence titling his collection "Miscellaneous Poetry" with *satura* standing not for the individual poem but for a book of poems.

But this was not the only reason for Ennius' deciding upon *Saturae* as a title. He chose it also because it put the collection in its proper place in the hierarchy of literature. Though this poetry may not have been epic or tragic, at the same time it was not on a level with farce and mime. To indicate this the poet selected a term that had stood for an informal preliterary dramatic performance. Perhaps the fact that Naevius had used the word as a title for a comedy also influenced his choice. These were just the loose literary connotations needed to convey the idea of personal informality and variety that were important characteristics of this kind of writing.

Saturae was also an appropriate designation because it was a thoroughly Roman word designating a thoroughly Roman creation. A glance through the titles that Ennius chose for his other works reveals that they fall into two categories, one Greek and the other Roman, depending on inspiration and subject matter. The *Sota, Protrepticus,* and *Hedyphagetica* have Greek content, while the *Epicharmus* and *Euhemerus* are named from the Greek writers who espoused the ideas found in them. The tragedies might be added to these. On the other side are those works which have a Roman focus: the *Annals,* an epic poem on the rise of Rome, the *Scipio,* written in honor of Africanus, the *Ambracia,* which presumably celebrated Fulvius' victory in 189 B.C., and the *Sabine Women,* a play based on a well-known event in Roman history. According to this pattern and in view of the historical connotations of the word *satura,* the *saturae* might be expected to signify something basically Roman. There is a further parallel between the *Annals* and the

Satires in this respect. Ennius apparently drew the title of his epic
either from the name of the yearly records that the priests of Rome
kept (*annales pontificum*) or perhaps from the earlier historical
tradition of the annalists who began writing in Greek prose about
300 B.C. In either case, he adopted a word with semiliterary connections as a title for a new kind of national epic. Similarly *satura* has
semiliterary ties, though in the case of the *Annals* the title had
venerable religious or literary overtones which were especially appropriate to the lofty theme and purpose, while the connotations of
satura were those of the everyday life of the common man.

Before leaving Ennius it is perhaps worth emphasizing once again
that satire in its beginnings was not yet the vehicle for criticism that
it became later in the hands of Lucilius, Horace, Persius, and Juvenal.
The few fragments that remain and the few comments that the
ancient writers make regarding the genre suggest that Ennius' *Satires*
were a collection of poems on a wide variety of topics held together
by the personality of the poet. There are hints in the fragments of
many topics and many moods. The critical element was certainly
present, but there is no indication that it predominated.

II

LUCILIUS, THE DISCOVERER OF THE GENRE

No trace has survived of the satires which Ennius' nephew Pacuvius wrote, but from what Diomedes says it is clear that these poems were of a miscellaneous nature and so were firmly in the Ennian tradition. With Gaius Lucilius the outlook is a little brighter, although his satires, too, are far from complete.

Not a great deal is known about Lucilius' life. He was probably born about 180 B.C. at Suessa Aurunca in Campania and died at Naples in 102. He lived, then, during a period that was marked by a significant expansion of Roman power abroad, while at home the challenge to the aristocratic Republican government was becoming more pronounced. During this century Rome fought wars with Macedonia and continued to extend her sway in the east as Greece and Asia Minor became provinces under her control. In the west Carthage was at last destroyed forever and Spain was brought into the Roman orbit. It was also at this time that the Romans had their first contact with the barbarian Germans invading from the north.

These conquests had a profound effect on life at Rome. Roman soldiers, administrators, and travelers returning from abroad brought foreign ideas and institutions to the city with them, and this influence was reinforced by the foreigners who were now arriving in Rome in greater numbers than ever before.

There was also a continuing restlessness in politics at Rome during Lucilius' lifetime. The Senate maintained its power, but under successful challenge from popular leaders like the Gracchi, rights and privileges were slowly reaching the middle and lower classes. Late in his life Lucilius saw the dictator Marius come to power as a new and different kind of threat to the Senate and to constitutional Republican government.

Literature in this period continued its rapid development in the wake of Ennius' achievements. Historical writing began and oratory blossomed. Moreover, Terence presented Greek subject matter to a Roman audience in plays written in a pure Roman Latin. It was important for Terence, Lucilius, and the other writers and thinkers of the time that the younger Scipio, general, aristocrat, and savant, and his close friend Gaius Laelius Sapiens ("The Wise") actively promoted literature and intellectual activity in general. While they fully appreciated the Greek culture and encouraged its study at Rome, the spirit of the so-called Scipionic Circle was one of complete freedom, so that a writer like Lucilius could develop his potential as his talent dictated.

This was the atmosphere in which Lucilius lived and worked. Born into the wealth that accompanied senatorial rank, he probably came to Rome early in life to receive a thorough education in Greek and Latin. When and how his intimate friendship with Scipio grew cannot be known, but it is clear that the two were close friends by 133 B.C. when Lucilius served with Scipio at the Battle of Numantia in Spain. Two years later, the poet began writing his *Satires* and devoted the rest of his life to them.

There were originally thirty books of satires of which only a little more than 1300 lines or part lines survive. Not only is there no complete poem among these, but few of the fragments are more than three lines long. Like the remains of Ennius' *Satires*, they have been preserved as random quotations in the works of later writers, with the great majority of them coming from the grammarian Nonius Marcellus, who lived in the early fourth century after Christ.

The order in which the *Satires* were finally put together only partially reflects their original organization. The earliest part of the collection is Books 26 through 30 which were begun in 132 B.C. and published in 123. Next came what are now Books 1 through 21 which appeared together probably in 106, while Books 22 through 25 were added at or shortly after Lucilius' death in 102. In most cases, it is impossible to tell when the individual satires were written. The final arrangement of the books was based on an ancient metrical canon according to which the hexameters were put first (1-21), the elegiac distichs next (22-25), and the books containing a variety of meters last (26-29). Book 30, which is all hexameters and so should naturally fall with Books 1-21, presumably maintained its place as the last of the five books published together in 123.

It is also worth noting here that the four books of elegiacs were primarily honorary and so were not satires in the strict sense. In view of the miscellaneous nature of Roman satire, however, it is easy to imagine how they might have been appended to the collection, especially since they were published after the poet's death.

Lucilius' Views on Satire

Perhaps the best way to begin a survey of what is left of Lucilius' *Satires* is to try to piece together his views on the purpose and nature of the genre and to determine, as far as it is possible, where he felt it stood in the hierarchy of Latin poetry. The fragments leave the impression that Lucilius had done much thinking about literature in general and satire in particular. Besides making random comments from time to time, he seems to have talked in a relatively systematic way about satire in a poem prefacing Book 26, while in Book 30 he apparently defended himself and his poetry at some length against an outspoken critic. Thus began the tradition among Roman satirists of defending satiric purposes and explaining satiric methods.

From the latter poem (1061-92) it is natural to conclude that social criticism was a main thrust of satire as Lucilius wrote it, for one of his critics is heard loudly and clearly taking the poet to task for his "savage actions and gloomy words." The speaker is especially incensed at what he interprets as a certain delight that the satirist takes in spreading insulting stories. He all but accuses Lucilius of libelous intent as he insists that how he behaves is no business of the poet. In this critic's eyes, the satirist is nothing but a man-trap and a scorpion with tail raised to attack. It is interesting to note in passing that the poet has his attacker indulge in the same unrestrained invective that he criticizes Lucilius for.

Unfortunately, not much of the poet's rebuttal has survived, but he seems to have promised a brief reply and to have gone on to show that his opponent's charges were rash and perhaps even unfounded. This line of defense may have been elaborated by the observation that if a man lives a blameless life he cannot be criticized by Lucilius. The mention of the reprobate Musco was more than likely part of a comparison made by the poet to the detriment of his critic, for Lucilius is well aware of this man's faults and even makes reference to his huge expenditures of money in the brothels of Rome. What is left of his defense confirms the impression left by his opponent that one of the main purposes of satire as Lucilius wrote it was to draw attention to people's shortcomings by offering frank criticism.

But this apparently was not the only object that the poet had in mind. In a fragment from another satire in this book (1039-40), he speaks of honoring a woman's beauty in his poems, and there is no reason to see anything here but a positive, expository purpose for writing. This same implication can be read into two lines from an earlier satire (791-92) in which the poet insists that he is writing for the benefit of the Roman people and that he is doing this conscientiously and eagerly.

From what has already been said about his poem of defense it is perhaps clear that Lucilius considered the personality of the poet to be an integral part of satire. Other random comments confirm this. He knows what to criticize, and it is this as much as anything that makes a poet of his personality eagerly speak out (696). In fact, he has trouble controlling himself; at times the pressure is so great that he can hardly keep from bursting (763-65). It is no wonder that he will attack "with the angry look and open jaws of a dog" (1000-01). But this is not to say that the satirist recommends the extremes of violence and anger, for in another line he renounces these to the point of suggesting that it is a crime to show such feelings (664).

All of this leaves the impression with the reader that Lucilius and his satire are inseparable. The satirist is a strong, well-balanced personality who is confident that his point of view and actions are correct. He is not afraid to criticize or disagree with his contemporaries, and he does so with gusto when the urge strikes him.

Precisely where Lucilius thought the genre satire fitted in the hierarchy of literature cannot be determined with any precision, but some idea may be gleaned from the remains of the poem that originally stood at the beginning of Book 26. Four or five other fragments also help. According to Cicero, when Lucilius insists that he does not want Persius to read his *Satires,* but is willing to have Laelius read them (635), it is because he does not want the very learned—in this case Persius—or the very unlearned as an audience, but prefers men like Laelius who are between the two extremes. There is surely an implication here that satire falls somewhere below the most sophisticated poetry demanding intense study and analysis, but well above the lesser genres that anyone can appreciate with a minimum of mental effort. Presumably, epic and lyric would be part of the former, while fable, farce, and mime would stand at the other extreme. This middle position for satire is borne out by the implication in Lucilius' poem of defense that, unlike those who write inspired poetry, the satirist has not drunk from the fountains of the Muses.

Contexts in which the *Satires* are referred to directly help to reinforce this impression. In a brief and poorly preserved line Lucilius uses the Greek word *schedium* in the sense of something quickly knocked together to refer to the informality of his writing (1131). The same idea is present in the terminology of a fragment already mentioned, when he speaks of honoring a woman's beauty in his "playful conversations." This comment is particularly important, since the two words *ludus* ("sport") and *sermones* ("conversations") which are used to label the *Satires* here, emphasize the humor and informality that are characteristically present. At the same time, the plural "conversations" suggests a collection with certain common denominators running through it.

The fact that Lucilius also has his critic use *sermones* at least twice to designate the *Satires* (1085, 1086) suggests that he considered it an appropriate description of the poetry he was writing. In what ways was it appropriate? It must be noticed first that, while this Roman word could be relatively colorless, representing speech in the broadest sense, it more often than not was connected with the art of conversation in which the Roman gentleman displayed his sophistication, good taste, and wit in a congenial or even convivial atmosphere. For Cicero it is so important that in his *On Duties* he relates it to oratory and hints at the need for formal training that might be part of rhetoric (1.133-37). That Lucilius is aware of this kind of discourse is perfectly clear from a fragment in which he connects food that is well cooked and well seasoned with "good conversation" (206-07).

Cicero's comments in the passage of the *On Duties* mentioned above may be combined with observations of other Roman writers to suggest a number of reasons for Lucilius' using the term in this way. In the first place, the word reflects the proper degree of informality which is such an important characteristic of satire. Just as conversation is not on the same level as oratory, but is based on a certain culture and sophistication that raises it above the vulgar, so satire does not fly as high as epic, tragedy, and lyric, but neither does it fall as low as farce and mime.

Secondly, conversation and satire both presuppose a positive personality generating or participating in a discussion. The way a man speaks reveals his true self, and the point has already been made that a strong personality is mirrored in the *Satires*. Moreover, each is marked by a variety of subject matter and mood which embraces high and low, serious and humorous. The last is particularly important, for satire as Lucilius conceives of it reveals an urbanity of wit. In Cicero's eyes and in the opinion of other Roman writers, this is one of the most important constituents of urbane conversation.

A final point of resemblance lies in the fact that both satire and *sermo* are essentially Roman concepts. When the latter is discussed as conversation, it is a purely Roman phenomenon manifesting the culture of the Roman gentleman. It is particularly appropriate, then, that it should be used to designate a genre of poetry that had its origins and development in Rome.

To summarize: for Lucilius satire as a genre was marked by outspoken criticism, though other purposes and moods were often present. The satirist himself was an important part of the poetry, and his methods governed the nature of a poem in any given instance. The result in Lucilius' mind was a kind of writing that fell in the middle ground of literature, and because it did, he could call his *Satires* "conversations." That this was an effective way of describing satire and setting it off from the other forms of poetry is borne out by the fact that Horace later adopted *Sermones* as the title for his collection of satires.

Subject and Form

There is so great a variety of character and subject matter in Lucilian satire that it is not possible to give more than an impressionistic idea of them here. To put it simply, no personality, no type, no institution, no activity at Rome seems to have escaped the satirist's attention. Both rich and poor populate the fragments, and they are drawn from every vocation and every stratum of society: lawyers, magistrates, old men, young men, gladiators, slaves, prostitutes, gluttons, rustics, convicts, hawkers, to name only a few. Greeks,

Lydians, Syrophoenicians, Carthaginians, and Spaniards are among the many foreigners that appear.

Lucilius was not afraid to name names in his *Satires,* and many of the characters he mentions are types drawn from contemporary and near-contemporary society: Musco the thief, Phryne the whore, Lamia and Bitto the gluttonous prostitutes, Macedo and Gentius the homosexuals, Troginus the alcoholic, Granius the auctioneer, Artemo the Arab, and Aeserninus and Pacideianus the glorious gladiators. Many of them are to appear again in the satires of Lucilius' successors.

Especially interesting are the satirist's comments on leading contemporary figures. Lucilius' intimate friendship with Scipio led him to adopt his mentor's friends and enemies as his own. Scipio himself appears fairly frequently in the *Satires,* especially in those written before his death in 129 B.C. Most references seem to be complimentary, though there are indications that Scipio too came in for his fair share of criticism. Among the mutual friends that are mentioned are Gaius Laelius, the cultured leader in the so-called Scipionic Circle; Rutilius Rufus, soldier, lawyer, and orator who carefully combined Greek and Roman ideals; Manius Manilius, another soldier, lawyer, and legal writer; Scipio's brother, Quintus Fabius Maximus, consul, diplomat, and general; and Junius Congus, the legal and historical writer.

Enmities that were both political and personal appear in the *Satires.* Lucilius was outspoken in his criticism of Quintus Caecilius Metellus Macedonicus, the general and senator who was a political rival of Scipio with pro-Gracchan sympathies. The satirist also takes this man's son, Gaius Caecilius Caprarius, to task for his rustic accent and general boorishness. Other undesirables who should be mentioned as making an appearance are Quintus Mucius Scaevola, lawyer, consul, and arch-enemy of Scipio, and Lucius Cornelius Lentulus Lupus, the stern and harsh judge and leader of the Senate in 131 B.C.

The subject matter of Lucilius' *Satires* can only be described as vastly miscellaneous. Marriage and women turn up frequently, while philosophy and food are also favorite topics. Love and friendship are discussed, as are law, religion, and household affairs. Lucilius more than once criticizes greed, extravagance, ambition, pride, and drunkenness, and expresses himself in no uncertain terms about money-lending and the senatorial abuse of privilege. Literary matters also take up a good deal of his time. Here he not only passes judgment on the work of writers like Pacuvius and Accius, but he also discusses orthography and literary-critical matters in general.

This wealth of character and subject matter proves Lucilius to have been a keen observer and an intelligent and witty critic of the world around him. But it also shows something else about him, as Quintilian and other ancient writers observed. The rhetorician found in Lucilian satire what he called a "marvellous erudition" (10.1.94). Indeed, even in the few topics mentioned above there is an astonishing breadth of interest and knowledge which embraces subjects extending all the way from law, senatorial procedure, and international affairs through philosophy, medicine, and history to the proper spelling of Latin and the price of grain on the market in Rome.

Lucilius' "marvellous erudition" resulted not only from an eager interest in the world around him, but also from wide reading and careful study of ancient literature. The names of a host of earlier writers and thinkers appear in the fragments, ranging from Homer and Archilochus on the Greek side to Naevius, Ennius, and Accius in Latin. Influences have been traced from these as well as from Aesop, the Sophists, Aristophanes, Pherecrates, Demosthenes, Plato, Aristotle, Menander, Euclides Socraticus, Callimachus, Bion and the Stoic-Cynic diatribe, Panaetius, the laws of the Twelve Tables, mime, Plautus, Terence, Caecilius, and many others.

It should be pointed out in passing that Lucilius treats character and subject matter with striking individuality. His views on philosophy and literature reveal this most clearly. While he shows himself to be aware of Epicurean, Stoic, Cynic, and Academic doctrines, especially in matters of physics and ethics, the fragments leave the impression that his personal philosophy was an eclecticism flavored by Stoicism and developed under the influence of the practical thinking of the Hellenistic philosophers.

In his literary judgments, too, Lucilius was apparently no blind follower of anyone. Though his theories cannot be reconstructed in any detail from what is left of his writings, the fact that he parodies Homer and Euripides, criticizes Ennius and Pacuvius, and takes issue with his contemporary Accius on matters of style and orthography reveals him as an independent thinker who recognized the value of originality and the need for change. It should perhaps be added that he had a reputation in antiquity for having brought literary criticism to Rome.

Reinforcing the widely miscellaneous subject matter is the great variety of form that the satirist used. Lecture or diatribe, letter, dialogue, farce, philosophical discussion, autobiography, anecdote, mock-epic, travelogue, polemic, literary essay, and fable, as well as scenes from history, comedy, the courtroom, and the banquet, all appear at one time or another. Other satires are simply narrative and miscellaneous poems containing a number of unrelated themes or topics loosely strung together.

Although it is impossible to reconstruct any single satire with confidence, it is worth looking at a few whose fragments are extensive enough to suggest at least hypothetical reconstructions. Perhaps the best known and appreciated of Lucilius' *Satires* in antiquity was the *Council of the Gods,* which was a long poem making up Book 1 of the *Satires* (5-52). Here the poet in mock-heroic fashion describes a meeting of the gods to decide the fate of the notorious Lucius Cornelius Lentulus Lupus after his death in the mid 120's B.C. Lupus, who had been consul in 156, censor in 147, and had become president of the Senate in 131, was a leading patrician of the time, a stern judge, and a strong opponent of the Scipionic party in Rome.

The fragments suggest that in atmosphere and development the *Council* was not unlike Seneca's *Apocolocyntosis* which will be discussed briefly in a later chapter. It began apparently with a statement to the effect that the gods have been called together to deal with the most important affairs of humans. They have been specifically commissioned to look into methods of preserving Rome and its people for at least a little while longer. Presumably Jupiter presided, though no words can be certainly attributed to him.

In the opening speech of the prosecution there may have been mention of the miserable condition of men, money-grasping soldiers, the tavern with its bad reputation, and the influence of eastern societies on Rome with their softness that undermines as it insinuates itself into Roman society like a sickness. An immediate result of this influence may be seen in the fact that the Romans are losing the good, old Latin vocabulary as Greek replaces it. It has been suggested that Romulus as the promoter of custom and tradition utters these words, but no matter who the speaker is, there is a delightful irony in the fact that as he gives examples of Greek vocabulary that should be avoided he cannot help using other Greek words (*porro, semnos, anti*) to make his point (15-16).

How all this fits with an investigation of Lupus' activities, it is difficult to say. It is at least possible, however, that Lupus fostered

such influence and is being criticized for it. It is tempting to hear
Romulus in another fragment speaking as a newcomer to these
divine deliberations (20-22), where the heavy rhetorical flavor gives a
special irony to what he is saying, since such sophistication hardly
goes back to the beginnings of Rome.

Also part of the prosecution is a reference in metaphoric language
to the "storm" of Lupus' activities and a plea, perhaps to Jupiter, to
put down the storm. It is impossible to know who spoke these lines,
but they would easily serve as part of a witty and clever rebuttal
offered to Neptune who certainly participated in the deliberations.
Apollo also took part, and it may have been he who pointed out the
Romans' propensity for calling all their leading gods "father." At
some point in the deliberations he is accosted by a person or god who
questions the value of his power of divination.

It is possible, then, to reconstruct this poem, at least in broad
outline, and there can be no doubt that it was powerful satire. The
form is meant to poke fun at the council theme that had been used
seriously in epic by Naevius and Ennius, among others, while the
satire as a whole is a parody of a meeting of the Senate. Within it,
besides Lupus and his habits, many facets of contemporary life
come in for ridicule and criticism: religion and superstition, useless
pursuits, praise of the "good old days," rhetorical affectation,
philosophy, and the creeping influence from the east.

Equally interesting is the mock-trial that made up the second
book of the *Satires* (53-93). This was a humorous treatment of the
famous legal action brought by the Epicurean Titus Albucius in 119
B.C. against the Stoic Quintus Mucius Scaevola for misgovernment
in Asia during his praetorship there two years earlier. There was
evidently an introduction in which Lucilius informed his audience
that he wanted to tell a tale that had often been heard, and this
was followed by presentations from both sides. Albucius spoke first,
and enough of his speech has been preserved to show a strong and at
times violent attack. Scaevola is accused of killing a man and of
generally immoral conduct. He has robbed and pillaged others, even
taking a woman-friend's garments from her wardrobe. This may have
led to an obscene handling of his sexual affairs. His lusting after boys
and his gluttony round out the charges brought against him. Albucius
seems also to have commented sarcastically on Scaevola's legal
ability. Finally, there is a statement from the prosecutor's strongly
worded peroration that has been preserved: "I do not say 'he may

win his case'; rather let him wander a homeless exile and a man without any rights."

The rebuttal of Scaevola is a similar mixture of fact and personal attack. He takes exception to the meticulous oratory of Albucius with its Greek words and its imprint of Greek rhetoric, reminding him with a sneer that he himself has Crassus, a fine orator, as a son-in-law. Albucius' Grecomania is evidently one of the reasons for the strong enmity between them, and at this point Scaevola becomes quite explicit:

> Albucius, you preferred to be called a Greek rather than a Roman and a Sabine, a fellow-citizen of Pontius and Tritanus, of centurions and standard bearers, outstanding men and men of the first rank. And so when you approached me in Athens when I was praetor I addressed you in Greek as you preferred. *"Chaere,* my Titus," I say. And my lictors, my whole troop and chorus [chime in with] *"Chaere,* Titus." This is the reason why Albucius is both public and private enemy number one for me. (87-93)

Scaevola also answered the actual charges by attacking Hostilius, Catax, and Manlius who were either witnesses or informers against him. As to the alleged murder, he says that Hortensius and Postumius, who appear to have been voluntary witnesses or else representatives of the officials who had investigated the charges, found the wrong man in the casket. What part Nomentanus played in the proceedings it is impossible to say, though some believe that he was on trial with Scaevola.

It is not clear from the fragments where Lucilius' sympathies lay. If this satire was the inspiration for Horace's piece on Rupilius Rex and Persius, then it may be that the satirist participated as a story-teller only, with the idea of poking fun at both of the principals. In any case, Lucilius uses the poem for comic satire of a number of subjects: leading personalities, the judicial system, abuses of provincial government, thieving, immorality, gluttony, Hellenomania.

The single satire that made up Book 3 (94-148) was an account of a journey that Lucilius made to southern Italy and Sicily, addressed, perhaps in the form of a letter, to a friend. The reason for the trip is not clear, but it is likely that the satirist intended to inspect his land holdings which lay in that direction. Some idea of what the poem was like may be gained from comparing it with Horace's description of his journey to Brundisium, though the latter poem was probably not as long.

The trip as far as Capua was by road which was at times wet and muddy, but at other times both good and bad:

> But these things were mere play there, and everything was just up and down. They were up and down, I say, and everything was fun and games. But when we got near the boundary of Setia, that was hard work—mountains that [even] the goats had abandoned, all of them Etnas and rough and rugged Athoses. (102-05)

While staying at Capua, Lucilius and his entourage view a gladiatorial contest. One of the combatants, a creature from Bovillae, has teeth that make him look like a rhinoceros, while there are other references to the strength of one of them and to the doubtful circumstances of someone's birth. Of the description of the battle itself only meager traces remain.

From Capua Lucilius takes to the sea with Puteoli his point of embarkation and Messana or Regium as his destination. His course may be traced past the promontory of Minerva (the modern Cape Campanella), through Salernum, Portus Alburnus, and by Cape Palinurus. A little later the travelers witness an eruption, perhaps in the Lipari islands.

One series of fragments from this satire (123-39) provides a glimpse of Lucilius and his companions putting up at an inn for the night where the landlady, who apparently is Syrian, after putting on her shoes in the best mock-tragic manner, sets her slaves to work splitting firewood. The meal is a simple one, for there are no delicacies, but this does not stop the travelers from drinking a lot of wine and paying the penalty later. Presumably they get some sleep, since another fragment shows Lucilius bellowing for his slaves in the morning.

The form and subject matter of this satire are fairly straightforward with Lucilius recounting his journey in witty diary fashion. As in Horace's poem on the journey to Brundisium, the satire was probably light and informal, being loosely attached to and secondary to the narrative. The towns and characters that appear along the way—the two gladiators, for example—and the travelers themselves apparently provided most of the material for satiric commentary.

For a number of satires Lucilius chose a banquet setting. Sometimes the meal is simply a means of motivating a discussion on a number of topics. But in at least two cases Lucilius satirizes the banquet itself and the host who presides. One of these is the supposedly fine entertainment given by the rough, unsophisticated soldier, Troginus, which appears in Book 30 (1019-37). Here Lucilius is out to burlesque the whole idea of refined banqueting, and he does so with vigor.

The tone of the satire was evidently set early with mention of the fact that Troginus was known as "Beer Mug" (*calix*) throughout the camp. His furniture is something to behold! There is only one couch, and it is so old and dilapidated that it is held together with rope. Its coverlets are threadbare, and the table nearby is not only too small, but it also has legs that are rotten. The guests suit these surroundings. The prostitutes Lamia and Bitto are there "with their teeth whetted," and are described as being gluttonous, old, dishonest, and stupid. They also smell of the barnyard. Another guest who fits well in this atmosphere is the babbling boor from the country, who is seen joining in the conversation as everyone prattles on. Perhaps it was here that the alcoholic Troginus came out with a mock-heroic and not very pithy remark about the dangers of overdrinking.

As the night wore on, the two bawds apparently offered their favors to the guests and received rather vulgar, though surely not unexpected, rejoinders from their prospective clients. There is a hint in one line that the drinking may have gotten out of hand and ended in a brawl.

This poem is a delightful *tour de force,* clearly anticipating pieces like Horace's banquet of Nasidienus. The satire is so transparent that there is no need to examine it in any detail. It is worth pointing out, however, that lying behind this burlesque is a serious criticism of the greed and gluttony of the times.

Other satires contain a less than witty approach. One of these is to be found in Book 30 where love and marriage are the theme (1093-1110). Lucilius tells first how a man, caught in the hunting net of a woman, has provided her with a gift of jewelry. As might be expected, things do not go smoothly after they are married, and the household falls to pieces, presumably through the wife's negligence.

Finally, things get to the point where the husband has to leave in an attempt to make a new fortune. He returns at the first opportunity out of longing for his wife, but is not let into the house, since everyone is certain that he is long dead and gone. After becoming coarse and abusive, he must finally have made his point, for his wife embraces him and soothes him with words of love. Presumably the cycle now begins again, and at this point Lucilius may have ended his tale with a sardonic laugh at the gullible husband. Marriage and women play a large part in Lucilius' *Satires* and, as here, the poet was quick to outline the problems caused by both. Some of his best invective involves women.

Another satire written in a serious mood is that which made up Book 19 and dealt with the Cynic-Stoic idea of contentment with one's lot in life (584-94). Lucilius began by discussing discontent, apparently insisting, among other things, that everyone suffers from this malady. This is true, in spite of the advice of the gods that we concentrate on the day that is good and replace present misery with thoughts of that. It is because we cannot take this advice that the gods must warn us to put aside our childish ways, ways which even old men follow when they are pursuing profit. Instead of always striving after things that are useless, painful, or even harmful, we should, perhaps like the ant, gather up only what we need and will use.

And yet there are men characterized by avarice who never have enough and so play the fool; they debate between money and people and decide that money is more important. The philosopher, on the other hand, and the right-thinking man by implication choose people and so choose correctly. Lucilius ends on a light note with the assertion that he does not want to go on raving like the tragic actor who spoiled his Orestes because he became hoarse.

The connection in theme with Horace's first satire is obvious and suggests that this satire, like the later one, was developed in a diatribe form. It is also worth noticing that Lucilius seems to have ended this, and presumably other serious poems, with a light and flippant remark, thus adding a satiric touch that was adopted by Horace in many of his satires.

These attempts to reconstruct a few of the satires of Lucilius, imperfect though the results may be, combine with the impression left by the rest of the fragments to show that in form and in content Lucilian satire was of nearly unlimited variety. He had inherited from Ennius a form that was essentially miscellaneous, and he proceeded to develop this as an aspect of his satirical writing that was almost as important as the criticism found in it.

The Satiric Element

Even a cursory glance at the remains of the *Satires* leaves the distinct impression that censure and criticism pervaded them. Lucilius' literary successors, satirists and nonsatirists alike, mention this first when they speak about his poetry. In a letter to Cicero, written in 44 B.C., Trebonius makes reference to Lucilius' *libertas* or "frank outspokenness." Quintilian also mentions this after pointing to the poet's "marvelous erudition" and then goes on to suggest that this frankness was the source of a certain bitterness or harshness as well as an abundant wit. Other writers may put it in different ways, but what they say amounts to the same thing. Horace, for example, describes Lucilius as the first to draw away the pelt under which a man hides himself and his ugly acts. As he did this, Horace goes on to say, he "took to task the leaders of the people and the people themselves, tribe-by-tribe." A little later, Persius with typical hyperbole speaks of him cutting up—or perhaps "hacking up" is better— the city and describes him as breaking his jaw on characters like Lupus and Scaevola. Juvenal insists that Lucilius enjoyed a freedom to write whatever came into his "burning mind" and extends the metaphor a few lines later when he says he was on fire and raged around "as if with his sword drawn."

These later writers have simplified the situation to a large extent by concentrating on one aspect of Lucilius' satiric technique. It is not fair to Lucilius, however, to stress his use of invective to the exclusion of everything else. Actually, the criticism in the *Satires* took many different forms, depending on the content. Whole poems seem to have been filled with serious attack from beginning to end, while in other cases the criticism was probably limited to isolated passages or contained in a pointed word or vivid epithet. At the same time, the satire that is found in the remains is wide-ranging. There is relatively matter-of-fact narrative criticism and comment, moral judgment and warning, parody and burlesque, and what might be called out-and-out rebuke and strong invective. A look at each of these is necessary for a full appreciation of Lucilius' purposes and achievements.

Perhaps the mildest form of commentary indulged in by Lucilius is the straightforward, narrative statement that appears fairly frequently in the *Satires*. One of the best examples of this is to be found in the poem on orthography in Book 9 (366-410). The purpose here was mainly explication, since the poem was written to set things straight as far as Latin spelling was concerned. There are satirical overtones, however, in Lucilius' admonition to his reader that he need not worry about whether to write *accurrere* or *adcurrere* and in his observation that the other man does not know the real difference in meaning between *poesis* (an extended poem) and *poema* (a short poem or a passage from a long poem).

This kind of low-key satire is present again in Book 26 when Lucilius advises Congus against writing history (689-719). There is the implication in some of these fragments that the satirist is addressing him as a friend. But even at that, Lucilius does not hesitate to tell the younger writer that he finds his purposes quite displeasing and that he himself tries to avoid what Congus wishes to achieve. He evidently made an attempt to show the young man where he was going wrong and then went on to tell him to undertake something that might bring him praise and other rewards.

Finally, there is the letter in Book 5 in which Lucilius chides a friend for not coming to see him when he is sick in bed (186-99). He comes close to rebuking him outright, but controls his temper and maintains his veneer of urbanity, preferring to make his point by underlining the fact that another visitor, perhaps a friend named Fannius, did not forget him.

The fragments which take the form of moral judgment and warning and which for this reason may also be called philosophic and didactic, leave quite a different impression from the narrative type of satire just mentioned, though they are of about the same intensity. Lucilius' discussion of how a friend is to choose a woman (910-28) falls into this category. The poet, after criticizing him for his attitude to married women and questioning him closely on how he would behave with a virgin, went on to advise his friend to choose a prostitute for his purposes. Though the fragments are sparse, there can be no doubt that questions of morality were discussed rather thoroughly in this satire with the satirist criticizing the attitudes of the other man and offering him advice.

The same kind of moderate moral satire is present in the poem which concludes Book 29 (962-73). Criticism of lust and cupidity brings the observation that "cupidity is removed from a lustful person, but not lust from a fool." There are further didactic implications in what appears to be at least part of the moral of the story: "When you've come to recognize this, then go ahead and live out your life without worry." The atmosphere here is similar to that of the diatribe satires of Horace.

The same is true of the fragments of the satire in Book 19 (584-94) in which Lucilius discussed contentment with one's way of life. The satirist deplores the fact that for a fool nothing is enough, even though he may own the whole world. At another point he seems to have put the choice of money or man to his protagonist, evidently by way of criticizing the other's discontent and greed. Finally, there is the recommendation that a man, perhaps like the proverbial mouse, store his provisions against a hard winter. In all of this there is clear anticipation of the kind of low key moral criticism and advice that Horace offers in his first three satires.

As a final example of this kind of satiric commentary, Lucilius' sceptical attitude to superstition might be mentioned. The fragment which best illustrates this evidently comes from a satire in which the poet is praising philosophy:

> This fellow trembles at these things—the bugbears and the witches that our Fauns and Numa Pompiliuses instituted—and he takes them all very seriously. Just as infant children are convinced that all bronze statues are living and human, so those people think nightmares are real and they are certain that there is a heart inside bronze statues. These are just picture galleries, nothing true, everything imagined. (524-29)

The criticism here is quiet and the mood didactic. After pointing to the superstition of certain people, Lucilius precisely and concisely makes his point in the last sentence. Nothing more need be said.

When he used parody and burlesque for his satiric purposes, Lucilius was appealing to that facet of Roman literary taste which had made the broadly humorous farce and mime so popular. The unit of parody might be the complete poem, such as the *Council of the Gods* and the trial between Scaevola and Albucius, where criticism and entertainment were carefully combined by the satirist. Falling into the same category is the description of the gladiatorial contest that appears in Book 4 (172-85). This was a celebrated battle between the two heroes of the arena, Aeserninus and Pacideianus, which was perhaps held at the funeral games of the Flacci about 140 B.C. Exaggeration sets the mood as Aeserninus is described as a dirty, mean fellow and his opponent becomes "by far the best gladiator who had ever lived since man's beginnings." The broad humor that pervades this satire may be glimpsed in Pacideianus' account of how he will fight. First he is going to take a blow or two from Aeserninus, but then he will run his adversary through with his sword. It sounds as if he may be preparing himself psychologically for the contest which is imminent. This is a broad treatment of low characters and subject matter, not unlike the account of Troginus' banquet discussed earlier.

The satires which take the form of scenes from comedy show another dimension of Lucilius' use of parody and burlesque. The attack on a house in Book 29 (937-48) may have been a whole satire or just one of a number of episodes in a poem. Here Gnatho, perhaps modelled after the character in Terence's comedy, *The Eunuch,* leads the attackers to battle. In mock-heroic tones one participant announces that he is going to wreck the hinges "with crowbar and axe of double bit." It may be this same character, who, when asked his name, parodies a line of the *Odyssey* by insisting that he is "Noman" (940). The besieged make their appearance throwing pots and pans on the heads of the attackers. A large part of the burlesque in this poem was surely literary, as the parody of epic in general and Homer in particular shows. It is tempting as well to see a broadside directed at Terence, for the kind of humor that is present here is good-natured, rollicking, and Plautine, showing none of the restraint that is typical of Terentian comedy.

There is a lot of literary parody in the fragments—too much to cover here in detail. While apparently striking out at tragedy and comedy, Lucilius speaks of "a sad person from some complicated prologue of Pacuvius" (879). Again, the frequent direct quotation from the tragedies of Pacuvius that appear in a satire in Book 26 suggests that this poem was filled with such parody.

The impression that other fragments leave is that subtle and not so subtle literary allusion appeared incidentally in the *Satires* as well. Lucilius mentions an aged Tiresias, for example, coughing in the hall before entering to partake of a rustic meal (228-29). The epic overtones are also unmistakable in the description of the tenacity of the bore who has accosted Scipio on the street (262-63): "whom neither bulls born and bred in the mountains of Lucania working in a team could drag away with their strong shoulders." Finally, Lucilius uses a kind of personal parody when he criticizes Caecilius' broad, rustic accent by calling him "a rustic pretor" (232) and when he imitates Albucius' Grecized Latin by using his own brand of Latinized Greek (84-86).

The rebuke that Lucilius offers ranges from mild to stinging, and it often overlaps with the other kinds of satire that have been mentioned. The relatively moderate reprimand of a friend who did not visit the poet when he was sick in bed and that directed against Congus for choosing to write history have already been discussed as part of a narrative criticism in the *Satires*. Again, there is the indirect rebuke of a Syrophoenician for eagerly going after money (540-41). A note of reproach is present in Lucilius' voice as he warns the man who has tendencies towards anger to keep his hands off women (855-56). And there can be no doubt about the satirist's direct approach when he lashes out at someone for dancing with Greek effeminates (33) or when he pointedly tells Gallonius, the glutton, that he does not really know how to eat well (203-05). Elsewhere he censures men for bringing trouble down on their heads by getting married (644-45), and in the same satire he rebukes women, apparently for their grasping ways (642-43).

In view of the fact that rebuke seems to blend so often into other kinds of satire—the narrative, didactic, and invective—it may be argued that it is wrong to identify it as a separate kind of criticism. Perhaps this is so. But the important part that such direct, personal reprimand plays in Lucilian satire demands that it at least be singled out for special mention.

It was the outspoken criticism, the Lucilian invective, that caught the eye of later literary critics, and it was this that satirists like Persius and Juvenal used to justify their indignant and often angry outbursts at the vices which they encountered in contemporary society. Whether any of the satires took the form of sustained invective, it is impossible to say. But if the frequency of serious censure, vituperative attack, and out-and-out abuse in the fragments is any indication, then it is entirely possible that major portions of some satires were filled with it. The remains are full of epithets that are at the same time insulting and abusive. There are idiots, clowns, stupid rustics, depraved individuals, a slippery character out on bail, a madman cracked in the head, an old, foolish sophist, and an unfaithful, depraved household and foul home. Troginus' guests, Lamia and Bitto, "the stupid, old, dishonest lady gluttons," have already been mentioned.

Obscenities and obscene pictures are also used as attack or negative characterization. A gladiator's mother did not bear him, but dumped him out (111). Twice a woman engaged in intercourse is described as winnowing grain with her buttocks (302, 361). Again, a man hacks off his testicles out of spite against a woman, perhaps his wife (303-05). Nomentanus is told by Albucius to go to hell (82).

By now it is clear that much of the invective in Lucilian satire is of a personal nature. Now and then it is the frank expression of an opinion involving a group of people or type of person, as when Lucilius insists that an overcoat, a gelding, a slave, or a straw hat is more useful to him than a philosopher (507-08). The same mood is present in his description of an unnamed light-fingered character in Book 28 (846-47): "He'll grab everything with his dirty hands; he'll carry everything off—everything, believe you me! He'll cart off all the things, and violently, too." Even more to the point is the satirist's description of an agent of some kind, whose name has not survived (652-53): "He's a thick-skinned freedman Syrian in person and a crook with whom I change my skin and everything else, too." There is also the praetor who is "gutting" him (501-02). Lucilius even turns this kind of frank personal censure against himself when he has his critic in Book 30 accuse him of setting traps and behaving like a scorpion with his tail raised to attack.

But Lucilius' invective is most pointed and most devastating when it is directed at specific people. In the case of Caecilius, the satirist twists a spelling (*pretor* for *praetor*) and links two seemingly incompatible words (*rusticus* and *praetor*) to put this "rustic pretor" down for his countryfied accent. He also goes on to warn people not to look at the "beak" and feet of this praetor designate (232, 233-34). In his attack on Lupus in Book 28, Lucilius seems to be more subdued, but the passage in which the poet describes the retaliation that Lupus will take against the man who does not appear in court (805-11) shows that outspoken attack was almost certainly part of the satire.

One of the most effective and informative pieces of invective in the *Satires* is the criticism of Albucius that Lucilius puts in Scaevola's mouth in Book 2 (87-93). This has already been quoted and so need not be repeated here. Lucilius' censure of this lawyer's Hellenomania comes from the heart, for the satirist was a strong promoter of what was Roman. The mood of this passage is patentlysardonic and sarcastic, and the heavy spondees which predominate in the first three and a half lines help to create this impression. Here a neat contrast is set up between what is Greek and what is Roman with the latter receiving more emphasis, as might be expected. At this point the invective becomes layered, for Scaevola uses a sarcastic tone of voice to recount his sarcastic reception of Albucius in Athens. The final declaration of hostility is at the same time simple, straightforward, and hard-hitting. Albucius is laid low, and with this pointed remark the whole passage becomes an epigram with a sting in its tail.

If the impression left by the fragments is correct, then the long satire which made up Book 11 (424-54) would appear to have been filled with invective. In form, this poem was a series of anecdotes about well-known people. Though only thirty lines have survived, these are enough to show a wide variety of personal attack. The wicked Asellus attacks Scipio's house; a praetor calls Scipio "dirty-faced" because he has thrown out all of the camp followers "like dung." Again, Lucius Cotta is described as an old man, a conman, and thoroughly venal, inclined to pay no one what he owes him. He may be the person referred to in the next few lines as a paramour, a crook out on bail, and a brawling, hard-faced, wicked cowboy-type.

And then there is Gaius Cassius, who is described as a laborer, pickpocket, and thief. Lucilius says he is called Cephalo, which is presumably a Greek translation of Cassius' cognomen Capito and is meant to convey the meaning "bighead." This man's association with the informer Quintus Tullius also clearly brands him as a person of less than savory character.

The reference to Quintus Opimius in another fragment is also loaded with insult. He is snidely called "father of the Jugurthine," where there is a reference to his son's being bribed by the Numidian Jugurtha, the arch enemy of Rome in this period. Lucilius goes on to describe Opimius as "beautiful but bad," pointing out grudgingly that he has become better as he has become older.

What has been said is perhaps enough to show that Lucilius' satires were shot through with brilliant, outspoken censure. It was effective all of the time, but was most effective when Lucilius was naming names. Horace, Persius, and Juvenal apparently thought so, too, for they respected Lucilius for this and adopted the technique in their own satires.

Before leaving the criticism and censure that is so important a part of Lucilian satire, two points demand at least some attention. The satirist's use of irony should not be overlooked, since it appears so frequently in the remains. At the same time, something must be said about Lucilius' wit, not only because it too appears frequently, but also because people like Cicero and Horace felt that it was an important aspect of Lucilian satire.

The Greeks and Romans fully appreciated the effective use of irony, and Lucilius employed it to good advantage for his satiric purposes. He used it in conjunction with all the degrees of satire already mentioned. It might appear in a single word characterizing contemporaries, as when the poet speaks of "the revered Metelli" (637), a family that he certainly disliked. It is an integral part of parody and burlesque as well. The gladiator described as "the finest on earth since the appearance of man" has already been mentioned. There is also Lucilius' burlesque of Albucius' style:

> How delightfully are his words arranged, all of them
> cleverly like the little dice in a pavement and mosaic
> with an intricate wormlike pattern! (84-86)

The exclamation is itself ironic, and within this the sarcastic use of adverbs and Greek words as well as a general style that is supposed to imitate Albucius' preciousness leave no doubt about the mood. The line which follows these contains a further ironic slap at Albucius' Grecizing in the Greek word *rhetoricoterus* which Lucilius uses to designate Albucius, "the orator *par excellence.*"

A final passage in which irony and invective are combined is worth quoting at length:

> But now, right from morning to night, on holidays and
> workdays, all the people and together with them the
> Senators run energetically around the Forum, never
> leaving it. They've all devoted themselves to one and the
> same art—cheating as carefully as they can, fighting
> treacherously, vying in flattery, each one pretending
> he's a good man, and setting ambushes as if they're all
> enemies to each other. (1145-51)

In this case, the irony seems to tone down the attack, while the metaphoric language from military activity makes the criticism all the more pointed.

The irony which has been considered so briefly here was part of the wit that Cicero, Horace, and Quintilian admired in the satires of Lucilius. Cicero describes the satirist as very witty and includes him among the old Romans noted for their urbane wit. Quintilian says that he showed an abundant wit which came from his erudition. Horace calls Lucilius clever and genial and witty and says he rubbed down the city with a great deal of salty humor. When these observations are put together, they strongly suggest that cleverness and wit were an integral part of his satire.

It is not surprising that such refined humor should appear as a characteristic of poetry that was basically irreverent. Indeed, the very essence of much of the satire discussed above is a certain cleverness and wit. One need only think of Troginus' banquet or the scenes from comedy, the relatively light-hearted treatment of the august gathering in the *Council of the Gods,* and the informal and quiet humor of the journey to southern Italy and Sicily, to recognize the wide scope and the importance of sophisticated humor in Lucilian satire. To these may be added many incidental occurrences—the joke involving sex, the clever use of literary allusion, especially the mock-heroic and mock-tragic, smart plays upon words or upon character. These are but a few of the ways in which Lucilius' sense of humor manifests itself in the *Satires,* and it was this kind of thing which people like Cicero and Horace had in mind when they called him urbane.

Style

A careful look at the verse, diction, and figurative language that appear in the fragments indicates that part of Lucilius' purpose as he wrote must have been to develop an appropriate vehicle for the great variety of subject matter that he wanted to present. The first four books of his *Satires* show that he began in the Ennian tradition by using a variety of meters. But, as with the other hallmarks of satire, Lucilius could not accept this one without questioning it. Actually, his use of miscellaneous meters appears to have been largely experimental, for the poet moves from trochaics in Books 26 and 27 through trochaics, iambics, and dactylic hexameters in Books 28 and 29 to the exclusive use of hexameters in Book 30 and the rest of the

Satires. By 123 B.C., then, Lucilius had decided on the verse form that best fitted his satiric purposes.

Why he chose the dactylic hexameter it is difficult to say. Probably he found it to be a relatively flexible form and well suited to the mixture of narrative, informal comment, and direct quotation that filled the *Satires.* In some ways the choice was a bold one, for the most common and significant use of this meter to Lucilius' time was in epic, which was a far different kind of poetry from satire. Lucilius had to adapt the hexameter, then, to make it a properly informal vehicle for his loose and easygoing poetry.

He achieved this informality in a number of ways. Perhaps the most striking characteristic of Lucilian verse is the frequent elision that occurs in almost every line. This slurring together of a final vowel of one word and the beginning vowel of the next evidently was meant to simulate the slurring of words that is a natural part of everyday speech. Most lines have at least one elision, while many have three and four. The colloquial effect is heightened by the eliding of monosyllables, usually conjunctions and pronouns. Elision did not occur nearly as often in epic verse, and Lucilius' mock-epic lines with their minimum of elision show that he was fully conscious of this difference.

The caesura, or main pause, that is expected in each dactylic line occurs most frequently in the third foot, which is normal for the hexameter. At the same time, however, there is enough variation to suggest once again the freedom that the poetic environment of satire demands. Now and then there is no significant pause in a line, while at other times an elision in the third foot tends to bridge the gap and counterbalance the caesura. In at least one instance two consecutive lines have a caesura in each foot, with the caesuras of both lines corresponding exactly. This reinforces the repetition that is present in the vocabulary and thought of the passage.

The unit of sense is usually one or two lines, though now and then the satirist or his speaker will ramble on through three or four lines before completing the thought. It is difficult to say anything significant about the enjambment, since there are few fragments of any length. From time to time, however, there seems to be a conscious attempt to create a colloquial feeling. In one instance (1050-51) a monosyllabic conjunction is put at the end of one line following the verb it governs and the noun that is object of the verb appears at the beginning of the next line completing the sentence and the sense. A variation of this enjambment which achieves much the same effect consists of a conjunction at the end of one line and the clause it governs in the next.

Informality is also aided by the words Lucilius uses to begin and end the line. The monosyllables which appear fairly frequently at the beginning tend to produce a choppy effect. As far as the end of the line is concerned, the Romans recognized early that the more stately epic hexameter demanded words of two or three syllables to conclude it. Lucilius seems to have used monosyllables at this point frequently enough to keep his reader aware that this was not heroic poetry. He was not afraid either to use words of four, five, or even six syllables to conclude a line. This too set his hexameter off from that of epic.

The language of the *Satires* reflects the great variety of subject matter. At the one extreme are tragic, heroic, and lyric elements and at the other the slang and colloquial speech of the streets and camp. The poet seems also to have made up words to achieve the proper effect.

Lucilius' use of Greek is quite striking. He at times quotes it directly and at other times Latinizes it before he puts it to use. Here, too, the range is wide with technical philosophical vocabulary standing side by side with that from the tavern and brothel. In many of the fragments it is difficult to see how the Greek suits the context, although in others, such as Scaevola's criticism of Albucius' Helleno-mania, the effectiveness of it is quite apparent. Recent studies indicate that the frequency of Greek words in the fragments is about average for these times, so that Horace's criticism of Lucilius for what he considers to be an excessive use of Greek must be taken as an opinion based on later, Augustan standards.

The way in which Lucilius put his words together shows him to be a master poet. The puns and other word-play, the alliteration, asyndeton, hyperbole, and metaphor, to name only a few of the figures he uses, help bridge the gap between colloquial speech and formal poetry and make the *Satires* the unique literary creation that they are supposed to be.

But Lucilius was not without his faults, as Horace's well-known criticisms of his style show. The later satirist's views on Lucilius' Grecizing are actually just part of a feeling on Horace's part that his predecessor had written too much and that what he wrote was undisciplined and murky. If the *Satires* were better preserved, it would be easier to judge Horace's criticism. But the simple fact that Lucilius wrote thirty books, while Horace wrote only two is an indication of two different approaches to writing satire.

There are a number of passages that may represent the kind of thing that Horace could not accept. The fragment on virtue (1196-1208) with its uninspired and rambling style could perhaps have been improved if, in the words of Horace, Lucilius had cut away everything that was unnecessary and had spent some time scratching his head, chewing his nails, and using his eraser. But even more difficult for an Augustan to accept would be the seven lines addressed to Penelope in Book 17 (567-73), where the preponderance of long, heavy Greek words, the repetition of *m*'s and *n*'s, the rather harsh alliteration in the first line, the aside in lines four and five, the piling up of nouns in the last line, and the excessive elisions in the second and sixth lines produce a style that could be fairly described as murky and muddy.

There are other shorter passages scattered throughout the fragments that also appear overdone. The obvious repetition in the description of the journey to Setia quoted earlier (102-05), seven verbs strung together in a line and a half to describe the toilet of a prostitute (296-97), and the long verbs of similar sound used one after the other to describe the grasping nature of a woman (640-41) have no parallels in Horace's *Satires* and could easily be the kind of thing he is criticizing.

And yet it must be remembered that, pointed and important though his criticism may be, Horace is quick to put it in the proper perspective. In fact, this is his reason for returning to this point in the last satire of Book 1. Lucilius accomplished important things in satire—so important that Horace called him the discoverer of the genre. And he *was* the discoverer, inasmuch as he took in hand what was essentially a miscellaneous and personal kind of poetry and, while developing the element of variety and the role of the poet, gave it a clearer identity by focusing on the critical element and molding the dactylic hexameter to serve as the vehicle of expression. In this way he set the artistic balance between discipline and freedom that marks all Roman satire.

III

VARRO AND MENIPPEAN SATIRE

It is almost impossible to know where and when Menippean satire, that strange medley of prose and verse, originated. It may have had its beginnings in Greek folk literature or it may have come from a Semitic source. There is also the possibility that it was an independent creation of Menippus, a Hellenized Syrian of the third century B.C., after whom it was subsequently named. Wherever it came from, Menippus was apparently the first to use this form, and it is unfortunate that, except for a few allusions to content, there are no remains of the thirteen books that he wrote. We do know, however, that, while he was not a member of the Cynic sect, this writer used his satire to promote Cynic ideas and to attack other philosophers, especially the Stoics. Menippus' satiric approach has been described as seriocomic, simply because he combined the serious and the humorous to make the moral point of what he was saying more palatable and attractive to his audience.

A number of later writers, both Greek and Roman, adopted Menippus' form and techniques, and it is from these that our impression of the genre comes. The first to use these methods at Rome was Marcus Terentius Varro (c. 116-27 B.C.), who produced approximately 150 books of *Menippean Satires.* Born north of Rome at Reate, he seems to have been of equestrian stock. His family was wealthy enough to have him educated at Rome and later at Athens, which made him the first of the satirists to have received part of his education in Greece. Little is known of his personal life, though it may be assumed that he was raised in relatively moderate circum-

53

stances and was exposed to the strong moral and religious views of
the Sabines.

While he was not a professional politician, Varro was active in
affairs of state and served in various offices at Rome, rising as high
as praetor. In the late 50's and early 40's he took Pompey's side in
the struggle for power and after Pompey's death made his peace with
Caesar who subsequently appointed him head of the public library
that was planned for the city. When Caesar was assassinated, Varro,
like so many others, was proscribed by Mark Antony. He was
eventually taken off the proscription list, but not before he had
lost his villa and his books.

His literary production was so extensive that it is difficult to
assess or even categorize everything he wrote. In antiquity it was
said that by the time he was 78 years old Varro had written
"seventy times seven" books, and in fact he may have produced as
many as 74 different works in some 620 books. He seems to have
written on subjects as widely different as meteorology and education and to have treated topics from history, ethnography, mathematics, astronomy, and philosophy. In addition to his technical
writing Varro also made purely literary contributions with his
poems, speeches, and Menippeans. Unfortunately, his once volu-
minous writings are now for the most part in fragments, with his
treatise on farming and sections of his study of the Latin language
being the only works preserved anywhere near intact.

As was the case with Lucilius, most of the fragments of Varro's
Menippean Satires have survived as quotations in the treatise of the
fourth century grammarian Nonius. What is extant are 94 titles and
some 600 fragments. It is possible, then, to make general observations about the satires, although it is all but impossible to reconstruct
any individual satire with any confidence.

Varro seems to have written his Menippeans between 80 and 67
B.C., well before most of his learned works and at a time when he
was most active in military and public affairs. The satires, which in
number of books made up almost a fourth of his total literary production, were first published separately and were later gathered
together by the author under the title *Menippean Satires*. Apparently,
by calling them satires Varro intended to put them in the miscel-
laneous-critical tradition of Ennius and Lucilius and by labelling
them Menippean he meant to associate this kind of writing with the

prosimetric form which to the Roman mind was both older than verse satire and quite different from it.

It is important to realize that Varro was the first to designate this form of writing Menippean; earlier it had been known simply as Cynic satire. By using this term Varro was underlining a spiritual kinship that he felt existed between Menippus and himself by virtue of the fact that, like his predecessor, he too was using the so-called Cynic method of attacking men's moral faults in a witty fashion.

In view of the condition of the remains, it is fortunate that Cicero has defined and explained the content and purpose of the Menippeans. In the *Academics* (1.4-9) he says that up to 45 B.C. Varro had not written any formal philosophical works in Latin because educated men preferred to read contemplative philosophy in Greek. By using Menippus as his literary model and aiming at the less educated, Varro instead chose to put philosophy on a popular level by dealing with serious subjects in a light and witty fashion. Cicero goes on to say that none of this was to provide a complete philosophical education, but it was meant to stimulate people's thinking about moral problems.

The details of style, subject matter, and satiric method that may be gleaned from the fragments bear out what Cicero has to say. The most characteristic feature of this literary form is the mixture of prose and verse in which the poetic passages are inserted into a framework of prose. In the case of Menippus himself, the poetry was probably limited to parodies of Homer and the tragedians and was put in iambic and dactylic meters. Varro, however, did not feel restricted by his model, for in addition to the traditional meters available to a writer of Latin verse—dactylic hexameters and iambic senarii, for example—he made use of meters like the glyconic and ionic which had only recently been successfully adapted to the Latin language. In all, he seems to have used at least ten different verse forms.

It is almost impossible to know with any certainty precisely how the poetry was used. Some poetic passages seem to have introduced a topic which was then restated in prose, while others appear to be repetitions and summaries of prose passages that immediately preceded them. For the most part, however, the fragments suggest an indiscriminate use of poetry. Sometimes, for example, a character simply speaks in verse for no apparent reason, as in a fragment from *The Lyre Listening Ass,* where the introductory phrase is in prose and the quotation in anapaestic verse (359): "He began to scold and said: 'You know these things and you make them commonplace and practice a useless art.'"

On occasion, the poetry is used to exemplify a literary point. This is the case with a fragment of the *Double Marcus* which was a discussion of figures of speech (50): "As the buoyant water spider skitters across the cold pond ...." This trochaic line was apparently meant to be an example of a simile. Again, *The Lyre Listening Ass* opened with an iambic prologue delivered by Phonascia, the personification of voice teachers. Verse is also used for such things as typical comments about beautiful women and to reproduce the marching song of soldiers.

While it is difficult to account for the appearance of poetry in any given instance, the various levels of style are quite apparent in the fragments. The mock-heroic seems to have had an important part, and the lines from Varro's *On Suicide* which echo a passage of Ennius may be taken as typical:

> What should I say you are, who with savage hand
> open your body's bursting lakes of
> boiling blood and with iron sword
> release yourself from life? (405)

Parodies of dramatic passages are not uncommon, as the stork simile from *The Slave of Marcus* shows:

> But we, shipwrecked and fallen like storks
> whose wings the blaze of lightning has
> scorched, sorrowfully fell from on high
> to earth. (272)

On the other hand, some of the poetry is purely, but elegantly, descriptive (390): "The tall lotus-tree is cut down, the lofty crown of Pallas crashes...." Finally, there are lines that reflect relatively normal conversation and simple, straightforward narrative. The examples that are preserved, then, show that Varro was a master of Latin verse, both modern and traditional, and that he understood the ethos of the various meters.

Varro's prose displays the same control of style and the same rich variety as his poetry. At one time it may be full of the complexities of the Asianic style, while at another it is simple, straightforward, and Attic. Sometimes Varro imitates another writer, as when he attempts to recreate the unique style of Sisenna, a contemporary historian:

> Mr. Pretty Shoes orders for himself a mistress fine as nectar and Tarentine wax, which Milesian bees gather and make from all the flowers, without bone and sinews, without hide, without hair, exceedingly pure, ample, resplendent, soft, lovely. (432)

Legal idiom and formulas are also to be found (543): "If any one son or more be born in ten months, if they be insensitive to music, let them be disinherited." Varro also employs proverbial expressions to add color (539): ". . . and he has men worried because they fear him more than a fuller fears the screech owl." These are but a few of the instances which might be cited to show that Varro not only used prose effectively in any given instance, but also wrote in a variety of styles to achieve the miscellaneous effect that he wanted.

This effect was reinforced by the diction and figures of speech that he employs. Like Lucilius, Varro draws his Latin vocabulary from almost every social level. Moreover, Greek words appear frequently and may well reflect the admixture of Greek in common speech. Nor does the satirist shy away from archaisms, neologisms, and words formed by analogy, but even goes so far as to coin new Latin words from Greek roots. Again, as in Lucilian satire, most figures of speech appear, with the less formal ones like punning and alliteration having a prominent part to play.

Using this loose prosimetric format, Varro treats a broad spectrum of subject matter that is both traditional and novel. This is illustrated best by the titles which have been preserved. Some have philosophical overtones: *Know Yourself, The Socratic Hercules, The Battle of the Goats: On Pleasure, I've Got You: On Fortune.* Others take the form of proverbial expressions: *The Pot Finds its Top: On Married People, You Don't Know What Late Evening May Bring, Second Childhood, He Flees Far Who Flees His Own.* Still others seem to involve characters that are comical or provoking: *The Blind Gladiator, Three Phallused: On Being a Man, Old Fed and Ready Fit to Fight.* The influence of dramatic subject matter is reflected in titles like *Oedipothyestes* and *The Furies.*

One group of titles shows the author capitalizing on the fact that in popular and derogatory etymologizing the word "Cynic" was connected with the Greek root for "dog." The result is a series of dog titles, such as *The Cynic, The Dog Teachings, The Dog Judge,* and *Beware of the Dog.* In some the stem is compounded with another to form an ambiguous title which reflects a typically Cynic humor. One of these is *The Water Drinking Dog* which can also be taken as *The Dog That Waters.*

The fragments themselves also show Varro's far-reaching interests and the wide range of his subject matter. Gluttony, envy, ambition, luxury, dishonesty in government, foreign superstition and the old Roman religion, sexual excesses of youth, and the disintegration of patriotism are among the problems discussed. Other subjects range all the way from a practical treatment of child-rearing to religious and philosophical discussions involving the surveillance of men's activities by divine beings and the propriety of suicide. Varro also includes literary taste, aesthetics, and music among his topics.

While the development of the individual satires must have varied with the subject matter, it would seem that most fell into two general classes. One group, which may have had enough direct quotation to be called narrated dialogues, was made up of narrative moralizing often related in the first person. The other kind were in essence didactic essays, closely resembling diatribe in form, content, and frequent use of an adversary.

The settings of the individual pieces show great variety, for Varro not only made use of the situations traditionally available to the satirist, but he also created many that were new and unique. Of those which he inherited from his satiric predecessors the banquet scene is quite common. *The Funeral Repast of Menippus* and *The Endymions* both fall into this category. The latter satire is enlivened by the appearance of a divine being in a whirlwind who tells of how men's actions are scrutinized from above.

But Varro with his rich imagination conjures up many other scenes and situations as well. In the *Double Marcus* he seems to have a discussion, if not a debate, with his other self on a subject involving matters of literary criticism. *The Furies* is a story told of the adventures of a sane man as he wanders among fools. At least part of the dramatic setting of the *On Suicide* is, appropriately enough, the underworld, where famous suicides like Hannibal are interviewed. Some satires, such as *The Sexagenarian* and *Ulysses and a Half,* apparently showed Varro himself moving about in Rome and

outside the city as well. Finally, at least one satire involved a flight
through the sky.

It is all but impossible to reconstruct a Menippean with any confidence. There are, however, a few indications of structure. If the
fragments are to be trusted, then the internal arrangement of each
satire seems to have been carefully worked out. There are transitional
markers like "first," "next," "finally," and "I now come to . . ."
which indicate changes of subject or action. In the case of the satire
titled *You Don't Know What Late Evening May Bring,* Varro used a
fourfold arrangement consisting of people, places, times, and things.
This perhaps anticipates his fourfold division of subject matter—who,
where, when, what—which he used in some of his technical writings.

Perhaps at this point a reconstruction of one satire, hypothetical
though it may be, will give some indication of what a Menippean was
like and at the same time will show a few of the problems that must
be faced in dealing with such scanty remains. There are a number of
fragments of *The Sexagenarian* (485-505) which suggest at least a ten-
tative reconstruction. Most of the story is narrated in the first person
by Varro, who, like a Roman Rip Van Winkle, has fallen asleep for
fifty years. When he opens his eyes, he discovers first that he himself has changed:

> He looked at himself and found out about himself. When he had
> first fallen asleep he was as smooth-headed as Socrates. Now he
> had become a baldpated, hoary bristled hedgehog—with a snout,
> too.

After this prose description, he upbraids himself in poetry: "Oh
foolish sleep of my watchful heart! You who took me as a beardless
boy!" Now he returns to the city to discover that it too has changed:
"When I returned to Rome I came across nothing there which I left
behind when I fell asleep fifty years before."

He apparently wanders about the city elaborating on the sad way
things have changed. He complains that "Where they used to have
elections then, now there is a market place" and points as well to
social changes that he finds unpalatable: ". . . in those days modest
men lived in Rome moderately and without taint; now we are in
upheaval." His criticism extends to what he calls "the foreigners—
Ungodliness, Falsehood, and Lewdness," to "the greedy judge who
kept thinking the accused was a *lucky find,*" and to people who

behave and think in a selfish manner: "What the laws demand they do not do. Everybody is completely eager *'to give in order to get.'*"

Eventually the people grow tired of the old man's perpetual complaining and his insistence that "the good old days" were better, and one of them tells him so in no uncertain terms: "You are wrong, Marcus . . . to attack us while you muse on old rubbish." This fellow, or someone else from the group, warns Varro: "We have been summoned to throw you off the bridge." And they do just that, for "He had scarcely spoken when, according to the custom of our ancestors, and without being asked, they grabbed him and threw him off the bridge and into the Tiber." The irony and humor in the ending stems from the fact that there was a time-honored annual religious ritual in which an old man was actually cast from a bridge. And so Varro's complaints of how things have degenerated are vividly disproved, much to the author's discomfort, by his being included in one of the old rituals which was still practiced.

Some of the remaining fragments are difficult to place in the satire, but are interesting enough to consider by themselves. One seems to have come from a context in which luxury or extravagance was being discussed: "If you had bought a four-footed mare to mate with my Reatine ass, would you have given me as much as I demanded for a stud fee?" There is also a simile, perhaps from a discussion of how children are raised: ". . . in the same way a dog grows from a pup, in the same way a kernel of grain springs from the stalk." Another colorful poetic passage containing many compound words must be quoted for its remarkable style:

> . . . and not where in the dark of night you
> follow by torchlight the feather-shaking,
> oar-footed, boxwood-pale-beaked ducks like
> cattle in the marshes. (489)

Finally, a line of poetry with a feeling of urgency and excitement in it may be related to these lines: "He is here, he is here with a torch enveloped in flame."

The Sexagenarian is a particularly good choice for reconstruction, since its fragments illustrate a number of the more important features of Varro's satiric technique. Perhaps what strikes the reader first is the author's witty and lighthearted approach to topics that are really quite serious. This humor appears to a greater or lesser degree throughout the remains of the Menippeans. A flute player from Thebes, for example, flows like a bubbling spring, while in another fragment a Roman matron spins away at her wool, keeping her eyes on the porridge so that it does not boil over. Again, someone heads dauntlessly for the underworld to question Hannibal and other famous suicides. Women in hunting costumes with buttocks bared, a comic slave with a "begoated" brow, thirty Jupiters without heads, and Infamia or Miss Disrepute with her hair in disarray, all appear at one time or another. There is even speculation as to whether the round Stoic god has a head or foreskin. Finally, mention must be made of the fragment in which Varro or one of his characters insists that a surfeit of gourmandizers has virtually done away with Rome's supply of thrushes and fat "fig-pickers."

One of the more common devices of argumentation that Varro uses is what might be called the then-now dichotomy, in which the good old days of the past are contrasted with the less healthy contemporary situation. Frequently adverbs of time are used to underline the comparison. "Then," for example, women lived a simple life and tended to their housework, but "now" they refuse even to accept the womanly role of childbearing. At times the contemporary part of the contrast may be lost or implied. Slaves "then" were put in their place if they misbehaved, the implication being, presumably, that "now" they rise up in revolt. Several whole satires, among them *The Sexagenarian* and *The Old Man Teaches,* were based on this dichotomy and were developed with this balance of past and present in mind.

At times there is no temporal word, and the contrast is simply implied. Numa is reincarnated to participate as an informed onlooker in one fragment (537): "If King Numa were to see these things happening, he would know that neither a trace nor a vestige of his ordinances remain." In much the same way, Varro often makes the very Roman appeal to "the custom of our ancestors" or to "our forefathers." In the *Double Marcus* he says (63): "Our grandfathers and ancestors, although their words smelled of garlic and onion, were noble fellows in spite of it." In *The Old Man Teaches* there is an appeal to the simplicity of the Roman of bygone days (186): "How often did the old-time country-dwelling Roman shave his beard between market days?"

Another important characteristic of Varro's approach to satire is what might be called the realistic nature of his criticism. It is always to the point and related to a Roman situation. This is per-

haps to be expected of a writer whose most important contribution
to the thinking of the time involved a systematic approach to things
Roman. In this respect he differs significantly from his model,
Menippus.

Varro does not, like a moral philosopher or diatribist, attack
luxury, greed, and similar faults as general and universal failings.
Rather, he attacks specifics such as the importation of sumptuous
foods from abroad, corruption in elections, dishonest behavior among
politicians, and bad taste in clothing. But none of his satire is finally
negative; besides offering criticism, he offers a cure. For he believes
that a return to simplicity and to the ways of the past can change
and correct the wrongs and evils of contemporary society.

Finally, there is the personality of the satirist which, as in verse
satire, is an integral part of Varro's Menippeans. This device of
speaking in the first person convinces the reader that the author is to
be believed and heeded. At times Varro simply uses it for effect as
in the *Double Marcus,* where he discusses literary figures with his
other self. In other satires, however, such as *The Furies, Ulysses and
a Half,* and *The Sexagenarian,* he speaks in the first person to relieve
the reader of the onus of criticism. He makes himself part of the
situation or actually sets himself up as the comical object of the bad
behavior being censured.

In view of what has been said about the philosophical overtones
and the moral and popular orientation of the Menippeans, it is
natural to speculate about Varro's personal philosophical beliefs.
When the remains of all of his writings are taken into account,
Varro appears to have been a thoroughgoing eclectic. As he turned
to write his formal philosophical works late in his life, he seems
to have felt that all philosophies differ only in terms of what they
consider to be the supreme good.

In the satires there are references to many philosophers. The
Cynics are mentioned by name and their ideas are alluded to in
many titles. In spite of these references, Varro was in no way an
adherent of Cynic ideas to the exclusion of others. Stoic philosophers
are named, and the Stoic wise man is ridiculed. Among the other
philosophers mentioned by name are Carneades, Democritus, Epi-
curus, Aristotle, Heraclides, and Empedocles. At times these thinkers
and their ideas are treated sympathetically, while at other times they
seem to be the objects of Varro's satire.

It can safely be said that Varro borrowed from any philosophical school of thought that he felt offered healthy and helpful approaches to solving the moral problems that the satirist was treating. He even went so far as to pay attention to physics, which was never very popular among the Romans, since it was a tool that could be used to attack superstition. Casuistry and pedantry were, however, rejected outright and exposed in satires like *Shadow-boxing: On Delusion* and *The Furies*. Varro was essentially a moralist, then, not a dogmatist, looking for any ethical direction which could have a salutary effect on his Roman contemporaries in a period marked by a general upheaval of society and its values.

There remains the question of why Varro wrote his *Menippean Satires* and what he meant their function to be. There is no good reason not to believe Cicero when he says that the satirist intended these writings to serve as a means of presenting much needed moral enlightenment in an attractive and palatable way. To accomplish this, Varro deserted the stern and serious approach of the philosophers and the personal invective of verse satire as Lucilius had written it and sugar-coated the moral truths that he was presenting with a light-hearted, witty approach that at times verged on sheer exuberance. Perhaps some pieces were written for their entertainment value alone; it is difficult to say. But in the Menippeans as a whole it is clear that by turning to the genre that had come from Menippus as a medium to spread ethical thought, Varro was attempting a new approach to contemporary problems. The satires were meant, then, to be a response to a need for moral direction in trying times, and they came from a man who was at heart a patriot and one who sincerely wanted the best for his country and his fellow Romans.

IV

THE DISCIPLINED SATIRE OF HORACE

With Horace (65-8 B.C.) we come to a writer whose *Satires* have been preserved intact, so that it is at last possible to see Roman verse satire in all its facets. Born at Venusia in the province of Apulia in southern Italy, Horace came to Rome at about the age of ten. Accompanying him was his freedman father who was apparently concerned that his son receive a good education. Not a great deal more is known about this period of Horace's life, though it is probable that he was exposed to the training in grammar and rhetoric that was normally enjoyed by young men of high rank only.

After a period of study in Athens, Horace joined the army of Caesar's assassin, Brutus, and served his losing cause at the Battle of Philippi in 42 B.C. In the meantime his father died and his family property was confiscated. As a result, Horace began working as a scribe assisting the Roman magistrate in charge of finances and public documents, after he returned to Rome.

When Horace began writing poetry it is difficult to say, but upon his return to Rome after Philippi he apparently kept company with various young poets of the day. One of these, the epic poet Vergil, introduced him to Maecenas, Augustus' unofficial minister of culture, who eventually brought him into his circle of friends. The fact that he now had a patron assured Horace of financial security, and, because of Maecenas' connections, it was just a matter of time until the poet was introduced to the emperor Augustus. Sometime afterwards Maecenas gave Horace his Sabine farm, a piece of land which was a source of great personal joy to him, as references in his later writings show.

Other useful personal details are few and far between. Horace never mentions any of his family except his father; he seems never to have married. As far as physical appearance is concerned, the poet admits to being short in stature and prematurely gray. It is perhaps worth pointing out as background for the *Satires* that he describes himself as irascible, but easily mollified. Horace died on November 27, 8 B.C. and was buried on the Esquiline Hill in Rome near his patron Maecenas.

Horace began his career with his *Epodes* and *Satires* which were probably written simultaneously. The *Satires* were published first, however, with the first book appearing about 35 B.C. and the second some five years later. The *Epodes,* which also appeared in 30 B.C., are a collection of iambics, modelled spiritually and metrically on Archilochus and full of the invective that was part of the satiric tradition.

The first three books of the *Odes,* which appeared about six years later, were a significant departure from Horace's earlier writing. These short poems, in which the poet adapted Greek lyric meters to Latin verse, were the climax of the artistic development of the lyric poem in Latin literature, and it is on these that Horace's fame for the most part rests.

The *Epistles* represent Horace's last new literary direction. At the same time, they are reminiscent of the *Satires,* and the poet himself points to the connection between them when he refers to both as "talks" or "conversations" (*sermones*). Apparently, once he had mastered the artistic competence necessary to produce the *Odes,* Horace felt the need to return to the moral problems that had preoccupied him in the *Satires.* But he did not return to satire. He chose instead the epistle form, which resembled satire in its easygoing narrative form and diction and in its hexameter verse, but which actually allowed the poet to take a more positive and less Lucilian view of the world he was describing.

Book One

The individual satires of the first book do not appear in the order in which they were written, but are arranged with some purposeful imbalance to suggest the relaxed course of cultivated conversation. The subjects flow from three diatribe satires to a fourth poem in which Horace expresses some of his artistic and moral ideas about the genre. In Satire 5, which is a description of a journey with friends to Brundisium, there is a dramatic change in tone, for here Horace's autobiographical persona is introduced in a lighthearted way along with an account of his relationship with his famous friends.

This personal emphasis continues in Satire 6, where the subject is a defense of the poet's relationship with Maecenas which also in effect serves as a rededication of the second half of the book. Satires 7, 8, and 9 balance the first three, inasmuch as they form a unit that may be designated "entertainments," just as the others were diatribes. The tenth satire, the last in the book, is a poetic self-defense which in a sense is an expansion of Horace's arguments in the fourth satire.

Other explanations for the arrangement of the poems are of course possible, so that it is perhaps best not to press the relationships suggested above. Most people will agree, however, that there is a studied informality in this first book.

The Diatribes (1.1, 1.2, 1.3)

The first three satires are diatribes, that is, literary adaptations of the Cynic-Stoic sermon form popularized by Bion the Borysthenite who lived in the third century B.C. In its literary transformation in the hands of the Latin writers the diatribe assumes a thoroughly Roman character. It tends to be specific rather than general in content, aimed as it is at definite vices and people. Moreover, it for the most part involves Roman situations. When the diatribes are examined closely it is clear that their themes are to a large extent drawn from the store of popular philosophical topics employed by the earlier street preachers and philosophers.

Some of the common marks of the diatribe as it is used by the satirist are coarse language, a tangential approach to the subject, examples from history, epic, comedy, and everyday life, sketches, illustrative scenes, and vignettes. Quite prominent is the use of an "adversary," fictive or real, to whom the satirist directs questions, charges, and comments which may or may not demand an answer.

Horace's first satire is programmatic only by implication, for he does not cite the varied themes he will pursue or lash out at vices that motivate his satiric verse. Instead, he begins the collection with an undatable poem, the form and theme of which set the standard for much of what follows. Its length is comfortable for the reader and contrasts sharply with the extremes represented by some of the later satires. While varying the tone in a smooth and polished way, the poet paradigmatically shows what is to come as he probes the follies and vices of human social behavior and "tells the truth with a smile."

The question with which Horace opens the satire not only motivates the discussion, but also serves to dedicate the collection to his patron Maecenas. There follows a series of examples of discontent which, the poet suggests, is caused by love of money and avarice. It is typical of Horace's satiric technique that in the major part of the poem he uses a digression to make his point (41-105), which he sums up (106-07): "There is a Middle Way in things; there are in fact certain fixed boundaries on either side of which uprightness cannot take a position."

At this point the satirist returns to the original question of discontent. Now, however, the cause is greed which makes men strive and compete unhappily, although an Epicurean contentment can be found by accepting life, just as a guest accepts what is offered at a banquet. Because he feels that he has said enough and does not want to chatter on like the hack Stoic Crispinus, Horace at this point brings the satire to an end.

In his second satire Horace considers the problem of adultery and the satisfaction of pleasure. He begins with what seems to be a pompous eulogy of the recently deceased singer Tigellius, but it soon becomes clear that Horace is out not to praise, but to criticize this fellow's extravagance. From here the topic shifts to other extremes of behavior such as pathological fear and extravagant parsimony. After still another shift to other enormities of conduct, the direction of the discussion is made clear in typical diatribe fashion with an anonymous participant suddenly asking a question (23): "What is this concerned with?" Horace replies by summarizing the moral of the story: "It's that while fools avoid one vice, they run into its opposite." After a few more examples, the point is made through a negation of the Golden Mean that "There is no middle ground."

Now that the problem has been established as one of excess in every direction, Horace gives force to his argument by concentrating on examples that are sexual and personal and by noting behavioral extremes. Finally, he suggests a simple solution to everything. Physical desire, as he sees it, is the originator of the problem, and if we look at the situation carefully, it is soon obvious that the whole problem amounts to nothing more than a need to satisfy physical urges which are at the same time necessary and pleasurable. The solution offered, then, is both healthy and typical of Roman peasant morality. The satire closes with a comic re-emphasis of the perils of adultery which Horace avoids by consorting with freed-women.

The third satire, on the commonplace of fault-finding, falls naturally into two sections. The first part (1-75) begins with a discussion of the uncontrollable inconsistency of the singer Tigellius. As in the preceding satire, however, Horace shifts his theme at a point where the reader might expect a general discussion of inconsistency and turns to the problem of leniency towards the faults of friends, especially their inconsistencies. Those who criticize others while ignoring their own faults deserve, and in fact receive, criticism. The best procedure, then, is to weigh virtues against faults while remembering our own failings.

In the second section (76-142) the poet proceeds to a more general discussion of the nature of the problem. The subject is still leniency towards the faults of others, but now Horace investigates the intellectual basis for being angry with a friend out of proportion to his misdeeds. In this context there comes to mind the absurd Stoic moral saw that "all sins are equal," which if left unquestioned could undermine friendship which means so much to Horace.

By way of refutation, the poet turns to the Epicurean explanation of the origins of social justice, according to which utility is the mother of justice and right. Given this reasoning, it is absurd to punish a temple robber and a petty thief with the same penalty. Instead, Horace proposes a sensible alternative for dealing with wrongdoing (117-19): "Let there be a rule to give just punishment to crimes, so that a person does not lash what deserves to be caned." The only person absurd enough to act counter to this is the much touted Stoic sage, who is not only an object of ridicule, but is also virtually friendless. Horace, on the other hand, who is the diametric opposite of the sage, is rich and blessed in friends because he puts up with their shortcomings.

In all three of these satires Horace has used the techniques established by Lucilius. Perhaps the most striking of these is the habit of satirizing by name, although unlike his predecessor, Horace generally restricts himself to names of people who are insignificant or non-existent. He may do this because of his questionable social status, but it is more likely that it comes from personal preference.

While the approach in these three poems is obviously that of the diatribist, Horace is first and foremost a satirist. He takes advantage of this to ironically undercut himself from time to time. While he starts out in the first satire much like a Cynic-Stoic preacher, with elements of other philosophies freely mixed in, he soon turns to the Peripatetic Middle Way or Golden Mean in this and the second satire. Satires 1 and 3, however, conclude on an Epicurean note with the poet rejecting the absurdities of Stoic practitioners and some of their doctrine. And so the lashing preacher reverses himself and embraces a doctrine of quietude when common sense demands it.

After leaving these poems, Horace never turned to the pure diatribe form again. It appears that these were among his earliest efforts at satire, and after successfully proving himself with them he deliberately went on to other varieties of satiric expression. But the fact that he included these three poems in his collection and even put them at the beginning hints that he felt them to be an integral part of a satirist's store. As we shall see, diatribe does appear again in the second book of the *Satires,* but there it has been adapted by Horace to suit a particular satiric context.

Horace's Views On Satire (1.4, 1.10)

Horace wrote the fourth satire of the first book to express a number of his artistic and moral ideas about the genre itself, and ultimately to defend himself against some of his critics. Their criticism was probably based on his ridiculing by name, for a line from the second satire (27) in which Horace censures individuals is quoted here (92).

The discussion opens with an exaggerated literary genealogy tracing Lucilius back to the writers of Greek Old Comedy. The common features demonstrating their reputed relationship are censure of moral failings, metrical composition, and humor. As Horace sees it, however, Lucilius falls short of perfection because his style is not sufficiently polished and because he wrote too much. The two problems are, of course, related. Although Lucilius is criticized on technical grounds, Horace cannot criticize his freedom of speech, for, after all, specific censure is the basis for his critical approach in his own first three satires.

Closely related to the problem of style is the literary level of satire. In terms of diction, it is much like New Comedy which differs from prose only in its being metrical. A verse of Horace or Lucilius, the poet claims with some facetiousness, is unlike one from a real poet like Ennius. This is readily apparent if their words are put in nonmetrical order, for the dismembered limbs of the real poet will show through. What Horace is establishing here, in spite of the combination of exaggeration and understatement, is the fact that in literary terms satire falls somewhere below epic.

Horace has been charged with deriving some kind of sadistic pleasure from hurting people, but he can only deny this and ask for the evidence. Regarding the charge that he speaks with frankness, the satirist has to admit it is true, but it is a habit that the best of fathers taught him when he was pointing out specific negative examples to be avoided by his son if he was to live frugally and without scandal when on his own. Accordingly, his criticisms may be onerous for those at whom they are directed, but in his satiric role the poet is a firm, well-meaning, corrective force for society. Generally speaking, then, Horace and Lucilius are in agreement on the moral nature of the genre.

As was probably to be expected, the followers of Lucilius attacked Horace for the criticism expressed in the fourth satire, in spite of the fact that he was himself an avowed follower of the earlier writer. And so Horace felt it necessary to write another satire, the tenth, to amplify his earlier remarks and define the various stylistic features necessary for good writing. Perhaps the most important part of this satire is the poet's succinct description of the characteristics of the good writer:

> You need to be brief so the thought moves along without
> verbally ensnarling itself and weighing down the wearied
> listener's ears. Moreover, you need to vary your style,
> making it now serious, frequently humorous, at another
> point sober like the orator's and poet's. At yet another
> time it should be like that of the witty man who
> reserves his energies and keeps them under careful
> control. Often humor cuts through problems better
> and more directly than seriousness. (9-15)

From Horace's point of view, Lucilius may have had his faults, but congeniality and wit are not lacking in him, especially when the undeveloped state of the genre is considered. And, besides, Horace does say that if Lucilius had written under the Augustan discipline he would have corrected the problems of composition that are evident in his satires. With this last observation Horace cleverly upholds his view of Lucilius' faults, while at the same time allowing for his excellence in the proper historical context. Horace now sums up his basic principle for good writing (72-73): "Erase often if you are going to write something worth rereading and don't strive to impress the masses."

While both of these satires are to be taken as serious literary criticism, it is important to remember that writing in defense of a literary form and criticizing literary antecedents are commonplaces among the Romans. As a matter of fact, Horace was simply following in the tradition of Lucilius, who may have been the one who brought literary criticism to Rome in the first place. Accordingly, the attacks which were supposed to have stimulated the writing of these literary defenses may not have been very severe or very numerous.

Moreover, we must be careful not to take Horace too seriously when he insists that satire is the only field left open to him or when he observes that satire is not poetry. As a matter of fact, after insisting in the fourth satire that this kind of writing is mere prose, Horace at the end of the poem threatens to attack his adversaries with the help of his fellow poets, thus clearly suggesting that he himself is a poet and that satire is poetry after all.

The Autobiographical Satires (1.5, 1.6)

Two highly personal satires are placed at the center of the first book, in both of which the first person of the satirist predominates as he explores his social situation in autobiographical fashion. By this method Horace responds to his personal critics, whoever they are, and at the same time is able to point to the personal element as an important aspect of verse satire.

As if to further explicate his defense of the genre which filled the fourth satire, Horace selects a theme and form for his fifth satire that are purposely gauged to underline the variety that characterizes this kind of writing. The journey to Brundisium has as its literary model Lucilius' journey to Sicily, a story line involving personal incidents, both pleasant and unpleasant, experienced while traveling south from Rome. But Horace uses Lucilius' account only in a general way, and, though he parallels it in some details, he produces a work which is really quite different from it.

The actual trip referred to took place in 38/37 B.C. when Octavian sent a party led by Maecenas to Brundisium to meet and make terms with Mark Antony. Though Maecenas' purpose was political, the entourage was made up mostly of literary people including Horace, who in his account plays down the political significance of the friendships involved and concentrates instead on the satiric possibilities of the trip. Accordingly, the poem is best appreciated as a story which affords a convenient continuum into which the poet can insert various pictures, sketches, and vignettes.

Analysis of the satire's structure contributes little to our understanding of the poem. Although subdivision based on days travelled and other such criteria is possible, this does not really lead anywhere. What is of greater literary interest and importance are the individual episodes described by Horace which, because they involve a wide variety of satiric material, give the poet ample opportunity to display his versatility.

Two themes seem to work their way through all of the episodes. One of these is the emphasis on friendship which moves the satirist to rhapsodize when Plotius, Varius, and Vergil join them (43-44): "How we embraced and how we rejoiced! Never in my mind would I compare anything to a delightful friend." In fact, the arrival or departure of any member of the group causes an emotional climax.

The other theme is that of self-satire which is woven throughout the poem, especially in the satirist's complaints of eye and stomach trouble. The whole episode of Horace in Apulia, his native region, which he may not even have seen since he was ten years old, opens with a heavy irony as he notes that the wind still blows hard and hot. Both humorous and deflating is his vain wait for an Apulian girl to keep her nighttime appointment with him. These are just a few of the examples of Horace's playful treatment of himself and his relations with the powerful and not so powerful of his day.

Satire 6 was apparently written as a rebuttal to the charges of anonymous jealous critics that Horace was using Maecenas to climb socially beyond his proper place. The satirist's reply takes the form of a very personal satire—ninety-four lines deal explicitly with Horace and his life—which, inasmuch as it is a poem of self-defense, is unusual in its extended use of diatribe techniques. The poem actually has a more general message: we should apply common sense in judging individual worth and question the aristocratic ethic with its emphasis on ancestry.

The position and content of this satire are integral to the overall arrangement of the book. As the sixth poem it begins the second half of Book 1, and the mention of Maecenas in the first line along with the verbal reminiscences of the opening verse of the first satire in effect rededicates the whole of the first book to Horace's patron. In content it fits neatly with the two preceding satires. The fourth is a defense of Horace's poetry, the fifth explores in an understated style Horace's relationship with the great men of his day, while the sixth is a defense of the poet and a eulogy of his patron.

After the introductory salute to Maecenas, the satire falls roughly into two halves. In the first section (1-44) the fact that Horace finds himself disparaged because of his friendship with Maecenas leads him to consider the problem of social and political ambition. He quickly shows that the accusations brought against him are groundless, for Maecenas chooses his close associates on the basis of their worth, and it was by this standard that Horace was admitted into his group of friends.

Then the poet turns to the second major idea: the reason for his having the personal qualities that attract Maecenas. The answer, of course, is simple—it all comes from the way he was brought up by his father. This is the source of his high moral character, and it is the reason why he can now live a life free from care and without many pressing duties. Actually, the two halves of the poem fit together in a hysteron-proteron relationship. Because of his upbringing Horace has the personal worth which ultimately brings him to the attention of Maecenas, who looks only to a man's character. Thus the Roman patron of noble ancestry and the freedman father from Venusia are equal in their influence on and importance to Horace's life; they have both helped make him what he is.

The Entertainments (1.7, 1.8, 1.9)

Since too much of any one thing, no matter how well it is done, can eventually overburden the reader, Horace places three satires which are notable primarily for their entertainment value after the more serious pieces. All three have vexatious people as their subject.

In the seventh satire, a mock-heroic clash of East and West takes place when Persius and Rupilius Rex meet in court. The dramatic date of this legal proceeding was 43/42 B.C., when Brutus was propraetor of Asia Minor and Horace was serving under him as a military tribune. If, as has been conjectured, the poem was written before 38 B.C., then it is one of the earliest satires.

In form and content the satire is fairly simple. Horace uses the first person to describe the lawsuit between these two very unpleasant people who have presented themselves to Brutus' court for a judgment. Though the poet spends much of his time describing how formidable and witty the two men are, he presents only a few relatively ineffective examples of their verbal skills. Only the pun of the drunken Persius is worth citing:

> By the great gods, Brutus, I beg you, since doing away
> with 'kings' is a family habit, why don't you murder
> this 'king'? Believe me, it's right up your line. (33-35)

The word *rex* ("king") is meant to refer to Rupilius, of course, but it is also meant to recall Brutus' part in the assassination of Julius Caesar, who was virtually a king, and to remind the reader of the relationship between this Brutus and his ancestor of the same name who had helped expel the kings from Rome. The complexity and ineptness of all of this make it a suitable climax to a poem in which the combatants leave the impression of being helpless, pompous fools.

The novel topic of the eighth satire is an attempt on Horace's part to vary his subject matter and at the same time to extend the range of satire. He has actually combined some of the standard elements of a *Priapeum,* that is, a poem about the god Priapus, with elements of a binding poem, of which the second idyll of the Greek poet Theocritus is a good example.

The humor of the whole thing is generated by the Priapus statue which tells the story in its own inimitable way. This ridiculous looking piece of figwood talks like an artifact from the Greek Anthology, as he cites the details of his origin and appearance. Not only is he long-winded, but he is incongruously epic in much of his diction as he describes the superstitious gyrations of the hags. Finally, out of sheer terror at what he sees, this "accidental" god is unable to prevent a tremendous noise from coming from between his figwood buttocks. The witches disappear, leaving wig and false teeth scattered about his feet. It seems that those who can call up the gods are unable to withstand a god's intestinal energy.

This satire should be taken as sheer entertainment. It is true that when he has finished Horace has ridiculed superstition and its trappings. But he hardly wants his reader to spend a lot of time analyzing the poem. The whole thing is a comic story with a surprising, almost blasphemous, ending.

The ninth is perhaps the most popular of Horace's *Satires*, not only because the problem dealt with is common to most people, but also because Horace treats it in a delightfully humorous way. Here, while he explains the character and habits of a persistent social climber, the poet at the same time pays tribute to Maecenas by describing their friendship in ideal terms. This is one of the most successful, if not the most successful, examples of Horace's use of autobiography.

The largest part of the satiric fun lies in the way the moral is presented. The sycophant comes under careful scrutiny, but the moral judgment is only implied as Horace encourages the reader to find amusement in his predicament as the unwilling and at times bemused object of the bore's attention.

The content of the satire is straightforward enough to need no detailed explanation. Horace is casually walking to a friend's house when he is unexpectedly accosted by a garrulous man he scarcely knows. It soon becomes clear that this fellow is not interested in Horace, but in Maecenas, and in the rest of the poem the satirist describes his efforts at getting rid of the character. In the end Horace escapes through divine intervention.

In structure the satire is essentially a drama in four acts. In the first three (1-20, 20-43, 43-74), the likelihood of Horace's escaping this man's grasp decreases to the point where he is in complete despair. There is even an abortive messenger scene in the third act when Horace reminds his friend Fuscus, who has happened by, that he has something to tell him, and Fuscus, seeing his dilemma, leaves the poet to his own devices. Horace's sudden escape in the final act comes about as a result of coincidence and divine intervention, as so often is the case in ancient drama.

The whole of the dramatic action is framed by physical contact. It begins with the pest seizing Horace's hand and ends with a plaintiff dragging Horace's malefactor off to court. There is even a little squeezing of Fuscus' arm in the third act which raises the question of whether Fuscus would have been more willing to come to Horace's aid if the latter had squeezed harder.

From time to time Horace hints at his indebtedness to Lucilius. Part of the opening line—"I was by chance walking"—seems to echo fragments from two different satires of Lucilius (258, 559), while the last part of the last verse—"in this way Apollo saved me"—also recalls a verse of the earlier satirist where a Homeric phrase is quoted in Greek (267). By using the same expression, but rendering it in Latin, Horace at the same time acknowledges Lucilius' work and yet criticizes him by implication for using Greek in a Latin poem.

Book Two

In contrast to Book 1, there are only eight satires here, which suggests that Horace is continuing the tradition of artistic variation. But as far as the number of lines is concerned, the two books are almost the same length. It does not seem possible that this symmetry could have been accidental.

The book falls naturally into two halves and shows more balance of form and content than Book 1. The second and sixth satires both have country settings, at least in part. Satires 3 and 7 are on Stoic topics, contain diatribes directed at Horace, and have comic endings, although the third satire stands out as being much the longer of the two. The fourth satire and the eighth satire have food in common, and the overdone Epicurean sympathies expressed here seem to balance the fun poked at the Stoics in three and seven.

Satire 1 continues the literary theme of the last satire in Book 1 and in form anticipates Satire 5, since both have a setting where one person asks for and receives advice from another in relatively rapid and informal dialogue. By way of contrast, however, the first has Horace's autobiographical persona, while in the fifth the satirist is completely absent. It should be pointed out that, as with the first book, more details of internal arrangement can be discovered and other groupings of the individual satires may be as cogent as that outlined above.

Since all the satires in Book 2, with the exception of the second, have a dialogue format, it has been suggested that Horace was here trying to put together a new type of satire based on the form of the philosophical dialogue. This opinion is strengthened by the fact that the introductions of Satires 2, 4, and 8 are similar to the opening sections of many of Plato's dialogues. A further indication of the philosophical intent is the Socratic irony that pervades the book.

Horace tends to be less the preacher now and more the object or observer of moral lessons. Some think that as he grew closer to Maecenas, and especially Augustus, it became less socially acceptable for him to attack or criticize in the first person. While this view has its interesting aspects, it seems more likely that Horace is altering his satiric approach as much out of a desire for artistic variation as from any social and political pressure. But, whatever changes in approach may characterize the second book, Horace is still writing very much in the tradition of Lucilius. His aim is still moralizing, and the satiric targets and objects of instruction remain human vices and bad behavior.

Two Consultations (2.1, 2.5)

Horace uses the dialogue technique twice in this book for what might be called mock-consultation. The similarity between these two satires ends with the form, however, for not only is the satirist himself present in the one and missing from the other, but the scenes and subject matter are also quite different. The first satire is a literary-critical study set in the present, while the fifth satire is basically socio-critical and is placed in a legendary setting.

Horace begins Book 2 by reopening questions about the nature of satire. He investigates the legal and moral problems encountered by the satirist by representing himself as conversing with Gaius Trebatius Testa, an eminent jurist of the time. By employing the figure of Trebatius Horace establishes a model that was to be used by Persius and Juvenal in their introductory poems. Both of the later writers present a fictive adversary who functions as a vulnerable foil as they discuss the motivation and ethics of the genre. Unlike his successors, however, Horace makes Trebatius a worthy adversary, thus giving the poem more liveliness and feeling. Trebatius is no straw man for Horace to knock down, but is rather a clever and intelligent opponent whose arguments Horace at times avoids only by purposefully misunderstanding them.

The charges which have been leveled at Horace form the occasion for the satire and for his seeking advice from Trebatius. These are, first, that Horace writes badly and, second, that he is too acid and goes beyond both the law of the genre and the law of Rome when he ridicules by name. The ever helpful Trebatius has a ready solution: stop writing, or at least write things that are socially acceptable. Under the present circumstances, the satirist is simply going to get into trouble for censuring people by name.

While Horace, of course, rejects the advice, it is the clearest statement we have of the objections that were being raised at this time against his satire. And yet his facetious defenses—he must write to avoid insomnia, frontier stock always strikes back in self-defense, nobody can complain about good poetry—prevent any overly serious interpretation of the poem. Like Lucilius, whose satiric directions he follows, Horace has lived with the great and is artistically and morally on safe ground. Accordingly, Trebatius at the end of the poem can only agree that there is no case against Horace.

If, as it is generally argued, this satire was written in 30 or 29 B.C., then it is the last of the *Satires*. And so it takes on a special importance from the fact that it tells us clearly where Horace stood literarily and socially when he turned from satire to work in the other genres. His quick dismissal of the criticism of the censorious aspects of his satire reveals a poet who is confident about his poetry and about his social position. The fact that he rejects this criticism in an offhand, joking manner and not in any sinister and serious way reinforces this impression. His confidence is shown as well in his willingness to equate himself with Lucilius, while readily admitting his own humble origins. In the ten years that have intervened since the first of the *Satires,* Horace has become secure as a poet and as a person. Accordingly, nagging complaints, bothersome people, and testy literary critics can be dismissed with a pun and a laugh.

In the fifth satire Horace rather incongruously has the Greek characters Ulysses and Tiresias discuss the Roman practice of legacy-seeking as a solution to the problem of acquiring wealth. The dialogue develops quite naturally with the underworld scene picking up where Book 11 of Homer's *Odyssey* leaves off. Ulysses, who has learned that he will return to Ithaca only after he has lost everything he owns, is in the process of consulting the prophet Tiresias to ascertain how he might regain his wealth. From this point on the satire becomes a blueprint and methodology for legacy hunters.

The technique used by Horace in this poem anticipates *The Art of Love* and the devices Ovid uses there to instruct the novice lover. In other words, it is as much a satiric treatment of didactic poetry as it is of anything else. The only element missing here is Ovid's claim to be teaching from experience, although Tiresias even approaches this by giving an example that occurred in his native Thebes before he died.

Once again, formal analysis of the poem is not necessary, except perhaps to point out that it divides generally into two sections. The first half (1-50) is mainly instruction in how one gets his name into a will as heir, while in the second half (51-110), particulars are given and difficulties are presented with hints on how to handle them.

The satiric humor of the poem lies, at least in part, in the anachronisms involved in shifting back and forth between a Greek and a Roman world. The poem begins in a Homeric atmosphere and then moves into a Roman social setting replete with household gods. After a brief backward reference to Ulysses' performance at Troy, the Roman world continues to be the scene of action until Ulysses is addressed by his patronymic. Then there is an abrupt shift from things Roman to things Greek when Tiresias suggests that Ulysses make use of the services of Penelope, his supposedly virtuous wife, to win over old woman chasers. This setting is continued as the seer recalls a bizarre incident from his native Thebes. The satire closes with Tiresias being called back to the dead by the Roman deity Proserpina.

The satiric touch is also to be found in the depreciation of the epic heroes. Ulysses was often portrayed in literature as a type of ideal man who has the resources to meet every situation. Here, however, not only does he put money above his social scruples, but he is also at a loss as to how to go about getting it. Perhaps even more amusing is the treatment of Penelope who, it is discovered, has remained faithful to Ulysses only because the suitors were not as interested in her as in their stomachs. If, however, she discovers the ease with which her body can bring in money from old men, she will be as firm and resolute in her newly found devotion to legacy-seeking as she was formerly in her chastity.

Country Scenes (2.2, 2.6)

The similarity between these two satires lies not so much in form as in content. Both present what is meant to be a sort of simple country wisdom coming directly from the mouths of rustics. In form, however, the earlier satire stands apart as a diatribe, or at least a monologue with some diatribe elements, while the sixth satire is a combination of two narratives.

In the second satire Horace recounts the words of the rustic Ofellus, who applies to gastronomic problems the standard of the Middle Way or the Golden Mean. This theme recalls the second satire of Book 1, where it occurred in connection with extremes of sexual behavior. As might well be expected of a homely country sage in the works of Horace, Ofellus' recommendations steer a middle course between the polarities of penuriousness and gluttonous prodigality. If this principle of the Golden Mean is followed, it will have a sort of insulating effect against the vagaries of life. The actual thoughts presented by the rustic are an interesting combination of restrained Epicurean sentiments and observations on gluttony and the frugal life that might have been expected from someone like Cicero, who was well educated in the various philosophies.

Two points must be made about this poem. In the first place, it appears that Horace is here foreshadowing devices and subject matter that he will use in the later satires. Damasippus and Davus in the Stoic satires, as we shall see, take essentially the same stance as Horace does in this poem when they insist that the wisdom they have to pass on is extremely important and worthwhile. The concern with food here clearly anticipates the subject matter of the Epicurean satires. It has been pointed out that the rustic philosopher appears again in the sixth satire.

It should also be noticed that the poem, in spite of its generally serious tone, has been put together on less than serious premises. Is it really possible, for instance, that Horace could recall in such detail these weighty observations that had been presented to him when he was a mere youth? Moreover, the skeptic might ask how a simple rustic could be so well acquainted with urban problems, moral philosophy, and Latin literature. When these details are noted, it can be seen how well this satire fits with the other satires in this book, most of which are based on preposterous circumstances.

Sometime around 30 B.C., after he had received the Sabine farm from Maecenas, Horace wrote Satire 6, in which he developed the contrast between the idyllic country life and the bustle of the city. The poem falls naturally into two halves. In the first section (1-76) Horace recounts the busy and harassing life that is characteristic of the city and contrasts it with the peace and quiet of his Sabine farm. The second half (77-117) is a rustic's treatment of the popular moral problem of blessedness in human life. Here the discussion is not developed in philosophical terms, as it was in the second satire of this book, but in the form of an old wives' tale which fits well in the mouth of a simple rustic.

But the artistic balance of this poem goes well beyond this. While the first half has the city as its subject, the second part contains the story of the mice in the country and then in the city. This episode also breaks in another way, for while he is himself attending a banquet, the rustic Cervius tells of the two banquets of the mice, thus neatly fitting two miniature banquets, so to speak, within a normal one.

There is also the parallel between Horace in city and country and the mice in city and country. But this symmetry is pleasingly disturbed by the facts, for the country mouse returns completely to his simple rustic ways, while Horace, the avowed country mouse, really loves the city and needs the two life styles to be truly happy.

In addition to this artistic balance, there is in the sixth satire what might be called an intellectual balance, and this is in many ways the climax of the *Satires*. Horace had spoken in his earlier satires of people who vacillated as far as preferences and goals were concerned. Here he shows himself resenting the city, but unable to find peace in the country alone. He has come to realize that the Middle Way can be applied in his particular case by balancing the complexity of one life form against the simplicity of the other. Accordingly, his moving back and forth between the two does not mean that he is vacillating, but rather that he has found for himself the peculiar form of balance which means personal happiness.

The Stoic Satires (2.3, 2.7)

When the diatribe form reappears in the third and seventh satires of the second book, it has undergone changes that make it a less austere satiric device. The popular wisdom is still there as subject matter, but the diatribe proper is encircled with dialogue. Moreover, Horace has become the adversary, not the preacher, and the tables have been turned with humorous results.

The popular wisdom that is presented in these two satires has a natural appeal for a satirist. In both poems Horace employs the Stoic teachings called "paradoxes" as texts for his sermon, that is, ethical truths which are contrary to popular opinion and are stated in a short, pithy form designed to shock the hearer. In the third satire the paradox is "all fools are mad," while in the seventh it involves the Stoic belief that "all fools are slaves." The fools, of course, are those who have not achieved total enlightenment through the Stoic philosophy, and it almost goes without saying that the universal category "all fools" includes Horace.

In both satires there is a preacher who lashes out at Horace from a rather strange tactical position. In the third it is Damasippus, antique dealer and former madman, who bursts uninvited upon Horace to convince him of his insanity. In the later satire it is the poet's slave, Davus, who takes advantage of the license of the Saturnalia to tell his master who the real slave is, at least in moral terms. In each satire, however, the quality of the wisdom has been altered by age and handling, for both Davus and Damasippus pass on to their victim tralatitious wisdom whose ancestry they cite, rather than something of their own composition.

As in the first three satires of Book 1, both of these poems end with a sort of joke. But here it involves the satirist's reassertion of self over his preachers, and in neither case does Horace stop the proceedings until the preachers begin to focus on his writing poetry as one indication of a morbid condition. It should also be noticed that each satire is heavily loaded with the commonplace devices of the popular preacher. The most frequent of these are the vignettes, pseudodialogue, rhetorical questions, and everyday speech. The purpose of the popular preacher is to use every means possible to prod, poke, teach, and convert, and both Damasippus and Davus maintained the tradition.

A question which must be asked about these two satires is whether Horace regards the paradoxes as serious moral truths. The nature of the characters that preach here—Damasippus the madman and Davus the past-present-future slave—seems to speak against a serious interpretation. So also might Horace's impatience with them at the end of the satires. But if, for instance, the discussion of avarice in Satire 3 is compared with the parallel discussion in

Satire 2 of Book 1 where Horace presumably is serious, the similarities indicate that while the truism in the mouth of Damasippus becomes bizarre and even ridiculous, a kernel of truth remains. The same can be said of Davus who puts together most of the already common Horatian themes, such as adultery, inconsistency, discontent, and gluttony, and now redirects them at Horace.

What happens in both of these satires, then, is that Horace tells the truth with an ironic grin that stretches from ear to ear. He had felt uncomfortable with the persona of the Cynic-Stoic preacher at the end of satires such as that which begins Book 1, although he wished to offer basically the same sort of moral truth. Now Horace can have his truth and feel comfortable at the same time. Diatribe and popular thought have thus become a truly useful tool, and the satirist is completely at ease with them when, as here, they are modified and qualified with irony.

The Epicurean Satires (2.4, 2.8)

As though he felt he had to provide equal time for competing philosophies, Horace follows each of the Stoic satires with a satire in which the popularized form of the Epicurean philosophy plays a dominant role. And once again he chooses the bizarre and outlandish aspects as part of his targets while leaving the possibility that the basic idea may be good. Unlike the Stoic satires, however, these two seem to be serial; that is, Satire 4 shows how to prepare a meal or banquet, and Satire 8 shows what a disaster it is when it is given.

In the fourth satire, Horace stands in the background while someone else, in this case Catius, does the speaking. What he says is framed at the beginning and end by dialogue with the satirist. Horace meets Catius, whose name has become synonymous with Epicurean tendencies and a paramount interest in fine cooking, as he is returning from a lecture on gastronomic affairs. Like a good student, he is working on his notes, and at the request of Horace he gladly repeats verbatim, much like Damasippus in the preceding satire, the wisdom of his anonymous master.

The stance of the satirist is ironic at the beginning and in the final dialogue of the poem. The opening line, "Where are you coming from and where are you going, Catius," is quite like the opening of Plato's *Phaedrus*. Catius' reply, however, with its note of haste, is

better suited to the running slave of Roman comedy. Horace's
compliments to his powers of memory, "whether an acquired skill
or a natural one," add to the humorous tone. The elaborate close
with its hyperformality and Epicurean verses parodying Lucretius
completes the ironic encirclement of Catius' report and is in humorous agreement with the student's feelings about the importance of
his academic speciality. The real satiric ridicule, then, is not in the
basic description of a meal. Here, as in the preceding Stoic satires,
the excessive and enormous are the satirist's target.

Just as Horace began his collection of satires with a diatribe
modelled after Lucilius, the inventor of the genre, so in the last
satire he returns to one of the most common of Lucilian themes. In
his description of the banquet of Nasidienus the poet uses the menu
and the other trappings of an elaborate meal to criticize the behavior
of the newly rich who have money but do not really know how to
use it wisely and gracefully. The host Nasidienus is not unlike Catius
of Satire 4, who initiated Horace into the mysteries of his master's
philosophy of food.

In content the satire moves progressively through examples of
bad taste beginning with the unusually early hour of the meal. As far
as the table is concerned, there are too many wines available and the
appetizer outdoes decent standards of taste. When the lamprey is
brought in, the unfortunate company is regaled with details of its
preparation, all of which, to the reader's relief and amusement, comes
to an abrupt conclusion when the wall hanging falls in a great cloud
of dust. After an ironic philosophical consolation from Nomentanus,
the host leaves the room, and his guests cover their amusement by
whispering among themselves. Nasidienus soon returns, however, with
renewed resolution to make the rest of the dinner party a success. But
his efforts are too vigorous, and as he begins to expound the philosophy of the latest dishes, the company, consisting, at least in part, of
Maecenas, Viscus, Fundanius, and Varius, take their revenge on him
and his show of poor taste by deserting him.

Except for the people already mentioned, those who were
present at the banquet are unknown. The names of several, however, have comic connotations that suit the scene. Porcius ("Piggy"),
for instance, is only too perfect for a man who stuffs his mouth
with whole cheesecakes, and Balatro ("Buffoon") neatly fits the
character who gulps down wine because he finds it humorous to help
drain his host's bank account.

Characteristics

When the poems which are now called *Satires* were originally published Horace gave them the title "Talks" or "Conversations" (*Sermones*) which was surely meant to underline their informality and their satiric disposition. There can be little doubt that in doing this Horace was following Lucilius. While his contemporaries probably recognized and referred to the poems as "satires" (*saturae*), the poet himself seems to have pointedly avoided this title because of its association with the censorious aspects of Lucilius' writings and with the earlier satirist's standards of composition. Instead, in the first book Horace makes use of periphrases such as "these things I toy with," and "this kind of writing," when he wants to refer to what he is producing. It is not until Book 2, when he has established his own standards for the writing of satire, that he employs the word *satura* to designate the genre satire and the individual poems.

Ancient authors commonly indicate their literary antecedents by such techniques as literary imitation, quotation, allusion, or citation by name. Horace follows this practice in his *Satires* when he claims with unusual boldness that he is writing in the tradition of Lucilius, whom he regards as the inventor of the genre (1.10.48). He also acknowledges his debt to his predecessor both by quotation and adaptation of Lucilian lines and phrases. It is clear, however, from Horace's observations in the fourth and tenth satires of the first book that he did not accept everything Lucilius did, but rather used what pleased him and what he considered basic to the genre, while modifying what he had to in order to meet the standards of contemporary literary taste.

Indeed, there is more than a simple span of years separating the two satirists. Between their respective ages there intervened the whole of the neoteric movement and a revolution in literary standards and tastes, so that by Horace's time there had evolved that appreciation and demand for greater polish in all aspects of writing which is usually called the "Augustan discipline." Accordingly, the informality and roughness of Lucilius' style was not acceptable to the literary arbiters whose standards Horace desired to meet. The younger satirist was himself in agreement with the contemporary criteria for good writing, and these formed the basis for his attacks on Lucilian style. Instead of following his predecessor's exuberance and lack of restraint, Horace achieved the flavor of informality and daily speech,

the primary idiom of the *Satires,* by creating a refined literary illusion
of these qualities.

Of the formal elements which are to be found in both writers
the most obvious is their meter. Lucilius had settled on the dactylic
hexameter, no doubt because of its versatility, and Horace continued
this tradition. Another feature common to the two of them is the
habit of ridiculing by name which in Lucilius is directed at his
contemporaries, both great and small, while in Horace it tends to
involve fictitious names and the names of those who are not prominent or are no longer living. Furthermore, Lucilius made his writings
a "mirror of life," as Horace calls them, and this characteristic is one
of central importance to Horace.

This impression of reality and topicality is reinforced in both
writers by the presence of the author himself who moves through
his writings either as a participant or an observer, although on
a few occasions he is present only by implication. But in matters
of satiric tone Horace went his own way, for he found irony, understatement, and good humor to be his most effective tools, and
he avoided the fierce attacks and invective that characterized Lucilian
satire.

Metaphysical and casuistic quibblings have no place in Horatian
satire. The satirist deals with the ethics and personal morality of men,
and the genre in which he writes is a medium designed to criticize and
correct vices and errant behavior. To do this Horace tries to please
with his poetry and humor while at the same time pointing out
human follies. The whole technique is well encapsulated by the
poet in his phrase "to tell the truth with a smile." But there is also a
serious side to his satire, for, as the reader himself begins to smile, he
is warned: "Why laugh? If you change the name, the story being told
is about you."

Much later in his career, while writing his *Epistles,* Horace
expressly declared that he adhered to no particular school of
thought. This is also true of his *Satires.* He was a poet primarily
interested in useful ideas, and for these he would turn in any direction
and to any school. To categorize his thinking as though he were a
systematic philosopher is to ignore the nature of the man and his
poetry. If Horace seems at one moment a Cynic, at another an
Epicurean, and at yet another an eclectic, this is all the reflection of

a man who refuses to allow systems of thought to overrule common sense and good judgment.

Furthermore, it is apparent that Horace actually delights in combining such varied offerings as Epicurean and Ciceronian thoughts on a given topic and making a cogent whole of them. To take another possibility, he is quite ready to find an Epicurean solution to a Stoic problem, or vice versa. About the only philosophical tenet that he is consistent in promoting is his particular adaptation of the Peripatetic Golden Mean or Middle Way.

Variety, implicit in the meaning of *satura*, is one of the more prominent features of Horace's *Satires*. In content alone the poet takes the reader through a maze of topics, some traditional, some not, though all to some degree involve ethics. There is no need to resurvey his *Satires* to show this; it is enough to note that he may move from a Lucilian diatribe on the problem of sexual excess to a discussion showing contemporary aristocratic thinking about class distinction, or from a rustic's thoughts on frugality to a wretched dinner party with a pretentious host. In language, too, he varies his offerings, as can be seen from the mixture of colloquial, mock-epic, philosophical, and comic diction and vocabulary that mark the *Satires*.

There is also the mixed arrangement with the individual satires carefully juxtaposed to create the impression that the poet knows the general direction in which the book is going but not its precise destination. The expected diatribes are provided, but there are not too many of them. More relaxed poems of entertainment, highly autobiographical pieces, and dialogues intervene. All of this variety is reinforced by the differing length of the individual satires and by the number of satires which make up each book.

The satires in which Horace speaks of himself and those in which he participates directly show another important dimension of the poet's satiric technique—the personal and autobiographical. It is a Roman idea that the literary representation of the author's person and daily life should be interesting to a reader, and it is as a result of this that Roman satire becomes a mirror of the poet's life. Furthermore, realism is gained by this device, so that the satiric experience, especially when it is stated in what resembles everyday speech, is something that can be identified, examined, and accepted. Once the poet has become believable and realistic, he can expect to be more effective in his role as the ethical instructor of society. When employing this convention, however, Horace takes great care to avoid making his own life a pattern to be followed by others. For if he did this, his own failings could be brought up as criticism against him and what he is saying. And so Horace concentrates attention not on himself, but on the lives of those around him, at times even becoming the butt of the behavior that he is trying to criticize.

An integral part of Horace's personality and satiric approach is the clemency and forgiveness that tempers his criticism. He considers real moral problems and passes serious judgment on them, but he judges by an ethical standard that is fixed by no dogma except that of a thoroughgoing humanity. The moral principles that he promotes are such that no man can fail to meet the standards set forward after receiving the satirist's apotropaic and protreptic advice.

When Persius compares his satiric predecessors he describes Lucilius as aggressive and violent and portrays Horace as gentle, subtle, and ironic. Persius is certainly right. From Horace's point of view it makes sense not to club people but to tease them and make them smile. And so in his hands satire becomes a social instrument which, as the opening satire of Book 2 shows, can be justified if you believe in people and take seriously the poet's role of responsible citizen-teacher-leader.

To write satire that is more than just a literary exercise the satirist must be part of the world he writes about. During his lifetime Horace remained an active member of Roman society. He had a part to play in the civil wars and was a close friend and confidant of men in power. Apparently the same personal qualities of wit and flexibility which make his writings so attractive also made him attractive to Maecenas and Augustus. In many ways the pull was mutual. Horace was the sort of person and wrote the sort of thing that Augustus wanted, and in turn the emperor's support enabled him to continue doing what he did best. The temper of the times, then, was on Horace's side, and Horace's temperament was suited to the times. The result was a reciprocal and symbiotic relationship which encouraged the Horatian transformation of satire into a socially useful device and enabled Horace to bring a new level of perfection to satire as a literary form.

SENECA AND PETRONIUS:
MENIPPEAN SATIRE UNDER NERO

The *Apocolocyntosis* of Seneca

There is hardly anything about the Menippean satire which goes by the name of *Apocolocyntosis* that is not problematical. This is at least partly because it is without parallel in Latin literature. Since it is a Menippean satire, it would be logical to expect similarities between it and Varro's Menippeans, but the remains of these show so little resemblance to Seneca's satire that attempts to draw comparisons can only end in futility.

Even the attribution of this work to Seneca the philosopher has been called into question, in spite of the fact that he is named as the author in the manuscripts. Apparently, some people feel that this kind of parody is not to be expected from the pen of a Stoic philosopher. But it is easy to misjudge Seneca, as even a quick reading of his philosophical essays and *Moral Epistles* shows. For, besides the serious Stoic purpose and outlook that pervade these works, there is often an ironic wit and even a playfulness that show a complex personality lurking in the background.

Moreover, we should not forget that, besides being a moral philosopher, Seneca was also an accomplished writer of epigrams, tragedies, and other poetry. And so it is possible to imagine his genius extending as far as a Menippean satire on the death of the emperor Claudius. Besides, why should a philosopher not have his joke against a man for whom he had no love anyway? Even if this makes the satire mean-spirited, it is hardly a reason to refuse the attribution to Seneca.

During his lifetime the philosopher was in an ideal position to observe the vagaries of the various emperors, and of Claudius in particular. Born about 4 B.C., by the time of the accession of Caligula in A.D. 37 Seneca had already been quaestor and had gained enough of a reputation as orator and writer to move in court circles. But in 41, at the instigation of his enemy, Empress Valeria Messalina, he was banished by the new ruler Claudius to Corsica on a trumped-up charge of adultery with Julia Livilla, Caligula's sister. Surely this was enough reason for Seneca's eventually putting pen to paper to parody the monarch.

Eight years later the philosopher was recalled from exile and assigned to tutor the young Nero, and at his accession to the emperorship in 54, Seneca became his most influential political advisor, cabinet minister, and speech writer. For the next five years he and Afranius Burrus, the sole praetorian prefect, directed state policy for the young emperor. Soon, however, Nero asserted himself and, brushing aside his family and advisers alike, he proceeded to indulge his appetites. Finally, in A.D. 65 a number of leading men, among them Seneca and his nephew, the epic poet Lucan, were implicated in a conspiracy to overthrow the emperor and were forced to commit suicide.

The most popular title of Seneca's satire, *Apocolocyntosis,* is not found in any of the manuscripts. There the work is titled either the *Apotheosis of the Divine Claudius* or the *Joke on the Death of Claudius.* Actually, it was Hadrianus Junius, a sixteenth century editor, who found mention of the *Apocolocyntosis* in the writings of the late historian Cassius Dio and attached it to this work. Dio says simply that Seneca composed an *apocolocyntosis* of Claudius after his death.

No one really knows what the title means. A common translation is "pumpkinification", since the *colocynthe* is a type of gourd, and the word is an obvious parody of the expected *apotheosis* or "deification." Since Claudius undergoes no physical transformation in the satire, however, some have resorted to free interpretations of the title. Perhaps the most popular of these is the view that the *colocynthe* is slang for "idiot" or "blockhead." But the ancient evidence for this is very slight, and translation of the title as "bumpkinification" is unsatisfactory, since the emperor is already a fool who is trying to become a god, but fails and suffers damnation instead. There are many other less convincing conjectures as to the meaning of the title, but these can be ignored for present purposes.

As far as content is concerned, the satire is essentially a mythological farce, which in a number of ways anticipates the Menippeans of the second century Greek writer Lucian. The satire divides naturally into a number of scenes with the writer beginning on a mock-historical note as he insists that he is telling the truth about Claudius' ascent to the gods. He then proceeds to describe the details of the emperor's death as if the Fates were performing an act of euthanasia. After these three ladies have woven an elaborate account in dactylic hexameters of the destiny of the new emperor, Nero, and the new Golden Age that his accession promises, Claudius finally dies after messing his pants (4).

With this introduction the satirist sets the mood and leaves the reader in no doubt as to his purposes and methods. In an atmosphere that can only be described as informal, colloquial, and at times even vulgar and crude, Seneca plays the iconoclast. He parodies historians and poets, jabs at philosophers, and treats religion with irreverence. He also begins his caricature of Emperor Claudius by having Clotho, the Fate who is supposed to cut off his thread of life, make sarcastic reference in Mercury's presence to the emperor's generosity in granting Roman citizenship to the provincial peoples:

> My god! I wanted to give him a little more time so that he could give the citizenship to those very few who are still left. For he was determined to see that all the Greeks, Gauls, Spaniards, and Britons had it. But since you've decided that some foreigners should be left for seed and these are your orders, so be it! (3)

The action now shifts (5-7) to Mount Olympus where Claudius' arrival is announced to the gods:

> It was announced to Jupiter that a certain tall man with white hair had arrived; he was threatening something, for he constantly shook his head; and he dragged his right foot. The messenger had sought his nationality, but the man made some reply which was incoherent and unintelligible; his language was unknown and he was neither Greek nor Roman nor of any known country. (5)

The Olympians send out their most heroic and knowledgeable monster-slayer, Hercules, to face this creature. But the hero is uncharacteristically perplexed. In an attempt to discover who the newcomer is, he uses a line from Homer's *Odyssey,* which strikes a responsive note in Claudius. He would have won over Hercules with his Greek, had not the goddess Fever, who had been the emperor's constant companion in life, set the record straight by identifying him as a native of Lyons. When Claudius bridles at this, Hercules "becomes 'tragic', in order to be more fearsome" and proceeds to threaten the emperor in iambic trimeters. Claudius begins a rebuttal, but an apparent lacuna in the text leaves what he says incomplete.

In this part of the satire Seneca continues his irreverent treatment of myth and religion by portraying the hero and demigod Hercules as quite unheroic. He is described as "hardly bright at all" (6), and, though he threatens the emperor in tragic verse, he at the same time "fears a blow from the fool" (7).

The characterization of Claudius begun earlier is continued. Besides the physical shortcomings that are parodied in the passage quoted above, there is sarcastic treatment of his learning and snide commentary on his Gallic ancestry. Mention of his willingness to put men to death and reference to his propensity for presiding over law cases take on a special irony in the particular circumstances. While nowadays we might not be as receptive as the Romans were to the insulting personal satire that Seneca exploits here, we can appreciate the scene as a delightful parody of a typical epic encounter between a hero and a worthy protagonist.

Apparently Claudius won Hercules over to his side, for the satire takes up after the break in the manuscript in the middle of a divine discussion of what kind of god Claudius should become. Jupiter interrupts to say that the emperor should not be present at this debate involving his fate, and he is quickly removed.

Janus now rises to speak and moves that from this day forward divinity be voted to no human being. Diespiter, on the other hand, recommends that Claudius be made a god and that this fact be duly added to Ovid's *Metamorphoses.* It looks as if Claudius is going to win, and Hercules makes the rounds of the gods lobbying for support by stringing proverbs together (9): "Don't deny me this; it's my thing that's under discussion. Whenever you want it, I'll do something for you. One hand washes the other."

But Augustus puts an end to the debate with a typically sane, level-headed, and well-reasoned speech against Claudius. He re-counts the murders perpetrated by him—the two Julias, Lucius Silanus, Messalina, Caligula, Crassus Magnus, Scribonia, the Tristonias, Assario—and points out that all of these people died without a hearing of any kind. He moves (11) "that Claudius be severely punished, that he be given no continuance, that he be removed as soon as possible, and that he be banished from heaven within thirty days and from Olympus within three." The motion is carried unanimously.

Here there is more satire of the various philosophies and poets, as well as humorous treatment of the deities as they attempt to cope with the situation. Actually, the whole debate is a burlesque of a meeting of the Senate. Father Janus, who, we are told, had been consul designate for the afternoon of July 1, delivers a speech made eloquent by virtue of the fact that he lived in the Forum. There is also Diespiter who carefully couches his proposal in the official senatorial jargon. Finally, like an old-time Cicero, Augustus rises and delivers a speech full of the rhetorical devices expected of those speaking in this august gathering. Once again, Claudius comes in for criticism, which this time consists of an enumeration of his murder-ous activities.

In the next scene (12-13) the emperor is taken to hell by Mercury, and on his way he sees his own funeral. "It was the most handsome spectacle of all with great care lavished on it, so that you'd easily know that a god was being taken to burial." In view of what is hap-pening to the dead Claudius, it is impossible to miss the irony here. Dishonest lawyers are seen lamenting his death, but the people as a whole and honest advocates in particular rejoice.

From the funeral train comes a dirge in anapaestic meter which is not unlike a chorus from a Greek tragedy. It contains the usual list of accomplishments described in an exaggerated way, but soon degenerates to an ironic appraisal of Claudius' legal activities:

> Weep for a man than whom no other could decide
> cases more quickly with only one side heard—and
> often neither side. Who now as judge will listen to
> cases all through the year? (12)

Claudius enjoys hearing his praises sung, but almost immediately Mercury wrenches him away and hurries him on to the underworld.

On the way they meet the emperor's freedman Narcissus who runs ahead to announce Claudius' coming. After passing by Cerberus, the emperor finds himself among a throng of people that either he or his henchmen had put to death during his lifetime. He greets them as friends, but they will have none of it, and Pedo Pompeius, their spokesman, sees to it that Claudius is taken directly into court for sentencing.

Claudius' descent to the underworld is, of course, a direct parody of epic descents like those of Odysseus in the *Odyssey* and Aeneas in Vergil's *Aeneid*. The trip here is not a voluntary one, however, and there is to be no return from hell for Claudius. The fear that is routine for the visitor when he catches sight of Cerberus is here burlesqued:

> He was a little frightened—he usually had a white-colored bitch as a pet—when he saw the black, shaggy dog which you'd really not want to run into in the dark . . . . (13)

The friends that the hero usually encounters in the underworld turn out to be the victims of the traveler in this context.

In a sense, the theme of murder that has appeared from time to time reaches a climax here when names are named and the cross section of the population that Claudius has put to death appears before him—Roman knights, a mime, freedmen, two prefects, friends, and relatives close and not so close. Through it all Claudius is portrayed as a fool who bumbles along without really comprehending what he has done or what is happening to him.

The judgment scene (14-15) is a fitting climax to the satire. It is at the same time appropriate and anachronistic that the mythical judge Aeacus just happens to be holding an inquiry under the Lex Cornelia which covers assassins and murderers. Claudius' murders are summarized—35 senators, 221 knights and others "as many as the sands of the sea and the dust of the earth."

No one wants to defend Claudius until Publius Petronius makes a haphazard effort. But even then poetic justice prevails, for Aeacus listens only to the prosecution and immediately passes judgment. All the souls stand amazed at this. But "to Claudius it seemed more unfair than strange."

After some debate it is decided that a new punishment should be devised for the emperor. He is to shake dice forever in a dice box with holes in the bottom. But after eight lines of mock-epic description of his plight, Caligula suddenly turns up and claims Claudius as a slave. When he gets him, he hands him over as a present to Aeacus who in turn gives him to his freedman Menander as his legal clerk.

In the final sentencing of Claudius the burlesque of the epic underworld scenery and action is continued. The anachronistic mention of the Lex Cornelia, the suggestions that Sisyphus might be relieved of his eternal burden, that Tantalus might be dying of thirst and that Ixion has had enough wheel-pushing, and the lofty hexameters describing Claudius' problems with the dice box all contribute to the effect.

Some people have found the ending unsatisfactory, but the swift, efficient, almost sleight of hand transfer of the emperor from one person to another provides a neat anticlimax and a clever cap for the whole satire. Besides, what could be more poetically just than that Claudius, the great and unfair judge and proliferator of freedmen, should end as a slave doing legal research for a freedman?

Characteristics

Surely by now there is no need to comment in any detail about the range of satire that is present in the *Apocolocyntosis*. Seneca's main purpose is to have a laugh at Claudius' expense, but as he does so he scatters broadsides at many institutions and people: Greek and Roman literature, historians, philosophers, poets, astrologers, foreigners, gamblers, second-rate lawyers, the law courts themselves, senatorial procedure, the imperial institution of deification, mythological commonplaces, superstition, Roman religion, and funerals. Even the great Augustus' accomplishments come in for some mild parody. The satire stands on its own, then, as a clever and irreverent piece of literature, and the theories which insist that the topicality of Claudius' recent death is the only thing that gives it punch are unnecessary.

Because the *Apocolocyntosis* is so well preserved, it shows fairly clearly how prose and verse were used together in Menippean satire. The ratio is roughly 3:1 with prose predominating so that the satire is really a narrative essay with intermittent passages of verse. It should be noticed that the majority of the poetry—some 94 lines in all—is, so

far as can be ascertained, original with the *Apocolocyntosis,* with
the other 12 lines or part lines coming from easily recognizable
Latin and Greek sources.

There are six passages of verse made for the occasion, and except
for the first two, these are carefully spaced throughout the satire.
The two passages that appear towards the beginning are quite
closely related. The first of these, which consists of six lines in
dactylic hexameters, represents a kind of false start. It appears
immediately after Seneca's historical and to some extent digressive
beginning and is a high-flown mock-epic description of autumn. The
passage is rejected outright by the author who immediately goes on
in prose: "I think it'll be better understood if I say the month was
October and the day was the thirteenth." He now twits the poets
about not being content with hyperbolic descriptions of morning
and night; they even stir up things at midday.

The second passage, this one made up of three hexameters, is in
essence a mock-heroic description of noon. The use of poetry here
at the beginning serves as parody of the lofty, epic approach to such
matters as Seneca is about to discuss and at the same time underlines
the down-to-earth and basically irreverent attitude of the writer.

The 32 hexameters which appear a little later (4) are also mock-
heroic. But they are used to poke fun at the theme of the mythical
Golden Age. Clotho, Lachesis, and Apollo all get into the act in a
thoroughly traditional way which is completely out of place in the
context of the *Apocolocyntosis.*

The fourteen iambic trimeters which are next in order (7) are
delightfully humorous. Seneca says that here Hercules became a
figure from tragedy so that he might appear more fearsome. Any
self-respecting dramatic character can be expected to speak at
least sporadically in iambic trimeters, and Hercules does so. These
lines help to reinforce the mock-tragic atmosphere and underline
the fact that Hercules is really a fool.

The anapaestic dimeters (12) also contribute to the continuous
parody of the *Apocolocyntosis.* They are particularly appropriate for
a funeral dirge, and are carefully anticipated by the author: "When
Claudius saw his funeral he realized that he was dead. For they were
chanting a huge dirge *à la grand choeur* in anapaests." The point has
already been made that after a relatively routine beginning the lament
soon becomes sheer burlesque and ends with a catalogue of the
people who will miss Claudius most—quack lawyers, minor poets,
and gamblers.

The parody of epic that is present in the last piece of poetry (15) is perfectly obvious and needs little elucidation. For these eight dactylic hexameters, in which Claudius' trials and tribulations with his dice box are described, are a clear travesty of similar passages in Homer, Vergil, and the other writers of epic.

While each of these passages is well motivated by its particular context, it should be noticed that all of them could be omitted without disturbing the narrative. Each is either repetitious or digressive. The poetry is important to the satire, however, for the humorous effect that it produces. Moreover, the variety and careful spacing of these passages generate a series of contrasts and a liveliness that are integral to the piece.

When we turn to verses quoted from the poets, we find that there are twelve complete lines or part lines, three of them from Latin authors and nine from the Greek. In no instance is there more than a single line, and very few authors are quoted: Homer, Euripides, Catullus, Vergil, and Horace.

In most instances it is simply a case of a clever reuse of a line, with the author taking advantage of the double entendre thus created. But two quotations are particularly effective. When Mercury is telling Clotho that it is time Claudius died (3), he quotes a line from Vergil's *Georgics* (4.90): "Give him over to death; let a better one rule in the empty palace." If we remember, as an educated Roman would, that Vergil is instructing his beekeeper to do away with the inferior "king bee" when the bees swarm, the satiric overtones become apparent.

Again, when Hercules approaches the strange monster Claudius (5), he finally resorts to a line from Homer's *Odyssey* in an attempt to find out who this creature is (1.17): "Who are you and from where; where is your city and where your parents?" Claudius, who prides himself on his learning, is overjoyed at Hercules' erudition and replies with another line from the *Odyssey* (9.39): "A wind carrying me from Troy brought me to the Ciconians." What is more, he caps it with a verse in Greek that Seneca describes as being "truer and equally Homeric": "There I laid low a city and destroyed the people themselves." With these three lines Seneca satirizes Hercules and the Greeks, Claudius' learning, and this emperor's treatment of Rome and the Romans. Although Seneca uses quoted verse more sparingly than original verse, it is clear that it is equally well motivated, occurring just often enough to add a certain cleverness and sophistication to what he is saying.

The verse presents a pleasing contrast to the informal prose of
the *Apocolocyntosis*. This informality is achieved in a number of
ways. There are numerous proverbs, both in Latin and in Greek,
that provide a homely and down-to-earth touch. Contributing to this
effect are the frequent colloquialisms in vocabulary and grammar and
a number of instances of parataxis. There is also much slapstick and a
certain amount of punning. It is hardly sophisticatedly humorous,
for example, to point out that Claudius messed his pants and then to
say (4): "Whether he did this or not, I don't know, but he certainly
messed up everything [else]."

The personality of the satirist as he participates in the *Apocolocyntosis* contributes to the atmosphere. Seneca is careful to portray
himself in the introduction (1-2) as a smart, irreverent, iconoclastic
commentator. He is not part of the action, but at the same time he is
not a completely disinterested eye-witness. From this position he is
able to offer wry comment directly to the reader.

After the introduction, however, the satirist remains in the background and contents himself with the odd aside to keep his audience
aware of his participation. He does such a good job of impressing his
satiric persona on the reader that, even though he makes no reference
to himself for the last two-thirds of the satire, he leaves no doubt that
all the biting commentary is generated by a very real personality.

Finally, some attempt must be made to decide precisely what
purpose the treatise was meant to serve. It differs in spirit from
Varro's Menippeans in that it lacks any truly didactic element.
Certainly Seneca had a private motive for revenge on Claudius'
memory because of the lengthy exile that he had endured, and this
may have been his only reason for writing the satire. Moreover, when
we look for public motives, it is difficult to believe that the
Apocolocyntosis could serve any political or propagandistic purpose.
This is true, in spite of the exaggerated praise of Nero that is
incorporated in it.

It is interesting to notice in passing that the faults and crimes of
Claudius that are presented in the *Apocolocyntosis* are those that
were generally known and recognized. Many unpleasant facts of his
life—his womanizing, his incestuous marriage to Agrippina, and the
likelihood of his death by poison, to name only a few—are not
mentioned by Seneca.

In view of all of this, it is perhaps best to consider this satire as a relatively innocuous lampoon circulated among the imperial "in" crowd, which took on a particular cleverness and sophistication from its form and from the literary parody and allusion that was incorporated in it. It is probably wrong to view the *Apocolocyntosis* as a serious moral condemnation of Claudius' reign and a recommendation that this emperor's divine honors be rescinded. Everything points to its being nothing more than a piece of healthy, permissible irreverence directed at the imperial institution of deification and at an emperor who hardly qualified as a god.

The *Satyricon* of Petronius

Petronius is one of those literary personalities about whom we would like to know more. The historian Tacitus in his *Annals* (16.17-19) briefly characterizes him as a person who combined luxury with good taste and debauchery with refinement. As governor of Bithynia, Petronius had proven himself an energetic and capable administrator, but when he returned to Rome he slipped into a life of dissipation and pleasure. As one of Nero's closest friends and his Master of Good Taste (*elegantiae arbiter*), he exercised a certain influence in the court. But he apparently aroused the jealousy of Tigellinus, Nero's ruthless praetorian prefect, who arranged a trumped-up charge against him and induced the emperor to order his death in A.D. 66.

Petronius died with a flair. When he realized there was no escape, he opened his veins and ended his life in a leisurely fashion, listening to erotic verse and composing an impromptu exposé of Nero's sexual debaucheries and depravities. He actually sent this to the emperor as a final token of his independence.

Although Tacitus does not mention the *Satyricon,* it was no doubt during his brief career as a favorite of the emperor that Petronius composed this satire against contemporary affectation for the delight of Nero and his court. The pretentious attitude of the emperor to poetry, music, charioteering, acting, and other Greek pastimes outraged conservative Roman sentiment, and the combination of decadence, wit, and sophistication that is found in the *Satyricon* is perhaps meant to be Petronius' expression of feelings that Nero had about art and society.

What is left of the *Satyricon* appears to be a fragment, though there is more of a tendency nowadays to view it as representing the full scope of the original. There are some 141 chapters that have been arranged by modern editors and about 30 scattered fragments gathered from the ancient commentators. It seems that what remains comes from Books 14, 15, and 16, but there is no agreement as to how many books were in the original.

The problem is further aggravated by the fact that even the remnant which has survived is a running selection put together by an ancient reader. As a result, it is by no means a continuous text, but is clearly full of gaps and interpolations. The best form of the title is *Satyricon,* probably a Greek genitive plural with the Latin word for "books" (*libri*) understood. In spite of the similarity, the title has nothing to do with the word *satura.* It is seemingly connected with the Greek adjective *satyrikos* ("wanton," "prodigal") and is meant to describe the satyr-like activities of the main characters. Perhaps, then, the title might be loosely translated "Books of Lusts."

It is difficult to reconstruct any of the events before the episode of the Banquet of Trimalchio. It is clear, however, that in the early chapters of the text as it now stands (1-26) the scene has been set and the main characters have been introduced. Two parasitic students, Encolpius and Ascyltos, and their young boy lover, Giton, have wandered, perhaps from Massilia, to a Greek town in southern Italy. Here they have a number of comic adventures with people like Agamemnon, a hypocritical rhetorician and teacher, and Quartilla, a nymphomaniac priestess of the god Priapus.

The Banquet of Trimalchio which follows (26-78) is the most extensive and the most complete episode in the remains of the *Satyricon.* But it is only one of many, and the length and complexity of what is actually a digression indicate how impressive an effort the whole work must have been. The banquet scene was, of course, a literary commonplace in Roman satire, but here it has Greek implications as well. The meal is actually a remarkable travesty of a Greek symposium, which provided an evening forum for display of erudition, philosophical discourse, and polite conversation. The host, Trimalchio, and his friends pretend to elegance, cultivation, and learning, but turn out to be nothing more than vulgar philistines.

Trimalchio himself provides the continuity for the whole episode. Although he plays the wealthy patron of culture surrounded by his huge household, most of the dinner he gives—both the food and the entertainment—could better be described as a circus. The dinner courses, which are exotic enough in themselves, are usually preceded by some obviously silly trick, and the dinner guests, in order to earn their supper, have to pretend astonishment at each one.

These incidents are accompanied by conversation containing example after example of Trimalchio's superstition, ignorance, petty tyranny, and extreme morbidity. It is these failings that have made him more attractive to readers than any other character in the work, but it is also these characteristics that finally drive Encolpius and his friends from Trimalchio's house to end the scene.

Actually, the banquet is a feast which turns into a funeral, an ending which has been anticipated throughout the meal. The last straw comes, however, when Trimalchio's entire household recites a funeral dirge over their master in anticipation of the gloomy event, and his final resting place, over which stands a gaudy monument, is described in glowing detail.

After the account of Trimalchio's entertainment, the story becomes fragmentary and difficult to follow. But it is clear that most of the incidents in what may be taken as the next section (79-99) involve the homosexual intrigues of Encolpius and Ascyltos as they vie for Giton's affections. When Giton chooses Ascyltos, Encolpius gloomily wanders into an art gallery and there makes the acquaintance of Eumolpus ("Good Singer"), a poor but unrelenting poet who remains a major character through the rest of the satire.

The first thing the poet does is to deliver a poem on the sack of Troy. This may be read as a parody of Seneca's tragic style, and Eumolpus himself is perhaps meant as a loose caricature of the tragedian-philosopher. The crowd that gathers is not fooled, however, and promptly drives the two of them away.

More sexual intrigues ensue during which Giton changes mates and Eumolpus starts a brawl with the inhabitants of the apartment building in which they live. After more pandemonium, the four of them—Ascyltos, Encolpius, Giton, and Eumolpus—escape and board a ship for Tarentum.

The outlines of the next episode (100-13) are clear enough. Once aboard ship, Encolpius is surprised to find that the vessel belongs to his enemy and pursuer Lichas, and Giton is dismayed to discover the presence of his quondam lover, the nymphomaniac Tryphaena. Both of these characters must have been introduced in parts of the *Satyricon* that have been lost.

Eumolpus tries to disguise his friends as Ethiopian slaves, but the trick fails and a brawl ensues with the rest of the passengers joining in on one side or the other. Tryphaena arranges a truce, mainly to rescue Giton, and in the brief calm that ensues, Eumolpus tells the charming story of the widow of Ephesus.

Now the labyrinthine plot takes another unexpected turn with another literary commonplace—a storm and a shipwreck (114-15). The three young men are saved, and so is Eumolpus, but Lichas has drowned. After burying him, the foursome go on their way (116-17) and encounter a local farmer, who informs them that they are in the neighborhood of Croton, an ancient Greek city. His description of the town is Swiftian in its logic:

> In this city literary pursuits are not honored: elo-
> quence has no status; there are no rewards and praises
> for good sense and decent habits, but whatever men
> you'll see will be divided between two groups: fortune-
> hunters and their prey. In this city nobody raises
> children, because whoever has heirs of his own gets no
> invitations to dinner or games but is deprived of all
> life's luxuries and lives in disgraceful obscurity. . . .
> You will enter a town that's like a land in the midst of a
> plague, where there's nothing but corpses being mutilated
> and the crows who are mutilating them. (116.6-9)

Eumolpus thinks he can turn the situation to a profit, so the group plans to enter the town in disguise with Eumolpus playing a wealthy but heirless man and the rest of the company his slaves. This will allow the greedy townspeople to compete for a place in his will by offering him presents of all sorts.

But the reader must wait to learn the outcome of the stratagem, since Eumolpus is overcome by his poetic mania again because of his captive audience (118-24). This time he offers an "art of poetry" as a theoretical justification of his lines and then proceeds to recite the first draft of an epic on the Civil War.

The final episodes of the *Satyricon* (125-41) are too fragmentary to reconstruct with any confidence. But what details there are indicate that Encolpius has become infatuated with another woman, whose name, significantly enough, is Circe. Somewhere along the way, however, he becomes sexually impotent and has to seek a cure by consulting Oenothea ("Wino-Goddess"), a drunken old hag who is also priestess of the god Priapus. After a number of failures, Encolpius is revived by the god Mercury.

Also in these final scenes the ruse of the disguise comes to a climax, as Eumolpus in the last chapter draws up a fraudulent will to satisfy the legacy-hunters. He attaches a condition that all who wish to share in his last will and testament must agree to participate in a cannibal feast and help devour his corpse. The Greeks—especially the Pythagoreans and Orphics—had developed the idea that cannibalism was the worst of all crimes against the gods and humanity, but the people of Croton, overwhelmed by their own greed, would not hestiate to break this most fundamental of all religious taboos. Thus the *Satyricon,* at least in its present state, ends on a note that is suitably grotesque.

Characteristics

About all that can be done with the *Satyricon* in a few pages is to point out some of its more important characteristics and try to recognize the spirit in which it was written. The form of the *Satyricon* has caused much confusion and comment, simply because it does not fit neatly with any specific genre of ancient literature. In fact, a reading of Petronius' work leaves the impression that it is a mutant which has no single source.

Some have viewed it as a novel or a romance mainly because of its length and because it has characters and plot that resemble those of later Greek Romance. But if it is to be catalogued in this way, then, so far as we know, it is a creation unique to its time, since its only predecessor, the fragmentary *Ninus Romance* of the first century B.C., has nothing in common with it. At the same time, there is no evidence to substantiate the theory that Petronius was consciously parodying a contemporary Greek novel.

The *Satyricon* has other literary affinities as well. The adventures of the heroes here remind us of epics like the *Odyssey* and *Aeneid* in which the hero wanders about experiencing similar strange and trying situations. But Petronius' creation can hardly be more than a parody of epic, for the heroic commonplaces that appear usually serve the primary purpose of travesty and caricature. When Lichas sees through Encolpius' disguise, for example, by recognizing the size and shape of his penis (105), there is clear burlesque of Euryclea's recognition of Odysseus' scar in Book 19 of the *Odyssey.* Again, there is a comical allusion to Odysseus' visit to the underworld in Oenothea's attempt to restore Encolpius' dead penis by performing a necromancy (135-38). Names like Agamemnon, Menelaus, and Circe that are scattered through the *Satyricon* also contribute to the atmosphere of epic parody.

It is perhaps not surprising to find that Petronius was also influenced by the mime, which had maintained its popularity from earliest times and continued to be performed in the first century after Christ. In the staged versions, as in the *Satyricon,* there was farcicality, sexual indecency, and deliberate artificiality. What is often described as literary realism in Petronius is actually the contrived domesticity of the mime. Indeed, the whole of the Banquet of Trimalchio with its series of tricks may be viewed as a mimic performance, and the last scene, in which Eumolpus plays his confidence game at Croton, contains a number of mimetic elements, not the least being the disguise which he adopts.

To complicate the issue, there are overtones of Seneca's philosophical writings in the *Satyricon.* His moralizing is often put in the mouth of a thoroughly unworthy character to be parodied by incongruity, while many Senecan conventions are mocked in the light of the Epicurean attitudes which set the tone of the *Satyricon.* There are times, however, when themes, motifs, and characterizations from the *Moral Epistles* appear with no satiric overtones.

Perhaps by now it is clear why it is almost impossible to find a satisfactory place for the *Satyricon* in ancient literature. Petronius drew freely on other literary forms, not only to provide subjects for parody and criticism, but also to build his work. But it is difficult to get away from the fact that the *Satyricon* is a satire from beginning to end. Even the title may be a sophisticated Greek-Latin pun on satyr-satire (*satyra-satura*), as some believe. If we admit the basically satiric nature of the *Satyricon,* then we surely must go the next step and recognize the fact that Petronius' greatest debt is to Menippean satire.

Mimic and mock-epic characteristics have been recognized in the *Apocolocyntosis* and in the fragments of Varro's Menippeans. So have literary allusion, imitation, and parody. All of these are found in profusion in the *Satyricon.* Varro and Seneca take a humorous approach to much of their satire. The *Satyricon* is so pervaded by humor, that the mood seldom becomes even remotely serious.

While the relationship between Petronius and his satire does not bind him to the Menippean tradition alone, it is important to notice that he is in essentially the same relationship as Seneca is to what he is writing. The author is a sophisticated commentator of whom the reader is aware but who keeps himself from overt participation in the action. Seneca for all intents and purposes disappears after the first few paragraphs of the *Apocolocyntosis,* while Petronius presents his satire through the person of Encolpius. This reminds us of what Horace did in his satires of burlesque (1.7, 1.8, 2.5). The comparison becomes more striking when we consider the mock-epic and erotic humor that these three satires share with the *Satyricon.*

A final obvious link between the *Satyricon* and Menippean satire lies in the mixture of prose and verse that is found in each. Although the ratio of prose to verse seems to be higher in the *Satyricon* than in the *Apocolocyntosis* (5:1), the verse is used in much the same way. It appears in the prose framework naturally extending what has been said without any clearly stated motivation, or else it appears as an example to illustrate something that has come up in a literary discussion. As in the *Apocolocyntosis,* some is quoted from earlier poets, but most appears to be original with Petronius.

In all of these respects, then, it seems fair to view the *Satyricon* as a Menippean satire. But Petronius was an original genius and produced a Menippean satire that was unique for its length and for the scope of its subject matter. This is at least part of the reason for the apparent differences. It is possible that if we had the whole of the *Satyricon* it would leave the impression of a series of Menippeans which had a common thread of character and a thin story line uniting them.

But the differences between the *Satyricon* and its literary predecessors may be a conscious reflection of a larger purpose of Petronius. He may have been out to have a literary joke at the expense of satirists like Varro. For in the *Satyricon* he uses satire for frivolous and comical purposes without intending it to be morally edifying. His completely humorous exposition of a popular Epicureanism of the most sensual kind, for example, is hardly what Varro was aiming at. In other words, it seems likely that Petronius was including satire among the targets of his satire.

One of the most striking features of the *Satyricon* is the marvelous variety that is found in it. This comes from the simple fact that the satirist is dealing with contemporary society in all of its facets. There is an almost endless parade of characters trooping through scenes and situations that are constantly changing. The action takes place on land and sea and in dining rooms, temples, baths, apartment houses, art galleries, whorehouses, and inns. Adventures are both real and fantastic and include brawls, banqueting, shipwreck, near-rape, and innumerable kinds of deception. Nearly everyone in society appears on stage at one time or another: young and old, male and female, rich and poor, educated and uneducated, freedmen and slaves. There are naive young men, moralizing poets, grasping women, hags, peasants, orators, chattering females, rhetoricians, seers, thieves, doctors, cooks, money-changers, and even a tombstone maker.

There is a variety of mood as well, although virtually nothing in the *Satyricon* as it stands can be called serious. For the most part the mood is a comic one, whether it be subtle humor, low farce, mock-epic and tragic, or slapstick. Now and then there is an underlying cynicism that surfaces in comments made by Encolpius, the poet's mouthpiece. Generally speaking, however, the moralizing, the tragic scenes, and the generally gloomy circumstances in which the characters find themselves from time to time are not meant to be taken seriously, but are part of what is being satirized.

The episodic nature of the *Satyricon* strengthens this impression of variety. When we think of Petronius' satire we tend to think of different stories—the Banquet of Trimalchio, the story of Quartilla or Circe, the episode with Oenothea, the tales of the werewolf, the straw corpse, and the woman of Ephesus.

This variety extends to the poetry that is found in the *Satyricon.* It ranges in quality and subject matter from mere doggerel on mundane subjects like baldness to what is supposed to pass for high-flown epic poetry. Petronius uses nine different verse forms, and in two cases he even produces hybrid poems. Agamemnon's views on the moral degeneracy of the times (5) are written in choliambs followed by dactylic hexameters, while Eumolpus' elegy on baldness (109) consists of three elegiac couplets and seven hendecasyllables.

Although the frequent gaps in the text make generalization difficult and dangerous, it appears that Petronius used poetry in two different ways. In some cases the passage of verse contributes directly to a particular scene or discussion as an example or a performance, while at other times it appears as part of the narrative with the context alone showing the connection. Examples of the former are Trimalchio's verses on death which he recites over the solid silver skeleton that lies on the table in front of him (34), Tryphaena's chant for peace (108), and Encolpius' prayer to Priapus (133).

But it is Eumolpus, the poverty-stricken, hack philosopher-poet, who creates most of this occasional poetry. His 65 lines on the fall of Troy (89) are bad enough, but it is not long before he adds a bizarre epic poem in 295 dactylic hexameters (119-24). In his Art of Poetry which prefaces this creation (118), he makes a plea for a return to highflown language, an avoidance of cliches, and a freedom to use historical fact with some license. He recommends as well that poets go back to using mythological backdrops, divine machinery, and legendary heroes such as are found in Homer and Vergil.

With this inauspicious beginning, Eumolpus rather short-sightedly sets himself the task of putting together an impromptu epic on the Roman Civil War. This is a mistake, of course, for good poetry, as Horace had pointed out earlier, demands much thought and much labor. Actually, Eumolpus has fallen victim to a bad habit of the contemporary poets whom he criticizes, and what he produces is no improvement on what he sees around him. Perhaps it is enough to say by way of criticism that his cliches are inexcusable, his language is grotesque and ineffective, and his distortion of historical fact goes well beyond any poetic license.

The second use of poetry in the *Satyricon* is more strictly Menippean. Here the author or the character speaking simply breaks into verse without prior announcement. This is already familiar from Varro's satires and Seneca's *Apocolocyntosis.*

The passages that are clearly in context suggest at least three different purposes for this Menippean poetry. Some of the lines are outright moralizing. Ascyltos, for example, breaks into elegiac couplets as he comments on the sovereignty of money over justice (14), and someone else, presumably the narrator Encolpius, uses the same verse form to develop this theme towards the end of the *Satyricon* (137). Quartilla's inferior elegiacs on victory and defeat also fall here (18).

Petronius also puts hendecasyllables, elegiacs, and dactylic hexameters in the mouth of Encolpius to convey euphoria or suicidal despair. This character uses verse to express the bliss he feels when making love to Giton (79) or Circe (127). At the opposite extreme is his dejection at losing Giton (80) and at becoming temporarily impotent (128).

Finally, there are four passages, one in sotadeans and the other three in dactylic hexameters, where the poet's purpose seems to be to create a mock-heroic effect for purposes of humor. Encolpius' elaborate description of Oenothea's simple house (135), the high-flown lines in which he compares his killing the goose with a labor of Hercules (136), and his description of his drooping penis where he combines three lines from Vergil (132) for purposes of parody are all meant to raise a smile in the reader. The exaggerated description of how he is going to cut off his useless member (132) combines strong emotion and the mock-epic to produce a situation that can only be described as ludicrous.

Just as there is a wide range of style and purpose in the poetry of the *Satyricon,* so there is a variety of language and idiom in the prose. It can range from a thoroughly polite and polished colloquial diction and idiom such as that found in Eumolpus' tale of the woman of Ephesus (111), to the drunken, stuttering, confused utterance of Dama at Trimalchio's banquet (41). Almost every one of Petronius' characters has a way of speaking that is peculiar to him. No other Latin stylist employed such a wide range of diction and style to portray individual characters.

Even Greek is authentically used to reinforce the impression of scenes set in the Greek centers of southern Italy. By this time many Greek words were regularly used as loan words by those who spoke Latin in towns like Croton and Tarentum, and Petronius capitalizes on this for purposes of atmosphere and characterization.

For these reasons the *Satyricon* has been of interest to historical linguists. Parallels have been noted between Petronius' prose and the Latin inscriptions found on the walls of the houses at Pompeii. This would appear to be significant, since this well-preserved city is located near the imaginary setting of much of the action of the *Satyricon* and was destroyed in A.D. 79, not long after Petronius' satire appeared. Such discoveries have led those interested in the Latin language to consider the *Satyricon* as a possible source of the common speech (*sermo vulgaris*) of the time which later became the basis for the modern Romance Languages.

But caution on this point is necessary, for the language of the *Satyricon* often seems common and everyday when it is not, simply because the content of the story is vulgar or because the characters are low and common. Trimalchio and his guests, for example, fall into two categories, the *nouveaux riches* like Trimalchio, who are simply crude and vulgar, and people like Encolpius, Agamemnon, and Eumolpus, who are cultured and educated, but thorough parasites. In contrast to the polite colloquialisms indulged in by

Encolpius and his companions, the parvenus among the guests expose their humble origins with their short, staccato sentences, their vociferously repeated oaths, excessive use of diminutives, Greek solecisms, mistaken syntax, peculiar metaphors, and just bad puns.

Often the damning evidence is simply style, rather than any item of vocabulary or grammar. An example is provided by Phileros' querulous reminiscences about the recently deceased Chrysanthus:

> He lived a decent life and died a decent death. What's he got to gripe about? He started with a dime and was ready to pick up a nickel from the garbage with his teeth. He grew and grew like a honeycomb. God! I think he left a solid hundred thousand, and had it all in cash. But I'll tell you the truth about it since I have a currish tongue: he had a harsh mouth, was all tongue, and pure trouble, not a man. (43.1-3)

Here the short sentences, lack of modifiers, and simple syntax create the illusion of small talk at the dinner table that Petronius wants, in order to give an aristocrat's eye view of the speech mannerisms of the lower class.

Rhetoric has an important part to play in the prose of the *Satyricon,* appearing most often, as might be expected, in the mouths of the characters who have at least some education. Declamation, or practice speaking, was an important part of the education of the time, and people like Encolpius or Eumolpus would surprise no one by breaking into a harangue at any time, especially in an emotional situation.

As a matter of fact, what is left of the *Satyricon* opens with Encolpius declaiming against declaimers and Agamemnon declaiming for them. In the art gallery, though he has just met Encolpius, Eumolpus, the shabby old poet, cannot resist telling the younger man a ribald tale of how some years earlier he had seduced the son of a quaestor, his patron, in Pergamum (85-87). Almost immediately he launches into a declamation on the decline of art as a decline in morals (88).

In most instances the persuasion and debate contribute to the humor of the situation. No sooner has Encolpius, for example, gone through the rhetorical gyrations of convincing himself to die well, than fishermen row out and save him from drowning (114). A little earlier the reader has been treated to a debate aboard ship between

Eumolpus and Lichas (107). Not only is the contest out of place in this atmosphere, but every one of the old poet's arguments is specious.

Finally, there is the satire of the *Satyricon*. But what can be said in a few paragraphs about a satire in which so many characters come dancing across the stage and where the writer's purpose seems to be to satirize virtually everything in society, including his own satire? At best we can only get a glimpse of what Petronius was trying to do.

Subjects for satire come tumbling from the satirist's pen: dishonesty, greed, wealth, extravagance, love, stupidity, superstition, naiveté, moralizing, philosophizing, flattery, hypocrisy, hypochondria, clientship, legacy hunting, the decadence of art and literature, rhetoric, legal agreements, shipwrecks, table talk, puns, and even tombstone inscriptions. These are just a few of the topics that are treated in one way or another, and the characters mentioned earlier are just a few of the types that are satirized.

But to provide some overall interpretation of the *Satyricon* as satire requires caution, for it is easy to miss the fact that Petronius is satirizing moral commonplaces rather than the corruption of his times. Perhaps the idea that crops up most often in the writers of this period is that of the degeneracy of contemporary times in comparison with the glories and virtues of old Rome. This rhetorical argument from ancestral custom is exploited by all Romans of good will, and Petronius' characters ostensibly fall into line as praisers of the past who lament the loss of ancient religion and the time-honored virtue. But at the same time they are themselves thieves and cut-throats who exemplify perfectly the contemporary age of moral decadence and materialistic extravagance.

And so Petronius uses this rhetorical commonplace for brilliant satirical effect by permitting such unworthy characters as Agamemnon, Eumolpus, and Encolpius to exploit thoroughly the philosophic sentimentality inherent in the notion. The satirist in this way ridicules artificial moralizers by showing that their views of good and evil are both trivial commonplace and moral hypocrisy, just as the rules and norms of society tend to be viewed as so many clichés.

And so Petronius' characters, both those that are supposed to raise a spark of respect in the reader and the comically deviant and criminal types, suggest a moral relativity, if not a topsy-turvydom. This impression of instability is reinforced by the nature of the travels of Encolpius and his friends. Instead of a well-defined epic quest, as in Odysseus' twenty-year journey back to Ithaca, the antiheroes of the *Satyricon* wander aimlessly, wherever chance or the moment directs. Many times it seems as if a narrow escape from some comically perilous situation forces the heroes along some unknown and unanticipated route, until another adventure bounces them in another direction.

Still another reflection of this instability is to be found in the checkered careers of Trimalchio and his guests. The humble, vulgar origin of a character is usually contradicted by his present affluence. But the chance accumulation of wealth has established a precarious status quo, and the message for those who base their existence on wealth alone is perfectly clear.

As a romance of roguery, the *Satyricon* offers a world of moral subjectivity filled with well-delineated characters more suggestive and morally ambiguous than any in all of ancient literature. But Petronius treats what is potentially a depressing theme with consistent humor. He never allows any attitude of bitterness or hostility to override his emphasis on the good cheer of the popular Epicureanism that he is promoting. Petronius' characters are rogues who arouse no moral indignation over their misdeeds, but are actually lovable because of their vices, not in spite of them.

But this is not to say that Petronius does not offer overt comment on the passing scene. Quite the opposite, there is much commentary, most of it coming from the satirist's spokesman, Encolpius. During the banquet of Trimalchio, for example, he gradually becomes less tolerant of what he sees happening around him. When the ladder slips and the boy falls on Trimalchio, Encolpius provides an editorial comment or two:

> The household shouted out, and so did the guests, not because of this fellow so rotten, whose neck they would gladly have seen broken, but because of the [possibly] bad outcome of the meal. They were afraid they would have to mourn a dead man they didn't cotton to. (54)

A little later Encolpius expresses his disgust at a chicken dish (65) and then makes his feelings known in no uncertain terms about the antics of Habinnas' slave and the food course which follows these (69). In quick order he criticizes Trimalchio and his drunken friends, comments on the terrible voice of the cook, and says he is ashamed to describe what came next (70). These are but a few examples of the running commentary in the banquet scene that leaves the reader fully informed as to how Encolpius feels.

Petronius also uses other characters to convey his satiric comment. Ascyltos, for example, breaks out laughing at the too elaborate device of drawing slips of paper from jars to announce dishes that are imminent (57). Earlier Echion had grumbled at Ganymede's pronouncements of doom and gloom on the high cost of living (45). Farce and satire come together as the people who have been listening to Eumolpus' poem on the fall of Troy promptly throw stones at him (90). There is much comment of this kind in the *Satyricon*, and there can be no doubt that Petronius is using it purposefully as part of his satiric method. But it all takes a special irony from the fact that those who pass judgment in this way are themselves at other points the butt of mordant satire.

By now it is perhaps obvious that in Petronius' hands Menippean satire had become something quite different from what it had been earlier. This is at least partly because much time has intervened since Varro adapted the Greek form to Roman needs. But literary evolution is not the whole answer. Seneca's *Apocolocyntosis,* which is roughly contemporary with the *Satyricon,* suggests an alternative and much more conservative development for Menippean satire. How, then, do we account for the peculiar form of the *Satyricon*?

The answer surely lies in the genius of Petronius. The point has been made often enough that Roman satire is subject to personality. This seems to be the case with the *Satyricon*. It is all but impossible to find predecessors and exact parallels for Petronius' work because he adapted the Menippean tradition to suit his own personality and his own needs. The creation that resulted was so different and so successful, that it brought an end to Menippean satire in its traditional form. And yet this was not too surprising, since the Menippean tradition had never been very strong at Rome.

But Petronius' personality had another important influence on the form and content of the *Satyricon*. The author was a sophisticated man, so much so that he was given official recognition at Nero's court for his refinement and elegance. The *Satyricon* is a product of this sophistication. It fairly exudes cleverness. In the first place, it is completely the reverse of what it should be. It is an epic with characters and activities that are low and mundane; the hero is

cared for him. Thrasea Paetus, the husband of Persius' relative Arria, a doctrinaire Stoic who had written a panegyric on the elder Cato and who as the leader of the Stoic opposition was eventually condemned by Nero, also had a profound influence on the satirist. This education and these influences could easily have left Persius a man of careful and gentle ways, so that there is no reason to disbelieve Probus when he says that the poet was modest, temperate, and respectful and loving to his mother, sister, and aunt.

On November 24, A.D. 62, Persius died at the age of twenty-eight, while visiting his estate eight miles south of Rome on the Appian Way. The cause of his death is mysteriously described as a stomach ailment. Persius' ancient biographer says the satirist was quite wealthy at his death and that he left the bulk of his money to his sister and mother, with the request that a substantial sum be given to Cornutus along with the books which he had accumulated. Among these were some 700 volumes of Chrysippus' writings. Characteristically, the philosopher accepted the library but refused the money.

After Persius' death Cornutus convinced the poet's mother that his early writings should be suppressed. As far as the *Satires* were concerned, after excising some verses from the end and polishing them in other minor ways, he gave them to Caesius Bassus to publish at the latter's request. They appeared soon after Persius' death, perhaps as early as 63, and were apparently an immediate success.

Subject and Form

Probus says that Persius wrote slowly and infrequently. This may be an inference gathered from the first few lines of Satire 3, though the labored style of the *Satires* as a whole and the fact that the corpus consists of only six satires and a prologue amounting to some 650 lines also suggest that this was the case. It is impossible to tell when the *Satires* were written, but it seems likely that they were not begun more than a few years before the poet's death, since Probus indicates that he was still working on them when he died. Neither is there any way of knowing whether or not Persius wrote the satires in the order in which they appear now.

Though in some manuscripts the fourteen lines written in choliambics appear at the end, in the majority they form a preface and for this reason appear in most modern editions as a prologue. Some scholars have rejected these verses outright because the meter is foreign to Roman satire, while the abrupt ending has led others to feel that the poem is incomplete. Still others take the fact that there is no clear connection between the first half and the last half as showing that there are actually fragments of two poems here. A careful, unprejudiced reading of these lines, however, shows that, regardless of their meter and seeming discontinuity, they do make a complete and coherent poem which serves an important function.

In this brief preface Persius is trying to indicate where he as a satiric poet stands in relationship both to the poets of the past who have gained a reputation for writing loftier poetry and also to those of his contemporaries who aspire to such loftiness in their poetic efforts. In the first half of the poem, then, he carefully disassociates himself from the poets like Ennius who are in a direct line from the Greek by disclaiming any designs on Helicon and Pirene and by insisting that he is going to leave the inspiration that these names imply to those who have proved themselves capable of drawing successfully on such sources. While he admits that he is himself a half-rustic (*semipaganus*), he is after all bringing forward poetry—he uses the word *carmen*—that is worth consecrating in the shrines of the poets.

The adjective *semipaganus* not only puts Persius' satire in the same relationship to epic, tragedy, and the like as earlier satire, but with its Italo-Roman connotations places it squarely in the non-Greek tradition. The word *nostrum* ("our") which brings this half of the poem to a solid conclusion may also remind the reader of things Roman, but it serves the more important purpose of concentrating attention on Persius as having a place between the poets of the past whom he has been discussing and his contemporaries whose appearance is imminent.

When he turns to his fellow writers, he criticizes them as crow and magpie poets who, in spite of a general lack of talent, have been driven by their bellies to attempt the inspired poetry that he has rejected. Persius' repudiation is made clear not only by the tone he takes, but also by the structure of the poem, for he isolates himself completely from the undesirables by keeping himself out of the last seven lines. The strong "I" of the first half of the prologue becomes a "who," an "it," and a vague "you" in the second half, with "our poetry" in the middle underlining the contrast. It should be noticed that "the nectar of Pegasus" in the last line is an echo of "the nag's fountain" in the first line and shows the poem to be complete.

These lines serve as an appropriate introduction to the *Satires* for a number of reasons. In addition to putting these poems in the proper literary perspective, they prepare the reader for the disjointed style and the irreverent, sarcastic tone that pervades them. Persius is out to catch the attention of the reader by startling him, and he does this not only with his thought and language, but also by using a meter which by now is unexpected in a collection of satires. And yet choliambics were not entirely inappropriate, since they were commonly used in poems of an introductory nature and had long been associated with poetry of criticism.

Satire 1 takes up where the prologue leaves off, since it is essentially a condemnation of contemporary literary tastes and habits. Persius begins with an exclamation: "Oh the concerns of men! How much emptiness there is in things!" This is adapted from two lines of the Epicurean poet, Lucretius (1.330; 2.14), and serves as a theme for this poem and the *Satires* as a whole. As he speaks to his unnamed adversary, he professes a compulsion to criticize and proceeds to lash out at the prevailing taste that promotes unnatural recitation of artificial verse for an affected audience. The poetry that is being written is foamy and puffed up like bark that has dried out, so that for the most part it is weak and artificial. He calls it "the kind of thing that floats weak and lifeless on the spittle that dribbles off the lips." It is the poets who are to blame for this sad state of affairs, since none of them devotes the time and effort to composition that it demands.

The adversary's lame suggestion that the truth should be avoided because it tends to hurt brings the expected reaction from Persius, the dedicated satirist, who insists that he is sincere in wanting to write satire and feels driven to express himself in this way. After all, Lucilius and Horace did it, and besides, Persius has something that he is bursting to tell, if only to a hole in the ground: "Who doesn't have the ears of a jackass?" This is his secret and this is his laugh, and, though it may seem to be nothing, it is worth more than any *Iliad* that any of his contemporaries may write. As far as his audience is concerned, it will hopefully be made up of those who have no patience with low wits and dimwits, but who appreciate writers like Eupolis, Cratinus, and Aristophanes, for Persius is offering the same pointed, well-distilled satire that is to be found in Old Comedy.

The writer accomplishes a number of objectives in his first satire, the most important being to express his feelings about contemporary literary standards and the social and moral shortcomings that these reflect. But within this framework he is also giving an account of his own poetry and satiric purposes, and as he does so, he takes an opposite tack from Horace. For the earlier writer had defined his satire in terms of Augustan discipline, while Persius disassociates himself and his satire completely from the literary atmosphere of the times.

One of the most important points he has to make is that he is a sincere and independent writer, genuinely concerned about the emptiness and gloominess of human life which makes all people no better than jackasses. These are the things he must talk about, regardless of whether his listeners are repelled or not, for this satiric drive is part of his make-up. Out of Persius' forthright approach to satire comes a serious outspokenness which, even when it is colored by humor, is not a Horatian smile but an uncontrolled guffaw (12) with more of the sardonic, sarcastic, and bitter than of any healthy belly-laughing. It is important to notice that what Persius says gains a certain identity of its own and so an extra validity from being presented in a concentrated style. As far as justification is concerned, he carries on the tradition begun by Horace of marshalling the earlier satirists and Greek Old Comedy in support of what he is attempting.

Those who feel that this poem is Persius' most successful effort usually make the point that it is the only real satire in the collection, while the rest are Stoic diatribes or at best essays with Stoic themes. It must be admitted that this is closer in form and spirit than any other satire to what Lucilius, Horace, and Juvenal wrote. But, in view of the broad limits within which the genre was defined by the Romans, it is unfair to single it out as being the only true satire in Persius' collection.

The second satire is a birthday poem addressed to Macrinus, about whom nothing is known, except that he was a man of wide learning and apparently loved Persius as a son. Unique though the form may be, the dedication is little more than a formality, for after the first few lines Macrinus disappears completely, and the poem becomes a study of right and wrong prayers with the emphasis on methods and purposes. Though Macrinus will not make the same mistake, most of those who belong to the upper classes have prayers that can only be uttered and muttered in secret—the death of an uncle, a crock of gold, the death of a ward who stands in the way of an inheritance. People think they can fool the all-seeing Jupiter and are sure they have when he does not strike them down immediately. But then this is not surprising, for, after all, they *have* bribed him with their plates of greasy offerings. When people think and behave like this, they have themselves alone to blame for defeat.

At the same time, man's materialistic outlook has affected his view of religion and, transferring his feelings about gold to the gods, he has come to gild statues and use elaborate instruments in his religious ceremonies because he thinks that this is what the deities want. It is time, then, to create the proper atmosphere, which can come only from honesty and purity of heart, mind, and soul. With this to guide and recommend a man's prayers there will be no need for hypocrisy and extravagance in matters of religion.

In theme and terminology the second satire is thoroughly Stoic, and it takes the form of a diatribe on the folly of men's wishes and prayers. The atmosphere thus created is reinforced by the paradox that all fools are impious and by the theory of the all-seeing deity, both of which are drawn directly from Stoic thought. The poem is topical, inasmuch as it is actually an attack on a serious problem of the times—the hypocritical, materialistic, superstitious habits of contemporary religion which leave souls "bowed to the earth, with no concept of heavenly things" (61).

At the end of the poem Persius insists that he would replace this cult of the external with an internal moral perfection which manifests itself in

> a soul where divine and human law are in harmony,
> a mind whose most secluded corners show a rare
> purity, and a heart filled with nobility and honesty.
> Give me these to take to the temple and I will enjoy
> a successful sacrifice with a handful of grain.

Though the thought and much of the terminology are Stoic, this is a noble statement of an idea that must have been in the minds of many, regardless of their philosophical leanings. Persius has distilled it into the fewest possible words while recommending an application that goes well beyond the immediate Stoic context.

In Satire 3 Persius sets wisdom against folly and once again gives what is essentially a Stoic theme a universal application. Though men are aware of the possibilities of living properly with the help of philosophy, most of them as a result of laziness, prodigality, and depravity—that is, because they are human and weak—are unable to bring themselves to follow those who are showing them the way. Persius plunges *in medias res* to present a dramatic picture of a teacher or preacher sitting beside the bed of a young man, chiding him for sleeping until noon. The latter is shown taking writing utensils in hand and petulantly throwing them down because the ink runs and the pen will not write as he wishes.

But this is just an excuse for not writing, and the satirist proceeds to criticize the young man for his laziness by telling him that now is the time to put aside the externals of lineage and wealth and to give up the life of vice and prodigality that blinds him to the truth. A child can be expected to avoid what is difficult, even though it may be beneficial, but a young man who has been exposed to the Stoic philosophy should know where to find instruction, for otherwise there can be no order or direction in his life. If he refuses to recognize this and insists on a life of prodigality and vice, then he is sick.

After introducing a centurion who scoffs at these ideas, Persius returns to the medical metaphor to show a sick man dying because he refuses to heed his doctor's advice and apply the proper remedies. The lazy, undirected man is like him, inasmuch as he is ill from greed, gluttony, fear, and anger, and knows but does not benefit from the proper remedy, which in this case happens to be philosophical. This kind of disease can only be described as a madness.

In the third satire both the theme and the metaphor from medicine which give the poem a unity are drawn from Stoicism. The poem falls naturally into three parts, the first of which, the explication of the disease, is the longest (1-62). After a close look at the patient (1-18) and an analysis of the symptoms (19-43), there is a statement of the seriousness of the problem/disease and an insistence that a remedy be found (44-62).

Diagnosis and description are followed by an outline of the cure (63-87), in which the complacency of the centurion who can only scoff at it serves to show how difficult it is to apply. In the final section Persius describes the consequences of neglecting the problem/disease by putting the physically sick man and morally sick man side-by-side (88-118).

The metaphor does much to relieve the monotony of the sermon, but Persius has also attempted to maintain the interest of the reader in other ways—by placing a dramatic scene at the beginning, by using examples such as Natta, the bull of Phalaris, and Damocles' sword, by making reference to his own childhood, by introducing a centurion, and by giving a final warning to the prodigal.

The fourth satire is a plea to "know thyself" addressed to those who avoid the unpleasant task of getting to know their limitations and capabilities and tend to delight and trust in their own vanity. Once again the dramatic situation is relatively unimportant, for in spite of the fact that Socrates speaks with Alcibiades, what develops is not a Socratic dialogue, but another monologue or diatribe. The philosopher asks the young man how he warrants the responsibility of governing when he does not have the genius, wisdom, and maturity to make the decisions that are expected of him and when his idea of the highest good is to indulge his expensive appetites.

Socrates advises him not to continue this charade, for relying on one's family to maintain such a position makes a person no wiser than a lowly herb seller peddling her wares. He goes on to observe that men do not really look into their own souls, so that they are quick to pass judgment on others without stopping to realize that they may be open to criticism. Alcibiades is a case in point, for he laughs at a Vettidius for being miserly, but is himself reproachable for a well-plucked effeminacy. Part of this young man's problem is the fact that he has given in to popular acclaim which represents the wrong estimate of him as a man. He should get to know his real self, then, and when he does he will realize that he is less than perfect.

Though this poem, which is at the same time the shortest and most obscure of the *Satires*, may have been inspired by Plato's *Alcibiades I* and by a passage of his *Symposium* (216A), it cannot be called a Platonic dialogue by any stretch of the imagination. There are actually a number of streams of influence that come together in the satire. Besides the connection with Plato, even a cursory glance once again reveals Stoic characteristics, inasmuch as Socrates is actually a diatribist delivering a sermon, in which he points to the folly of emphasizing exterior things and mentions the highest good. Similarly Stoic is the exhortation to philosophy which concludes the poem and which in tone and purpose recalls the end of the third satire.

But the rhetorical tradition is also exerting an influence in this satire, for the theme itself is by now as much a part of rhetoric as it is of philosophy. Moreover, the anachronistic nature of the situation suggests a *suasoria,* or practice piece, in which an Alcibiades might be given advice on how to use power by a budding Roman orator who no longer has the opportunity to reach such a position.

Satire 5, which is a treatment of the Stoic dogma on *libertas* or true freedom, begins as a kind of dialogue between Persius and Cornutus, but as with the satires before it, the dramatic situation is soon ignored. When the poet makes a facetious reference to the current literary habit of requesting a hundred voices, a hundred mouths, and a hundred tongues in order to do justice to a lofty theme, Cornutus reminds him that he should leave it to other poets to "chase after the mists of Helicon" and to squeeze their wheezing bellows. Persius is to write about familiar things in a less elevated style marked by smoothness and pungency as he rakes over diseased morals and pins vice to the mat. The writer quickly assures Cornutus that he is not pursuing trifles; he needs a hundred mouths to express his admiration for his philosopher friend.

Persius begins by describing how he came to Cornutus at an early age to be molded by him and how they grew together as if born under the same constellation. But the poet has in this respect been the exception, since, in spite of Cornutus' ability to offer the philosophic instruction and consolation that they need, most men do not take advantage of it, simply because they are too busy with their materialistic pursuits.

As he waxes philosophical at this point about the need that each man has for true freedom, Persius strongly implies that this is the main benefit to be derived from Cornutus' philosophy. It is not that liberty which results from some praetor's edict, but the freedom of soul which comes from knowing the truth and from being aware of what is right in a given situation. The man who has achieved this state has moderate desires, treats his friends fairly, and is generous and sparing at the proper times, while his unenlightened counterpart is simply a fool who cannot lift a finger without going wrong.

Though you protest that you are free by the laws, Persius tells his imaginary sceptic, avarice and luxury will pull you first one way and then the other. Consider the lover in a play. When he says very grandiloquently that he is going to abandon his passion for a young lady and succeeds, he comes to enjoy freedom in the Stoic sense. Usually, however, he is unsuccessful, and he is like the politician or Jew who may feel free, but who is actually a slave to his canvassing

or his superstition. In an abrupt final comment Persius smiles in the
direction of his opponents when he asserts that, if you talk like this
to a varicose-veined centurion, he will guffaw in your face.

It is difficult to disagree with those who say that this is the most
successful of Persius' Stoic satires, for the straightforward narrative
style and restrained diatribe prove refreshing and make the poem not
so much a sermon, as a *sermo* or conversation, one-sided though this
may be. There is also a satisfying alternation in thought between the
positive recommendation of the Stoic *libertas* and description of
those who have not accepted or cannot accept the idea of this ethical
and moral freedom. This atmosphere is reinforced by a wide variety
of dialogue that ranges all the way from the personal conversations
of the poet with Cornutus, the procrastinator, and the sceptic,
through the exhortations addressed to the unlucky moral slave by
Avarice and Luxury, to a scene drawn from comedy.

The drama and liveliness of this satire come also from the wide
assortment of characters who make their appearance: Cornutus,
trader, glutton, gambler, Cleanthes, procrastinator, Dama (who
becomes Marcus Dama), Brutus, Masurius Sabinus, praetor, camp-
follower, rustic, ditchdigger, Bathyllus, Crispinus, Davus, Chaeres-
tratus and Chrysis, Luxury, Avarice, slaves from Cos, politician,
mob, Herod and the Jews, and Cybele with her priestess and
followers. It may all still smack of the bookcase, and the poetry may
lack the spontaneity of Horace's, but the features just mentioned
combine to make this the most spirited of Persius' *Satires*.

The sixth satire is a letter written by Persius from Luna on the
Ligurian coast to Caesius Bassus who is on his Sabine estate. The
satirist is in a somewhat expansive mood; he is at peace with the
world and feels no need to worry about other people and their
successes or anticipate any misfortunes that may befall him. He is
going to enjoy life not by being too frugal or too prodigal, but by
simply living up to his means, though in special circumstances he
may use some of his capital. His heir is not going to like this for
obviously personal reasons, while others with less at stake will
shake their heads at what they consider to be an attitude fostered
by one or other of the foreign philosophies. But these criticisms are
nothing to worry about, for, after all, what can a beneficiary do to
you when you are dead?

At this point Persius turns to his heir and tells him that he is not
only going to spend some money on a donation of gladiators to a

triumphal celebration, but that he is also going to make a dole to the people. When the other threatens rather petulantly to refuse the inheritance, Persius informs him that he does not really care, since, even if there is no one left in the family, he can always find a beggar who will be willing to take his place. The satirist advises his heir to accept what is passed on to him and be thankful for it, even if it is somewhat less than it might have been, for Persius is not going to live a miserable life in order to leave his successor the means of living extravagantly. What is more, there is no end to this kind of greed, since the more a man gets the more he wants.

In this satire Persius comes close to recommending a happy mean, at least as far as the enjoyment of life is concerned. He can never become a Horace, of course, but at the beginning of this poem Persius is more genial and amiable than at any other point in the *Satires*. It is tempting to see here a mellowing of his rigidly Stoic outlook, which might have continued had he lived long enough to write more. The genial atmosphere does not last through to the end of the satire, however, for the thought of his heir's reaction leads naturally to a condemnation of prodigality and greed, and it is on this note that the poem ends.

If Probus is right when he says that Cornutus removed several verses from the end of Persius' book of satires, then the lines should logically have come from the end of this satire, leaving it unfinished. But the sixth satire gives every indication of having been completed; it even ends on the same negative note as the first, third, and fifth satires. Moreover, it is difficult to imagine what Persius might have added to round it off. If he had gone on to discuss greed at greater length, the whole thing would probably have degenerated into another diatribe, and the relatively relaxed and informal atmosphere that he works so hard to create would have been lost. As far as the thought is concerned, Persius has made his point about living correctly and has added a few observations on greed, so that there seems to be nothing more to say. It is perhaps better, then, to imagine the excised lines as coming from a seventh satire that had just been begun.

Characteristics

There is no need to make further mention of the fact that the *Satires* are pervaded by a Stoic outlook. It is important to notice, however, that they are not merely philosophical diatribes and that Persius is not preaching Stoicism. He is actually using his philosophical background and training to point out men's faults and criticize contemporary social conditions, so that if he is selling anything, it is not philosophy, but morality.

All of this becomes clearer from a glance at the themes of the various satires, for, in spite of the fact that they are heavily layered with Stoic thought, the content is by no means exclusively Stoic. The first satire, for example, has no more to do with any specific philosophy than does Juvenal's first satire on this topic. The same may be said of the subject matter of the second satire, which had been treated in Plato's *Alcibiades I* and had made its way into rhetoric as a standard theme on which an orator-to-be might speak. Moreover, in this poem Persius is dealing with a problem that transcends Stoicism—and all philosophy, for that matter—so that he quickly goes beyond the paradox that all fools are impious to plead for something basic and universal—an honest, reverent attitude to religion.

As far as the fourth satire is concerned, the point has already been made that the theme developed here is common to a number of philosophies and rhetoric. By the same token, the theory of the Golden Mean and the idea of enjoying one's resources that are found together in the last satire are not necessarily Stoic. It is wrong, then, to look upon Persius as a doctrinaire Stoic and to criticize him, as some have done, for giving a thoroughly traditional and unimaginative account of Stoicism. He is not so much a philosophical thinker as a social thinker and as such is not primarily interested in developing and elaborating Stoic thought, but in using it to discover and solve the ills of Roman society.

When Persius is judged as a poet with his eye on people and society, his true worth may be seen. Satire is poetry, and because Persius knew this he drew freely on his literary predecessors. In his poems there are echoes and imitations of writers as widely different as Homer, Plato, Euripides, Theocritus, Ennius, Plautus, Terence, Propertius, and Ovid. It has already been noted that two lines of Lucretius provided the pattern for the first line of the first satire, and it can be shown that Catullus and Vergil also had a strong appeal for Persius.

But the two most important influences on the *Satires* seem to have been Lucilius and Horace. As matters stand, most of the evidence for Lucilian inspiration comes from external comments in the ancient *Life* and commentaries. According to Persius' biographer, the poet was inspired to write satire by Lucilius' Book 10, in which the earlier satirist had commented on contemporary Roman literature and had attacked the early Roman poets. Again, an ancient commentator says that Persius' third satire imitated one from Book 4 of Lucilius which contained criticism of the vices and the prodigality of the wealthy. This authority also mentions the fact that the second line of Satire 1 (*Quis leget haec?*) comes from Lucilius' first book and compares two other lines of this satire (1.27-28) with two lines of Lucilius (1344-45).

A direct comparison between Persius' *Satires* and the fragments of the earlier poet suggests that his first poem is not unlike the introductory satire of Lucilius' Book 26, at least as far as purpose and subject are concerned. A passage of Satire 3 (88-109) has been compared to a few lines of Lucilius (678-88) by virtue of their having a description of sickness in common and also because of verbal reminiscences. There are other similarities between subject matter and vocabulary that may or may not be significant. When all the evidence is considered, however, it would appear that Lucilius' influence lay not so much in matters of detail as in inspiration and general tone.

Persius' debt to Horace is great, too great to cover in any detail here, for in the fifth satire alone there are over 100 quotations, imitations, and echoes. The influence is most obvious in the characters that reappear in Persius' poems. Bestius, the protector of morals, Dama, the slave who has risen to a position of power, Crispinus in his vocation of bath-keeper, and Cratinus, the doctor, all crop up again in their original roles. Nerius, who is a usurer in Horace, is transferred loosely as a man who is out after money, and Natta, who was originally a dirty old man, turns up as a prodigal.

But names are only a small part of Horace's influence. Though he quotes no line in its entirety, Persius uses many phrases and word combinations of his predecessor which he adapts to create interesting and even surprising effects. At one time he simply substitutes a word of his own for a key word of Horace, while in other instances he conflates two or more Horatian phrases. There are still other examples where Persius is obviously imitating a picture or thought of Horace without making any direct verbal connection.

There can be no doubt that Persius knew his Horace very well, but a glance at the many parallels shows clearly that he was no slavish imitator. For, in spite of the fact that his debt to his predecessor was great, by combining and adapting what he borrowed the satirist made the material his own and used it to create a poetry that was new and different.

Persius' style has at one time or another been described as harsh, angular, disconnected, grotesque, condensed, allusive, and crabbed, while some have contrived delightful new Persian combinations such as "contorted involution," apparently because they feel the traditional qualifiers are inadequate. While all of these terms are appropriate to a greater or lesser degree, it is better not to call his poetry obscure as many have done, for this implies that thought and imagery are difficult to penetrate and understand, and this is simply not the case. What Persius is attempting to say is usually perfectly clear, and, while his figures of speech may at times be contrived, they are with a few exceptions perfectly understandable.

Also, for the careful reader there is nothing vague and obscure about the organization which Persius employs within the individual satires. Each poem begins from an immediate dramatic situation of which the poet or his spokesman is a part, soon develops into a diatribe-like monologue in which the point of the satire is discussed, and ends with an epigrammatic comment that may contain the moral of the story, as in the first two satires, or may restate the problem by relating to it a typical example from literature, mythology, contemporary life, or philosophy.

It is true, however, that Persius' *Satires* are difficult to read. This is partly because of an uneven narrative style and partly because of the many unusual combinations of words. The problems that his narrative presents are especially evident in matters of transition. The example which springs to mind is the prologue in which the apparent lack of connection between the two halves has led some to be suspicious of the poem.

The third satire is full of such disconnection. The metaphor of the broken pot and unmolded clay (3.21-24) fits only loosely with what precedes it and hardly at all with what follows, making the movement from the reality of the episode with the pen (19) through this metaphor to the reality of the young man's landed possessions a little more than one can follow at a first reading. The transition from Natta to the tyrants a little later (3.35) is also unexpected, and then when the point of this has barely become clear, Persius jolts his reader on to a picture of himself as a boy (3.44), the purpose of which is again not immediately apparent.

There is the same abruptness in the appearance of the centurion, who is not organically connected with the rest of the poem, but is allowed to come and go as a character in a stream of consciousness (3.77-85). Moreover, when the physically ill man is introduced (3.88-106), it is without comment and without connection of any kind, and the morally sick man makes a similarly sudden appearance (107-18), though the other has at least to some extent prepared the way for him. In the third satire, then, Persius shifts gears suddenly and often, though a second or third reading clarifies most of the difficulties.

There is not as much of this kind of thing in any one of the other satires, but abrupt transitions do occur fairly frequently. The shift to Jupiter and then to Staius in the second satire (17-19), for example, is a little uncomfortable for the reader. Towards the beginning of the fourth satire there is a problem of transition and connection in the unexpected, almost jarring appearance of the old woman whose position does not become clear until two lines later (19). When Persius suddenly begins generalizing in the fifth satire about the many vocations of man (52) and appears to be getting to his philosophical point, he instead comes right back to Cornutus (62-64). Then, after this false start, there is a real shift to true freedom (73), which the reader must relate to the earlier praise of Cornutus by assuming that it is the most important lesson to be learned from his philosophy. Another unsignalled transition occurs in this satire when the poet suddenly introduces a scene from comedy (161).

The disruption of the train of thought caused by Bestius' appearance in the sixth satire (37-41) comes from the fact that Persius has a cavalier-like attitude to dialogue. He is not at all interested in exploring its dramatic possibilities and does not even bother to make it clear who is speaking. The reason for this is at least partly the fact that his serious, intense purpose keeps driving him in the direction of diatribe, sermon, and monologue and away from more relaxed devices like dialogue. In the case of the passage just mentioned, the words fall into place as soon as the reader realizes that the heir is speaking.

The many unusual verbal combinations that also make the *Satires* difficult reading occur both in brief phrases and in the larger units that form the imagery of these poems. With regard to his language, Persius insists that he has two purposes in mind—to practice an extreme economy (1.125) and to express what he has to say in as striking a manner possible (5.14). With the first he is running against the grain of the times, but he tacitly commits himself to such condensation when he expresses his criticism of the frothy, foamy, effete style of his contemporaries in his first satire. In his desire to present his thoughts in an eye-catching manner, however, he is very much a part of this times, as a glance at the rhetorical treatises of Seneca or Lucan's epic poem, the *Pharsalia,* quickly shows.

And so Persius' *Satires* are full of condensed and unusual expressions and pictures, some of which are successful and some not. The satirist's adversary in Satire 1 says in a much quoted passage that display of one's learning is justification enough for writing poetry (24-25): "To what purpose, then, is learning if this ferment and the wild fig tree that has been planted within you does not burst your breast and make its way out?" Here the metaphors of fermentation and fig tree are boldly placed side-by-side in a context entirely foreign to both and presented in starkly simple language, so that, while the result is perhaps a little too grotesque, Persius has vividly and succinctly made his point.

Somewhat similar to this is the satirist's description in Satire 5 of how he will set his critic straight (91-92): "Get ready to learn! But let that anger and wrinkled snarl drop from your nose while I pull your old grandmothers out of your heart." The passage is difficult to construe, but it seems to mean that the poet intends to correct some of the skeptic's outdated ideas. Once again, the picture is perhaps overdrawn, but the choice of adjectives and verbs, the use of the parts of the body, the striking figures of speech, and the general condensation of language produce a blend that can only belong to Persius.

There are some figures of speech that are similarly strange and exaggerated—the heart that sweats drops of blood that come from the left side of the breast, the avaricious man who flogs the stock exchange, Cornutus who is planting Cleanthes' crop in clean, receptive ears. At times Persius tries to pile too many of these metaphors together as when he has Socrates in Satire 4 introduce the scales of justice, the metaphor of the curved and straight lines, and the theta of condemnation close upon one another (10-13). In this case the irony is heightened, but the mind is distracted by such concentrated exaggeration. Perhaps the most obvious example of this kind of hyperbole occurs towards the beginning of the third satire, when the Stoic preacher addresses the young reprobate:

> It's your game that's being played; it's you who are
> dripping away like a madman; you will be despised.
> The pot half-baked and made of green clay when
> struck shows its flaw in the sound and gives a grudging
> response. You are damp, soft clay, and now, right
> now, you should be taken quickly and molded with-
> out stopping on the swiftly revolving wheel. (20-24)

Games, a leaky bottle, a cheap pot, clay on the potter's wheel are
all crowded together in such a way as to suggest that the poet was
carried away by it all. Again, as Persius describes his stage of development when he came to Cornutus for instruction, what could have
been a relatively straightforward account becomes a maze because of
the poet's search for the striking word and the brilliant figure
(5.30-36).

But this is not to say that Persius cannot put together successful
combinations of language and metaphor. His description in the first
satire of a typical reciter of contemporary poetry is quite effective
for the feeling of contempt that almost oozes from it:

> Here is someone with a hyacinth-colored shirt speaking
> something stinking through his nose; with a lisp he
> filters forth his Phyllises and his Hypsipyles and what-
> ever else of the seers is weepworthy, as he trips up
> his words on the roof of his delicate mouth. (32-35)

The criticism is devastating because of a concentration of metaphoric language of the senses and the images of filtering and wrestling
and also because of a careful use of adjectives and verbs.

Another passage that catches the eye in much the same way
occurs in the third satire when Persius asks the prodigal whether
he has any certain goal:

> Is there something at which you are aiming and directing
> your bowshot? Or are you chasing crows every which
> way with potsherds and mud, not worrying where you're
> going, and are you living life on the spur of the
> moment? (60-62)

The young man's lack of direction is neatly developed by the
metaphor from hunting, and the point is driven home in the last

three words. The much quoted comparison that Persius makes between the procrastinator and the rear wheel of a wagon in the fifth satire is similarly vivid and forceful (70-72).

But, as a rule, Persius is most effective in his shorter passages and individual words. His keen powers of observation are at work, for example, as he describes the illusion of the morning sun widening the crack through which it enters (3.2). He also has a talent for keeping close to the traditional while adding a new dimension to it, as when he speaks not of "knowing thyself," but of "getting down into oneself" (4.23-24).

One of his most striking figures is the metaphor of the curve that keeps recurring, but which never extends to more than a line in length. The best example is found in the second satire (61): "Oh souls bowed down upon the earth and empty of anything that smacks of heaven!" Here language, figure, and meter combine to produce a feeling of agitation, depression, and foreboding. Everywhere in the *Satires* there are eye and ear-catching turns of phrase and metaphor expressed briefly: the rare bird, a warty Antiopa, a [sizzling] frying pan of speaking, a stupid beard, glassy bile, a sick throat slowly giving forth sulfurous fumes, citizens made yesterday, chunks of hearty poetry, the varnish of colorful language, and a circumcised sabbath.

To create these effects, Persius draws on all levels of language from the colloquial to the literary. When he insists that he is using "words of the toga" (5.14), he seems to mean language that is in everyday use in Rome and vocabulary that is primarily Roman and not Greek. As a matter of fact, the mixture of idiom and vocabulary that is found in the *Satires* is the healthy combination that characterizes earlier Roman satire. Persius draws much from the colloquial language of the city, but at the same time is not afraid to adapt and quote even from lyric and epic poetry. The odd barbarism and solecism appear, and there are a fair number of archaisms, many of which are probably drawn from Lucilius. From time to time he will even coin a word for effect. The *Satires* also leave the impression that Persius avoided Greek vocabulary, for he uses such words sparingly, usually limiting himself to those which had by this time made their way into the everyday language of Rome.

One dimension of Persius' style that is often overlooked is the relatively straightforward narrative that occurs from time to time. There is a Lucretian simplicity about his charge to prodigal young men (3.66-76), for instance, and though the ideas expressed are not original and show a certain repetition, the simplicity of the Latin balanced against the loftiness of thought and purpose makes this one of the most attractive passages in the *Satires*. Persius' description of the man who enjoys true freedom leaves somewhat the same impression (5.104-12), while his warning to his heir is also free of erudite allusion and unnecessarily complicated language (6.52-60).

Part of this narrative technique is the bright and graphic picture that Persius paints on occasion. Both in the scene at the beginning of Satire 3, where the reprobate young man is visited by the sage while he is still in bed, and in the description a few lines later of the sick man who enjoys a sudden and unexpected funeral, the poet has presented the type under discussion with particular perspicuity. Especially attractive is the portrayal of the misdirected grandmother or aunt in the second satire. After inviting the reader's attention as if to a portrait, Persius goes on to show her superstitiously charming away the evil eye with saliva and her middle finger and impatiently praying for success for the newborn baby as she imagines him on the estate of a Licinus or in the villa of a Crassus. Persius makes her desires stand out even more clearly by quoting part of her prayer directly, and then almost as an anticlimax he personally requests Jupiter not to grant such prayers. With these lines the episode takes on an epigrammatic identity separate from its function as part of a satire and becomes a little poem in its own right.

Everywhere in the *Satires* there is a striking sense of climax that contributes to the effectiveness of Persius' style. Natta's final immersion in vice, for instance, where not even a bubble comes to the surface (3.34), and Jupiter's cry of "Good god!" at a preposterous prayer (2.23) are at the same time climactic and ironic. But perhaps the best example of the ironic climax is the cap which Persius puts on his description of a man who has squandered everything he owns on offerings to the gods in the hope of increasing his resources (2.50-51): ". . . until a dime disappointed and without hope gives forth a helpless sigh in the bottom of his money box." This is the result of all the man's striving, and the personification provides a nice twist, for his complete frustration and dejection are transferred to the coin and underlined by words of negative connotation: disappointed (*deceptus*), without hope (*exspes*), helpless sigh (*nequiquam suspiret*), the bottom (*imo*).

Finally, Persius' tendency to use *sententiae*, or brief pithy comments, for effect is typical of the period in which he is writing. Some of these have already been mentioned, but among the others that should be singled out are his espousal of an enjoyment of life without prodigality in the last satire (25-26): "Live right up to your crop and grind your granaries completely," and his comment on people's relations with one another in the fourth satire (42): "We attack and in our turn we offer our legs to the arrows." He also sums up the message of this satire in a striking way (52): "Live with yourself and get to know how sparse your furnishings are." The ending of the second satire where he recommends an honest approach to life and religion is equally pithy (75): "Let me take these to the temple and I will have success with just a little grain."

Though the hexameter that Persius uses displays a little more regularity, perhaps because of Ovidian influence, it is essentially the informal verse of earlier satire. The poet is careful to avoid dactylic and spondaic words at the beginning of the line, while at the end he uses words of four and five syllables only seven times all-told and seldom allows a monosyllable that is not part of an elision. Within the line there is no hiatus, and the male caesura in the third foot predominates, occurring in some 600 of the 650 lines. Informality is achieved by word grouping in the line and often by an enjambment that puts a conjunction, relative, or correlative at the end of one line and the rest of the construction in the next.

Before leaving Persius, some attempt must be made to give him his proper place in the history of Roman satire. It is not enough to say that he is inferior to the other writers in this genre, for the point has already been made that much of his poetry is effective and some of it is even striking. Nor is it fair to brush his poems aside on the grounds that they are not true satires, since as a matter of fact, the three elements of personality, variety, and criticism, that were such important constituents of earlier satire, are repeated here.

The poetic personality that pervades the *Satires* cannot be the well-rounded individuality that Lucilius and Horace present, simply because Persius is under the influence of a thoroughgoing Stoicism which leaves him a sincere and earnest moralist, but little else. Every now and then, however, there are flashes of feeling that suggest a greater depth of character. His honest admiration for and attachment to Cornutus in the fifth satire, for instance, and his near genial attitude in the sixth satire make it a distinct possibility that, had he lived longer and written more, Persius might have presented a better rounded picture of himself. But even if the poetic personality is incomplete, the moral earnestness of the *Satires* remains an important element of Persius' originality, for such an eager, serious, and at times almost grim attitude does not predominate in Lucilius and Horace.

The variety that has been mentioned from time to time as a feature of Roman satire is not as pronounced in Persius' poems as it is in the writings of his predecessors. At least part of the reason for this is the simple fact that Persius did not produce a corpus of comparable length. But a broad panoply of characters does make its appearance, and quite a number of human shortcomings and vices are criticized.

With Persius, however, it is a variety of style and language that predominates, and it is because of this that no two satires are alike, in spite of the similarities that have already been mentioned. Within the individual poems this miscellaneous element makes itself felt in rapid and unexpected changes of scene and metaphor and in the uneven alternation of narrative and dialogue, with the novel use of language reinforcing this illusion of diversity and variety.

But it is the element of sincere, outspoken criticism that so predominates in Persius' *Satires* that it might be called their essence. By combining the passionate approach of Lucilius with the language of the genial Horace and adding his own touch he has created a kind of satire that does not in the least resemble that of either of the earlier poets. He has produced an invective that may at one time be insulting and at another sardonic, but which most of the time is filled with ridicule and irony. Juvenal owed much in his satiric technique to Persius.

The *Satires* of Persius, then, have a vein of originality in them that gives them an identity of their own, but when they are put in their proper place in the hierarchy of satire, they most certainly fall below those of Lucilius, Horace, and Juvenal, simply because Persius' narrower outlook has produced poetry of more limited scope. This came at least in part from the poet's overwhelming commitment to moral teaching, which imposed certain restrictions on subject matter and methods and left little room for the informality and spontaneity of Lucilius, the relaxed and genial approach of Horace, and the honest and natural disgust of Juvenal.

But it is not entirely fair to judge Persius against the other writers of satire without recognizing the fact that he was in a sense a victim of the times in which he wrote. By now Lucilius' freewheeling approach was inconceivable and Horace's geniality was anachronistic, while Juvenal's indignation was not yet possible for both political and literary reasons.

Moreover, Persius had to cope with a situation which made satirical writing very difficult, and so he turned to the Stoic philosophy as the vehicle for his satire. This was a clever move on his part, both because the popularity of Stoicism gave a certain validity and even protection to his poetry and also because it enabled him to speak in more general terms about the vices of society and so avoid the risk of offending those in power. But Persius faced another problem, that of making his satire novel and forceful in a period when novelty was a byword in literature. He solved it by adopting and extending the outspoken criticism that marked much of Lucilian satire and by creating a new and colorful satiric style.

VII

JUVENAL: A RETURN TO INVECTIVE

The last third of the first century after Christ was fertile ground for satire at Rome. By now it was generally felt by Romans of the better class that the Augustan peace with its concomitant luxury and extravagance had had a generally debilitating effect on society. There had been too many emperors after Augustus who seemed determined to outdo one another in cruelty, depravity, and dissipation of all kinds. Many Romans believed that there was much to satirize by the time the emperor and archvillain Domitian died in 96, and the opportunity to do so came with the advent of a new, though still limited, freedom of speech under Nerva, Trajan, and Hadrian.

The result is that there are satiric overtones in most of the writing of the time. The historian Tacitus, for example, leaves no doubt as to how he feels about the various emperors and other leading personalities who had lived before him. A work like the *Annals* is so filled with running satiric commentary that the reader begins to wonder about the historicity of much of what Tacitus is saying. Again, in his biographies of the Caesars, Suetonius is not afraid to inject opinion both outright and by innuendo about the personalities and actions of the various people he discusses. Even Pliny the Younger in his *Epistles* with their sophisticated subject matter and carefully controlled style makes excursions now and then into the satiric, especially when he has occasion to reflect on the morals and habits of his contemporaries.

It would be interesting and valuable to pursue this satiric spirit in the writing of the Silver Age for the light it sheds on the social and literary atmosphere of the times. But this is above and beyond our immediate purposes and such tempting digressions must be saved for other times and other places. The most that can be said here is that at the end of the first century and the beginning of the second century the moral climate, the new freedom, and the Romans' natural propensity for satire combined to produce poetry and prose shot through with the satiric spirit.

Even though he is not a satirist by definition, Martial (c. A.D. 40-c.104) must at least be mentioned in passing both because of the obviously satiric purpose of so many of his *Epigrams* and because he had a considerable influence on his younger contemporary, Juvenal. The first eleven books of his *Epigrams* were written between 86 and 98 after Christ at the rate of about one a year, while the twelfth appeared perhaps in 102, three years after the poet had left Rome to live out the rest of his life in his native Spain. Books 13 and 14 were actually the earliest, appearing in 84 or 85. He did most of his writing under Domitian, then, and though there is much criticism in his poetry, Martial managed to avoid trouble for himself by taking a careful approach to his satire and by including in his collection many poems of flattery addressed to the emperor.

His primary purpose in writing the *Epigrams* was to entertain, and even a quick reading of these short, usually clever, often witty poems leaves the impression that, while they were written for an audience, they clearly served as a diversion for the poet himself. And so it is not surprising to find Martial calling his poems "trifles" and describing them as "playful" or "sportive." But this is only half the story, for he also insists that his page "tastes of mankind" (10.4.10) and that it is "life" which appears in his poetry (8.3.19-20; 10.4.8-10). And, as a matter of fact, his pages are filled with people of all kinds and with all their habits, customs, and institutions. Martial gets into every nook and cranny of Roman society to drag out subjects for his commentary.

By the time he wrote, criticism, parody, caricature, burlesque, and many of the other elements that together make up Roman satire were also an important part of epigram. In late Republican times, Catullus had given this satiric spirit a significant part to play in his epigrams, and though the works of his successors in the genre— Domitius Marsus, Albinovanus Pedo, and Lentulus Gaetulicus—are now all but non-existent, it is clear that they exploited it in their poetry, too. The increasing insistence on epigrammatic "point," the "sting in the tail" which usually contains a satiric thrust, is one evidence of this.

The connections between epigram and the genre satire are clear and obvious. Both show an almost unlimited variety which in Martial's poems extends even to the meters used. Dramatic elements, dialogue, commentary on contemporary people and affairs, mordant wit, irony, and the personality of the poet and his relationship to his poetry are other common bonds. Even the obscenity that plays so large a part in Martial's *Epigrams* can be paralleled to some extent in Lucilius, Horace, and Juvenal.

In many of his poems, Martial is out to draw attention to the foibles and faults of the people that surround him. Dishonesty of all kinds, the many abuses of wealth, perversion, ostentatious luxury, arrogance, greed, and the vanity of men and women are just a few of the shortcomings that catch the poet's eye. Nor does he overlook the many everyday problems of living in the city.

He carries out his satiric purposes for the most part by concentrating on individuals who exhibit these foibles and faults. By mentioning contemporaries he gives his satire a special vividness and topicality. But many of the names which appear in his poems are made up for the occasion, so that they tend to generalize his satire. In both cases he makes careful choices with the ultimate purpose of protecting himself against reprisal.

And so a cross-section of Roman society passes before the reader's eyes. There are women of all kinds, ranging from those guilty of too profuse a use of makeup to others suspected of poisoning friends and relatives. Men of all nationalities, professions, and callings appear—Charmenion the effeminate Corinthian, Cotta the fop, Caecilianus the mean and greedy host, as well as legacy hunters, wealthy auctioneers, swaggering ex-slaves, misers, plagiarizing poets, gossips, poverty-stricken dandies, prickly lawyers, second-rate doctors, talkative rhetoricians, and on and on.

It is almost impossible to know what epigrams to single out as being representative of Martial's satire. He needs to be read in his entirety. But perhaps a careful selection of a few of his poems will at least hint at the range of Martial's satiric criticism and will at the same time serve to illustrate some of the satiric methods that he uses.

Like Juvenal, Martial is a keen observer of life in the city. In one of his earlier epigrams he tells Fabianus why he should not come to Rome (4.5):

> You're a good but poor man and truthful in what you
> say and think. What is it, then, Fabianus, that you're
> looking for in coming to Rome? You can't be considered
> a pimp or a good-time fellow. Nor can you summon
> trembling defendants with a solemn and gloomy tone
> of voice or seduce the wife of a close friend or get an
> erection up for frigid little old ladies or sell imperial
> favor that is based on nothing and disappears like smoke
> or applaud Canus or applaud Glaphyrus. How, poor
> soul, are you going to manage a living? "A reliable man,
> a sure friend—" This is nothing. You'll never get to be a
> Philomelus that way.

In these ten lines, which are comparable to parts of Juvenal's third
satire, Martial not only manages to give a vivid picture of immorality
in Rome, but also adds a depth to his satire by jabbing at Greeks like
Glaphyrus who has found success in the city as a musician and the
freedman Philomelus who has risen to the top by following the
regimen that Martial has just described.

If we can almost hear Juvenal's Umbricius talking in this poem,
he has to come to mind again as Martial turns to discuss the noises
of the city (12.57). A poor man just can't get any sleep as a veritable
parade of noisemakers goes by—teachers, bakers, bronzesmiths,
money-changers, goldsmiths, soldiers, shipwrecked beggars, Jews, and
hucksters of all kinds. The contrast that Martial develops between
the poor man's life with all its harassments and that of the wealthy
Sparsus who enjoys complete tranquility illustrates an epigrammatic
comment of Juvenal (3.235): "Only with great resources does a man
manage to find sleep in the city." Then, as now, urban poverty was a
real and lasting problem, and Martial, too, can sum it up in a few
words (5.81): "If you're poor now, Aemilianus, you'll always be
poor. Wealth is given to nobody nowadays except the rich."

Martial also has much to say about the faults and foibles of
humanity in general. Caecilianus is taken to task in no uncertain
terms for his miserly gluttony (1.20):

> Tell me! What craziness is this? While the whole mob
> of guests whom you've invited look on, you, Caecilianus,
> all by yourself gobble up the mushrooms. What is
> there for me to pray for that suits your great big
> belly or gut? May *you* gulp down a mushroom such as
> Claudius ate!

The point becomes clear when we remember that the emperor Claudius was allegedly poisoned by a mushroom. Martial's technique here is typical of many epigrams, for in the last line he extends the satire to include a second personality and holds the ironic climax to the very last word (*edas:* "may you eat!").

A number of Martial's poems take the form of advice on how to avoid such faults. An epigram addressed to Maximus (2.53) in a sense complements the one to Caecilianus. For here the poet tells his friend that if he wants to become free he should not attempt to dine out, but should devote himself to living a simple, frugal life. Into this epigram once again Martial weaves additional satire by mentioning Cinna, the host, with his imported dishes of gold inlay (*chrysendeta*) and by making oblique reference to the expensive wines that appear on the tables of the wealthy.

The greed of legacy hunters also catches the epigrammatist's eye. Here, for example, is Gemellus who wants to marry Maronilla, not because she's beautiful, but because she has a cough and so is likely to die soon (1.10). Envy, hypocrisy, pride, and self-importance are just a few of the other shortcomings that Martial singles out to criticize in his contemporaries.

The various professions in Rome also come in for their fair share of satiric comment in the *Epigrams.* Doctors, lawyers, and poets were especially vulnerable. Diaulus who had become an undertaker after being a doctor is twice described by Martial as really not having changed his job. He still lays people out dead (1.30; 1.47). Again, doctors like Symmachus actually do more harm than good to their patients by making house-calls (5.9; 8.25). And so it is not surprising to find that even a healthy person like Andragoras should die in his sleep simply because he has seen Doctor Hermocrates in one of his dreams (6.53).

Lawyers seem to have been a favorite target of Martial. Among those who stand out is Sabellus who at the time of the Saturnalia is swelled up with pride at having received so many gifts from grateful clients (4.46). As Martial lists these, it gradually becomes clear that by urban standards they are really quite trivial—wheat, beans, sausage, olives, cheap pots, to name only a few. The last two lines of the poem, then, take on a heavy irony: "Why, Sabellus hasn't had a more profitable Saturnalia in ten years!" With this observation the whole poem becomes a delightful commentary on this fellow's qualifications as a lawyer.

Mention might be made in passing of the unnamed lawyer who is so surly and self-important that he cannot even say hello (5.51) and of Cinna whose eloquence allows him to speak only nine words in ten hours (8.7). In another poem there is a note of frustration in the poet's voice as he pleads with Postumus, his lawyer, to stop his lofty tirade on the Battle of Cannae, the war with Mithridates, the Punic Wars, and all the Mariuses, Sullas, and Scaevolas and get down to pleading Martial's case, which, incidentally, involves three goats (6.19).

Contemporary poets do not escape Martial's satire, and as might be expected, his main criticisms are that they write poorly and they write too much. In his two epigrams on Ligurinus (3.45; 3.50) he anticipates Juvenal by lashing out at this second-rate poet who invites people to dinner as a means of gathering an audience to hear him recite his poetry. And then there is Gallicus, the poet-lawyer who professes to want an honest appraisal of his accomplishments (8.76). Martial gives him the truth in the last two lines of the poem: "O.K., then, hear what is truer than the truth: you, Gallicus, don't really want to hear the truth."

There can be no doubt, then, that the epigrammatist's purpose in large part was to satirize the world around him. But even a glance through Martial's poems shows that the genre epigram is far different from the genre satire. In fact, the poet himself differentiates between the two as he takes Tucca to task for imitating him in epic poetry, tragedy, lyric poetry, satire, elegy, and epigram (12.94).

In the first place, Martial's collection is made up of brief poems of an occasional nature written in a variety of meters. As such they are a different literary creation from satire where the longer format and the single narrative meter give more scope for sustained rhetoric and development of more elaborate themes.

The variety of epigram is also different from that of satire. In the former it exists mainly between poems, while in the satires of Lucilius, Persius, Horace, and Juvenal it is found not only between poems but also within the individual satires. A comparison will perhaps make this clear. Martial and Juvenal both have a great deal to say about living in Rome. The epigrammatist presents his criticisms in a fragmented way via individual poems in each of which he deals with a single aspect of life in the city. Juvenal, on the other hand, puts it all together in his third satire and rushes his reader from one urban scene to another.

Finally, it should be pointed out that the purposes of epigram and satire are really quite different. Both deal with life, but Lucilius,

Horace, Juvenal, and, to a lesser degree, Persius sweep through life
pointing out the ills of society and the world, insisting that something should be done, and at least hinting that something can be done
to rectify the situation. By comparison Martial is like a gnat flitting
from one person or thing to another and biting here and there without any sustained purpose. In fact, he deliberately disrupts the satiric
effect of his *Epigrams* by including poems of adulation addressed to
the emperor and by adding others that are complimentary, consola-
tory, or descriptive. As we shall see later, Juvenal felt there was an
epic quality about his satire. Perhaps this is what is missing in the
Epigrams of Martial.

It has already been pointed out that Martial had an important
influence on Juvenal. After what has been said about satire in the
Epigrams, it should come as no surprise to find that the influence
lies in theme and details of language rather than in meter, rhetoric,
and other more general literary effects. But the influence is surprisingly strong, for throughout the *Satires*—even the latest ones—there
are reverberations and reminiscences of Martial's topics, characters,
and language—so much so, in fact, that deliberate and direct borrow-
ing can be assumed, in spite of the fact that Juvenal has reworked the
material thoroughly for his own purposes.

Decimus Iunius Iuvenalis is the last and, in the opinion of many,
the greatest of the Roman verse satirists. Very little is known about
his life. The *Satires* offer next to no help, the *Lives* appended to the
manuscripts are late and unreliable, and the three poems in which
Martial mentions him (7.24; 7.91; 12.18) provide no information
except that he is considered eloquent by the epigrammatist.

Typical of the problems facing anyone attempting a reconstruction of Juvenal's life is that presented by the famous inscription
which was found at the poet's home town of Aquinum about 80
miles south of Rome—and which, incidentally, was subsequently lost.
It may not even have referred to the poet, and if it did, because it
was a simple dedication from a young army officer to a local
goddess, it had no bearing on Juvenal's poetic activities in Rome.
The most that can be gleaned from it is the fact that Juvenal belonged
to the local aristocracy at Aquinum.

Juvenal was probably born sometime between A.D. 50 and 70.
This is at least a reasonable conjecture, since incidental references in
the *Satires* suggest that he was already middle-aged early in the second
century when his poetry first appeared. If, as the *Satires* also indicate,

he lived to be eighty years old, then he may have survived into the reign of Antoninus Pius who assumed power in A.D. 138.

The only other biographical item worth mentioning is the story of his exile. Supposedly Juvenal wrote a lampoon against the actor, Paris, a favorite of the emperor Domitian, who promptly banished the poet to Egypt where he died a short while later. Since the satirist could have been no older than forty-five in Domitian's reign, it is unlikely that any exile ever took place. The story was probably a fabrication by later scholars who had nothing to go on but the description of the Egyptian atrocities in Satire 15 and the antisocial nature of the satirist and his satire.

Book One (Satires 1-5)

There is no way of knowing when Juvenal began writing his *Satires*. The intense criticism of the activities of Domitian indicates, however, that the first of them could only have appeared after that emperor's death in 96. The first book may have been published soon after A.D. 100, since the prosecution of Marius Priscus which took place in that year is mentioned in Satire 1 (49). There is also the possibility that this book appeared as late as 110 or 111, if, as some scholars believe, there is a reference in Satire 2 (102-03) to the *Histories* of Tacitus which appeared between 104 and 109.

In terms of both form and content, the first five satires are best described as rhetorical invectives. Juvenal self-styles his poems as an expression of his overwhelming rage at the immorality and corruption that everywhere meets his eyes. Self-righteous indignation therefore determines the satirist's attitude, his poetic style, and the content of his *Satires*. He insists again and again, with seemingly deliberate exaggeration, that the world of the present is an incredibly evil place, ever moving toward apocalypse. Vice is at its highest point and ready for a fall.

Juvenal does provide an explanation for the existence of numinous evil, but in quasi-mythological terms. Rome has lost contact with her own sacred traditions, and this loss of the old virtues and customs has led to degeneracy and perversion. Juvenal's Rome is simply out of harmony with her own glorious past.

In his first satire the poet introduces the angry satirist and the evil world of contemporary Rome which he will deal with throughout this book. Here too are examples of rhetorical devices and poetic imagery which Juvenal will use as he moves to attack. Another important component of this satire is the criticism of contemporary literature that runs through it. While the moral criticism makes the poem programmatic for the first book, this aesthetic criticism makes it programmatic for the *Satires* as a whole.

Juvenal begins with the source of his vexation—the artificiality of contemporary literature, especially epic and tragedy, which have become sterile exercises in mythology. And as bad literature is a major source of his rage, so the satire that he writes is his means of taking revenge against poetasters. Not only is the satirist's criticism to be noted, but his poetry itself is also intended as an authentic, realistic literature to replace the cliches, monotony, and fraudulence of the recitations.

As it develops, then, the satire constitutes a defense of its own nature as opposed to the pretensions of contemporary epic and tragedy. Juvenal is careful to place himself within the literary tradition of satire and to point out how on the one hand he resembles his predecessors in the genre and how on the other he is creating something new.

At this point Juvenal suddenly insists that he is also a social critic, and with this the focus of the satire shifts from bad writing to bad men (22-80). Here descriptions of evil are extremely vivid, and the satirist makes two famous but paradoxical statements. First, given the circumstances of this society, it is difficult *not* to write satire. Secondly, anybody without the slightest literary talent could write poetry against these people (79-80): "If talent is lacking, indignation writes my verse, such as it can—the kind I can write or any old scribbler like Cluvienus." There will be no mythological fakery in his lines; his satire will mirror the very stuff of life.

For all his pretense to realism, there can be little doubt that Juvenal is at his rhetorical best here. The whole passage is actually a brilliantly developed rhetorical figure known as *enargeia* or "imagery," an imaginary imitation of events described as if they were right before the poet's eyes. He acts in these lines as though he has walked down to the crossroads with stylus and wax tablet in hand to describe the crimes and criminals of Rome. And so Juvenal has become as much a literary artist as the artificial writers he ridicules. It is almost as if he wants to emphasize this when in the next six lines he resorts to a mythological theme to explain the origin of human nature with its passion and vices:

> From the time when the storm clouds raised the water
> level, and Deucalion climbed a mountain in his ship and
> asked for a prophecy, and little by little the rocks grew
> warm and soft with life, and Pyrrha showed naked girls
> to men, whatever men do, their desires, fears, anger,
> pleasures, their joys and journeyings, this is the stuff of
> my satire. (81-86)

The content is the "stuffings of real life," while the form remains rhetorical commonplace. But it is a rhetorical commonplace used properly and effectively.

Instead of remaining at the abstract level with more universal condemnations of Rome, Juvenal now moves on to a vice which he feels is most representative of the corrupt Roman character. This is greed, especially that which appears in the patron-client relationship where the profit-motive has perverted traditional Roman honesty. A concrete example is given in the description of a day in the life of a poor Roman who must serve as client of a rich patron. Juvenal concentrates on the food dole and spends some time telling how the client-patron relationship is abused by the wealthy man who is at the same time greedy and gluttonous.

At this point the satirist develops a symmetry in his poem by returning to some of the key ideas of the opening lines. He now begins an imaginary dialogue (147-71) and criticizes his own original statements, saying that he cannot really deal with contemporary personages and events because he can get into trouble with influential people if he names them. This kind of a dialogue with an imaginary interlocutor or adversary, in which the satirist defends himself against possible charges of libel, is a satiric convention already developed in the works of Lucilius, Horace, and Persius.

Juvenal resolves his problem by writing against persons of history (170-71): "I shall try to say what I may be allowed to against those whose ashes lie along the Flaminian and Latin Roads." In the end, then, Juvenal reduces the scope of his pretentious program and resorts to another line of attack which seems ironically to subvert and contradict the original one.

According to the consensus of modern scholarship, the second satire is the earliest, simply because Domitian and his censorship play so large a role in it. Be this as it may, the real strength of the satire does not come so much from its social context as from its scabrous nature, for it deals with the theme of homosexuality in a humorous, not a moralizing, fashion. Some historical interpretations of the poem try to emphasize the role of Domitian, who played at being censor while conducting an incestuous love affair with his niece. This necessitates taking the theme of the satire as hypocrisy, and if this is the case, then the last two-thirds serve as a kind of afterthought. There is actually a better reason for Juvenal's attack on Domitian as censor. Beyond the question of hypocrisy that is involved, the satirist wants to demonstrate that Roman society is devoid of sexual morality and that consequently any censorship is sheer futility in a situation where the men of Rome have unmanned themselves.

The satire begins with an attack against hypocritical perverts who pretend to a philosophical and highly moral way of life, but who behind the stern guises are disgusting homosexuals. Here the poet introduces one of the most delightful characters of the *Satires* in the figure of Laronia. As a woman of pleasure, she represents natural vice as opposed to the unnatural vice of the philosophers. She delivers a lively invective (36-63) against this group of effeminates and in the process rhetorically strips them of their Stoic disguises. While it serves as a transition to and motivation for the treatment of undisguised homosexuality which fills the rest of the satire, her invective has broader applications as well, for in her examples she effectively ridicules all Roman men and claims they are all perverted weaklings.

Juvenal now turns to an example in the person of the transvestite and extends this theme in his hyperbolic description of the worship of the Bona Dea, a rite limited to women in the "good old days" but now taken over by the effeminates. This passage is actually an elaborate epic parody in which the implements used by the men to prepare their toilet are described like weapons of war. The section ends with a "modest proposal" from the satirist: why not carry this whole business to its logical conclusion and castrate yourself, since your privates are just so much useless flesh anyway?

After describing Gracchus, a decadent noble (117-48), who disgraces himself by a homosexual marriage in which he plays the female role and by fighting as a "net-man" among the gladiators, Juvenal invokes the powers of the underworld and has the glorious heroes of old Rome address themselves to the disgusting conduct of their descendants (149-59). This section of the satire takes on a special color from the fact that it is a comic inversion of Vergil's glorious vision in *Aeneid* 6, where the poet has Aeneas journey to the under-world to receive a prophecy of Rome's greatness.

The satire closes with a statement of the moral truth that has been proven satirically: Roman manhood with its sexual deviancy is its own worst enemy. An example is available in Zalaces, an Armenian youth, who becomes the lover of a Roman tribune and therefore his sexual conqueror. He returns to his homeland with the spoils of victory, namely the Roman habits and manners which no longer belong to Roman men.

The third satire, that on the city of Rome, has always been a favorite. This is at least partly because its organization is so lucid. It begins with a prologue in which Juvenal introduces his friend, the native Roman Umbricius, who is leaving his corrupt city for Cumae, the home of the prophetic Sibyl in Campania. Here are introduced all of the themes that are to be taken up in the rest of the satire.

Now Umbricius begins a lengthy invective against contemporary Rome in which he treats in order the worthlessness of honesty in a city where all values are purely monetary, the evil influence of Greeks and other foreigners who are flocking to Rome to usurp the places of genuine, free-born Romans, the abject poverty and frustrat-ing feelings of helplessness experienced by the lower classes, the frequent fires and collapse of buildings which make the city a dangerous place in which to live, the urban sprawl and congestion, and the thousand other everyday dangers and disasters that cannot be avoided. The cumulative effect of this description of Rome's horrors is that the city becomes a hellish underworld, which Umbricius is fleeing as if from the very image of death.

The epilogue which follows neatly balances the prologue, thus helping to form a frame for the attack. Here, as night falls, Umbricius reasserts his intention to escape from Rome, and he bids the satirist a final farewell.

Once again in this satire Juvenal is concerned with the decay of Roman tradition, a subject which he introduced in his first satire and elaborated in the second satire. The name "Umbricius" is carefully chosen to underline this fact. Because he is all that is left of traditional Rome, he is a "shade" or "shadow" (*umbra*) of her former greatness. His departure, which comprises the major narrative event of the poem, is meant to symbolize the departure and loss of all that was once truly Roman. But Umbricius is a shadow in another sense as well, for he is an *alter ego* for Juvenal and all righteous men who appear throughout this book. His sufferings are parallel to theirs, at times symbolically and at other times actually.

By the time this poem ends, Juvenal has developed a neat paradox: Rome is no longer in tune with its own traditions, but has become a foul Greek city. Umbricius is a native Roman with all the traditional virtues, but he must flee to Cumae for his new home, which, ironically enough, is the oldest Greek city in Italy. And yet this is the only proper place for the last scion of what is now an utterly corrupt city. Consequently, it was in no offhand way that Juvenal introduced Daedalus (25), who literally flew from Crete to Cumae to escape the evil labyrinth and its monster. Umbricius, like Daedalus, must save what is left of his life, even though he is already middle-aged. The magical escape, a solution Juvenal already proposed to himself at the beginning of the second satire, is his last hope.

Both the form and historical significance of the fourth satire have occasioned difficulties for some readers. The poem falls into two sections—a description of the purchase of a huge fish by the extravagant praetorian prefect Crispinus (1-36) and an account of a special meeting of Domitian's council of state called to discuss how to cope with another giant fish that has been given to the emperor (37-154).

In this satire Crispinus and the emperor Domitian are both examples of monetary extravagance. This is especially incongruous in the case of Domitian, since as perpetual censor he was responsible for checking this vice in particular.

It is more than a little grotesque to have a monstrous fish motivate these men's prodigality. Crispinus purchases one for an inordinate amount, while Domitian gets his from a lowly fisherman of the Adriatic, who brings it to him at the notorious Alban villa. In each part much ado is made about a trivial matter, and the fish are as much symbols of foolish and misguided interests as they are of extravagance.

The effectiveness of Juvenal's poem lies not so much in its social criticism—Domitian was long dead by the time of its publication—as in its mock-epic characteristics, since the satire is most likely a parody of a lost epic by the court poet Statius. In one instance, Juvenal delivers a sham invocation to the Muses (34-36), while at another point he presents a catalogue of vilified councilors (72-122) which is a clear parody of the list of virtuous heroes that appears so often in epic. Here the list becomes progressively more villainous instead of more heroic. The earliest members to enter the council are fawners and flatterers who are evil only by weakness and helplessness, while those who arrive later are more actively vicious.

The members vie with one another in reaching a decision about the fish (123-43), until Montanus in mock-epic fashion rules that a special deep dish should be prepared for it. He does not stop here, however, but goes on to point out that this will set a precedent for the future: never again will the emperor lack potters to assist him in imperial undertakings. Finally, the council is dismissed, and, jerking the reader away from the mock-epic atmosphere that he has created, Juvenal suddenly brings him back to reality with a final piece of personal invective directed at Domitian and his reign of terror (150-54).

In the fifth satire Juvenal turns to discuss the perversion of the client-patron relationship, which was another traditional Roman institution sanctioned by religion. Trebius, to whom the poem is addressed, is an example of a client whose role has actually become that of a degraded slave. His name takes a certain significance from the fact that, like Juvenal's, it derives from Aquinum. Trebius also calls to mind Umbricius of the third satire, for both are men of equestrian status who have been forced to degrade themselves and live beneath their natural dignity. The other major character in the satire is the patron Virro, who has obviously become a tyrannical master in direct proportion to Trebius' enslavement.

The satire begins on the general note that *anything* is better than being a guest at a rich man's table. Even if one has earned the right through many years of service to sit there, a wretched meal will be his only reward. In the central section of the poem (24-155) marvelous fun is made of the dinner menu, as two types of meals are presented, one for Virro, which is likened to mythological fare served to the gods themselves, and another for Trebius, which can only be described as thoroughly ignoble and disgusting.

As a prelude to his discussion of the meal, Juvenal describes a bloody, drunken brawl that will ensue between Trebius and Virro's freedmen. Through it all Virro sits at high table, transcendent, removed from the degrading conflict beneath him. Wine, fish, sauces, mushrooms, even the water he drinks are special.

The end of the poem (156-73) is especially unpleasant, since

Juvenal goes out of his way to mock Trebius, who, not even realizing the depths of his own cravenness, really deserves to suffer pain for his depravity. In other words, the satirist ridicules Trebius' degradation as much as Virro's loss of the traditional Roman generosity of character. The pursuit of money, carrying both men in its wake, has displaced time-honored values.

Book Two (Satire 6)

This satire, which was published by itself as a separate book, appeared sometime after A.D. 116. It is Juvenal's most ambitious effort, running to some 661 lines. This is without the so-called O-fragment which constitutes an independent problem and will be discussed later.

The poem is best read as an extension of Book 1, for its tone remains one of vehement indignation and its rhetoric is still invective, as Juvenal treats women and their faults. If he is not regaling the reader with details of women's promiscuity, he is parading other examples of female excess—their sickening religious frenzies, their greed, their pathological cruelty.

In formal arrangement Satire 6 seems to have a bipartite structure, with the first part (1-285) treating the loss of a positive ideal, chastity, and the second (286-661 and O-fragment) dealing with the presence of a negative concept, extravagance. The poem begins with a mythological prologue in which Juvenal describes the departure from the world of men of the goddess Chastity along with her sister, Astraea. This is another example of the withdrawal of a beneficent god, a motif which the satirist uses extensively to symbolize the beginnings of evil and the end of Saturn's Golden Age. Now turning to Postumus, a friend who is planning to get married, Juvenal humorously offers him two better choices, suicide or pederasty. There is clever inconcinnity in this juxtaposition, and Juvenal reinforces it by attacking the promiscuity of all Roman women.

The first examples are arranged in a climactic order with each case worse than the last: buxom country girls of ill-repute; actors and gladiators who drive women wild with passion; Eppia, wife of a Senator, who forsakes home, husband, and country to become the mistress of a gladiator; Messalina, Claudius' "harlot empress," who works in a brothel. After a climax has been reached here, Juvenal proceeds with a list of women who have abandoned sexual modesty in other ways, beginning with the woman who gives her husband a large dowry and so can get away with anything and ending with the lady of the salon who affects a knowledge of Greek, which is really a shameless tongue fit only for the bedroom.

Whereas the first prologue was quasi-mythological, the introductory lines of the second part of the satire (286-300) are quasi-historical. As long as Rome remained a poor, humble Italic city, she kept her original morals, but after Hannibal's defeat wealth softened her. Juvenal now plunges on to describe the results of extravagance. There are, first of all, women like Maura and Tullia, who, intoxicated by wine, wealth, and sex, urinate on the altar of Chastity. Then there are those with secret religious rites which have been transformed into sexual orgies. Finally, he presents Ogulnia, who satisfies her various perverted appetites by squandering her husband's money.

Here it is necessary to digress for a moment to mention the O-fragment which was found late in the last century in a manuscript of the Bodleian Library in Oxford. The discovery of a passage of Juvenal's *Satires* that was not otherwise known from the manuscripts was completely unexpected. Although these lines apparently belong to an inferior manuscript tradition, there is no good reason for rejecting them. They are usually placed after the passage in which Ogulnia is mentioned and contain a description of a pathic homosexual who acts as a Roman wife's factotum. The unfortunate husband has to put up with him, even though he knows in his heart that this pretended homosexual is really committing adultery.

After the O-fragment Juvenal continues his discussion of female excesses to the end of the poem. The panoply includes women who fall in love with musicians, gossips, alcoholic next-door neighbors, meddlesome women of learning, and, of course, those who use hideous mud-packs on their faces or turn their dressing rooms into private courtrooms.

The poet spends more time on women's involvement with superstition, which stems mainly from the perverted religions of the East with their highly sexual overtones. Although all women in Rome involve themselves in superstitious activities to a greater or lesser degree, depending on their social rank, Juvenal singles out horoscopy and numerology as the most dangerous and most frightening.

Of the concluding examples of excess, the most important is the empress Agrippina, a brutal murderess, who neatly parallels the nymphomaniac Messalina in the first half of the satire. With her appearance the poem reaches a final climax in abortions, supposititious children, and bloodthirsty stepmothers.

Book Three (Satires 7-9)

It is usually conjectured that this book of the *Satires* appeared sometime between A.D. 118 and 121. At this point in his career Juvenal seems to have taken a new approach to what he was writing, for he now avoids rhetorical invective and, except in the ninth satire, he plays down sexual humor. The outlook of the satirist is more philosophical, but less homogeneous than it is in the earlier satires, and the major task for the reader is to understand the irony which sets the tone from now on. Instead of the overt, hyperbolic attacks he employed earlier, Juvenal resorts more and more to implied attack. He is no longer the direct victim of the crimes he is describing, but has become a much more detached moral critic.

Like the first satire, the seventh is somewhat programmatic, dealing with literature among other intellectual disciplines and combining aesthetic observations with moral criticism. The first section of the poem (1-35) has occasioned some difficulties because it seems so unconnected with the rest of the satire. Juvenal says that all hope and prospect for liberal studies are in the emperor alone. The emperor, however, remains unnamed, and this gives rise to the historical problem of his identity. It is perhaps best to recognize the fact that, while the satire dates from the reign of Hadrian, the historical references used by the satirist imply Domitian, Juvenal's *bête noire.*

As patron of letters, the emperor is too powerful a personage and defeats his own purpose by putting too many stipulations on the artists who serve him. The most stifling of these demands is that of praising him. The artist, then, should look elsewhere for support. But because noble patrons are too miserly to assist the eloquent man, the only realistic course open to him is to try some other trade.

The example of the emperor actually serves as a point of departure for a discussion of what is wrong with the whole contemporary society of Rome when it comes to men of letters and their economic suffering. The poets themselves are one specific example that Juvenal describes in detail, while implying that the problem encompasses all the nine Muses and all the liberal arts. Once the satirist has disposed of the emperor as a possible patron, he treats the plight of learned men without such patronage. Here are included writers (36-104), both poets and historians, and speakers (105-243), who in turn comprise orators, teachers of rhetoric, and secondary school teachers.

It is worth noting that in this satire Juvenal seemingly contradicts his own argument by offering three examples of success as well as the many of failure. But the irony underlying the examples supports a cynical interpretation, for the popular epic poet Statius has really prostituted his art to gain success (82-86), while the actor, Paris, is a spoiled darling of the imperial court, and his blatant favoritism destroys the system of merit that Rome requires both at home and abroad to survive (88-92). Quintilian, the famous teacher and rhetorician, serves as an object of parody, for Juvenal sarcastically insists that he acquired his reputation by sheer luck and not, as the Stoic philosophers did, by any real achievements (186-94).

The satire thus turns out to be a sardonic statement, and not at all a praise of the emperor. It is an attack against prevailing social conditions which make true art, true literature, and true learning impossible, and it is a subtle attack, categorical rather than personal, against the emperor as a reflection of the times.

Satire 8 takes the form of a persuasive speech in the deliberative type of oratory, and it is therefore formally different from the satires of invective in Books 1 and 2. The poem is addressed to the Roman aristocrat, Ponticus, who is offered moral advice and exhortation. Juvenal seems more intent, however, on providing humorous descriptions of vice than positive moral directive, for he keeps attempting persuasion by telling Ponticus how not to behave and laces his arguments with negative examples.

Perhaps it is better to view the satire as an exposé of the unfounded arrogance that Roman aristocrats display. They are so concerned with the past glories of their families that they do nothing in their own careers. They are completely oblivious of the fact that the illustrious examples of their ancestors should be inspiring them to virtue and not to self-indulgence.

The persuasive form of the satire is therefore ironic. What Juvenal is really saying is not that Ponticus and his kind are morally curable, but that their belief in the excellence of noble birth is a false ideal. The poet's original question "Of what value are family trees?" is given the answer "none," and the poem concludes humorously with the satirist's feeling of shame that the nobles accomplish so little of merit and yet are filled with such pompous pretense to greatness.

Satire 9 is Juvenal's only poem cast in dialogue form. It is an argumentative and legalistic conversation between the satirist himself and a certain Naevolus who was once one of the most successful male prostitutes in Rome. But now something has made him gloomy, and the ruined beauty of his face can only be the mark of some inner torment. Juvenal accordingly asks him why his fortune has turned against him (1-26) and why he has changed a way of life that was previously so enjoyable.

Interestingly enough, the term that Juvenal uses for "way of life" is *propositum,* the same word he employed for Trebius' shameful behavior in the fifth satire (1). Like Trebius, Naevolus is not really an object of sympathy for Juvenal at all, for the satirist's words are intended as cynical mockery of this man's immorality. Juvenal is fully aware that the source of Naevolus' corruption is really a moral and spiritual one, but the addressee, blinded by materialism, never catches on to this fact.

Naevolus responds at length (27-90) with a bitter tirade against the cruelty and miserliness of his patron, Virro, who has the same name and habits as Trebius' malevolent patron in the fifth satire, but who is here specifically characterized as a homosexual and Naevolus' lover. The latter's lament, then, centers on his lack of remuneration for his "services" to his master. He has the nerve to complain that Virro has cruelly subverted the sanctity of the patron-client relationship, even though their whole homosexual arrangement is a perversion of the original meaning of "patron-client."

Juvenal ironically concedes that Naevolus' cause is just (90-91) and inquires of him what Virro has to say for his part. The other replies that his accomplice is afraid that their affair will be publicized, and so he has threatened him with violence. Virro hates Naevolus because he knows his crimes, and any personal enemy who is also a homosexual is especially lethal. "O Corydon, Corydon," Juvenal mockingly responds (102), in a comic allusion to the homosexual atmosphere of Vergil's second eclogue. There is no secret life for the rich, for every menial slave knows all about his master's behavior and will even improvise and add a few details to make the rumors more scandalous. The only way to live in all common sense, Juvenal says, is morally and uprightly (102-23).

Naevolus responds (124-29) that this common sense advice is mere commonplace. He wants real help because time is money, and he is getting no younger. He cannot afford to be deceived again as he was by Virro. The slavish client closes the satire (135-50) by discrediting himself once and for all with his absurd pretenses. He prays for the satisfaction of his humble wants and says his fate will be a happy one if only his stomach can be filled through the use of his sexual organs. His needs are actually extravagant, including cash money, silver vessels, two litter bearers to carry him to the circus, a personal engraver, and a painter.

With absurd self-pity, Naevolus shows how perverted his notion of justice is and how limited is the meaning of his life which aims only at wealth:

> . . . this is a wretched prayer, nor have I even hope
> for this. For when Fortune is called on my behalf, she
> sticks wax in her ears, taken from that very ship which
> fled the Sirens' songs with a deaf crew of rowers.
> (147-50)

This final complaint is a false claim, because the satirist went out of his way in the prologue to show that Naevolus was quite well off before his turn of fortune. These lines parallel the opening passage and complete the symmetry of the satire.

Book Four (Satires 10-12)

Once again, there is little indication of when these satires were published, though it is probable that they appeared sometime between 121 and 127. If anything, Juvenal has moved even further away from the invective that fills the first two books. No longer are his themes primarily Roman, but he now turns to write what may be called universal satire. He does not express his indignation; he completely drops playful sexuality. Beside this book, the satires of Book 3 appear to be transitional.

There are a number of programmatic statements at the beginning of the tenth satire, which seem to be part of Juvenal's plan of announcing formally his new style of satiric poetry. Immediately he declares that his new moral vision includes the entire world and all of mankind:

> In all the lands which stretch from Cadiz to the Ganges
> and Dawn, few can distinguish true goods and their
> opposites, with the clouds of error removed. (1-4)

It should also be noted that in this poem Juvenal's own emotional attitude changes drastically. He no longer accepts wrath and indignation as his means of expression, but resorts to irony and tranquility. Instead of censuring vice with uncontrolled anger, harsh laughter becomes his critical tool.

To make this point explicit, Juvenal introduces one of the standard literary conventions of antiquity and one which was transmitted through the Renaissance to appear even in Burton's *The Anatomy of Melancholy.* This is a comparison between Democritus of Abdera and Heraclitus of Ephesus (28-54), legendary philosophers who represented two contrary ways of viewing the foibles of mankind. Democritus, the scoffer, ridicules everything men do, while Heraclitus, the melancholic, weeps profusely at the very same things. Juvenal explicitly selects the attitude of Democritus for his own model.

Satire 10, which is the second longest of Juvenal's *Satires,* has always been a favorite. Its structure is lucidly symmetrical, and its language is not difficult. The satirist begins (1-27) by saying that men always pray to the gods for the wrong things, in fact for things which will later redound to their own harm. This recalls Persius' poem on the same subject, although the differences between the two satires are clear and striking. Juvenal briefly lists some examples of ill-advised prayers—military glory, eloquence, political power, physical strength—each of which will be treated at greater length later in the satire. Most harmful of all, of course, is a prayer for money, and the satirist insists that the wealthier a man is, the more his own fears possess him.

After the presentation of Democritus and Heraclitus, Juvenal begins a long series of examples which describe the misguided desires of mankind (54-55): "So what vain and dangerous things do men seek? For what things is it right for them to polish the knees of their gods with wax?" This rhetorical question brings a long answer that begins with the disadvantages and dangers of power (56-113). Here

Juvenal uses the example of Sejanus, Tiberius' praetorian praefect, who, at the height of his influence, fell out of favor and lost his life.

Then there are the disadvantages of oratorical eloquence (114-32), as evidenced by Demosthenes and Cicero, who met similar, violent ends. In the discussion of the drawbacks and dangers of military glory (133-87), he chooses Hannibal as an example of a great man who became a trivial example for posterity (166-67): "Run on, madman, and rush through the savage Alps, so that you may delight schoolboys and become a subject for declamation!" Alexander the Great and Xerxes also illustrate the vanity of the warrior's desires.

Now the satirist turns from wishes conceivably within man's control to those in the hands of the gods and of Fortune in particular. He begins with the problems caused by old age (188-288) and then moves on to the hazards of being beautiful (289-345). There is no need to list all the commonplace objections to these that Juvenal brings forward.

If, then, all the desires of men are erroneous, should they pray for nothing? Juvenal offers sound advice when he insists that the gods be allowed to give what they know is best (346-66). Yet if you must pray for *something* when you pray, ask for "a sound mind in a sound body" (*mens sana in corpore sano*); ask for a brave heart without fear of death and one that can endure hard labor, both physical and moral. The satire ends in paradox, then, since all the things men actually pray for are external and detrimental to themselves, but what they can and should pray for they already have within themselves, so that there is no need for prayers at all. As Juvenal says (363), "I merely show you what you can give yourself."

In the eleventh satire Juvenal continues to laugh derisively at men's failures. Most interpretations of the poem have not moved beyond the immediate social context, so that the question of moderation has been taken as the basic issue. The satirist defends a simple way of living and dining while attacking all manner of extravagance. While this is certainly true, there is much more to the satire.

The writer's views are framed by a traditional and commonplace reference to the banquet. Juvenal begins with an attack against those who waste their property to satisfy the excessive tastes of their dinner table (1-20). "Their whole reason for living is in their palate

alone," and "they seek after relishes throughout the four elements."
It is the ultimate paradox that when they have spent all they have in
a vain effort to acquire the finest foods, their debts finally force
them to sign themselves over to the gladiatorial school where they
have no choice but to eat the coarse fare of the training table.
Juvenal now turns to a contrasting theme of moderation and insists
upon the old wisdom of the Delphic Oracle: "Know thyself"
(21-38). In the case of both large and small, trivial and important,
moderation is a key idea.

These first two sections of the satire exhibit perfectly the wit
and humor of the poem. Juvenal takes an essentially trivial moral
problem of gluttony and deliberately overplays its evils:

> What end awaits you? Your purse is shrinking while
> your esophagus swells. Your father's cash and property
> have been drowned in that belly of yours, spacious
> enough for capital, heavy silver plate, herds, and whole
> estates. (38-41)

It is important to notice that the essence of the poem resides in
humorous, overstated, and distorted descriptions of this vice. Its
opposing virtue, moderation, is viewed by Juvenal as utterly doomed
to failure, simply because excess is rampant everywhere. In fact, in
one vivid passage restraint becomes a concrete substance that is
expelled from Rome leaving vice triumphant.

After his humorous attack on gluttony, Juvenal finally turns
to his dinner invitation and asks one Persicus to join him for simple
fare (56-182). Again there is brilliant irony in the invitation itself,
since the name Persicus implies luxurious excess.

The poet begins this description of the meal with a mythological
simile which sets the tone of all that follows when he says he will
play Evander to Persicus' Hercules or Aeneas. Here is another
reference to the Golden Age motif so prevalent in the *Satires*.
Throughout these lines Juvenal idealizes the Roman past and fills
his menu with crude, rustic fare, even more grotesque and indelicate
than the "banquet" which Baucis and Philemon set before Jupiter
and Mercury in the eighth book of Ovid's *Metamorphoses*. In attacking luxury, he dredges up traditional examples of hardy temperance
like Cato the Elder, the Fabii, the Scauri, and the Fabricii. Even
these are exaggerated, however.

As a matter of fact, the satire leaves the impression of being a subtle mockery of the philosophy of moderation. Throughout this poem the comic disproportion between Juvenal's restraint and society's excesses is only too evident.

Although the twelfth satire is the shortest of the complete poems, its obscure structure, peculiar syntax, and exotic language present serious difficulties for the reader approaching it for the first time. The poem is actually bipartite in structure with the first part being a description of an escape from shipwreck (1-82) and the second a commonplace treatment of legacy hunters (83-130). The problem is to determine how the two parts are related.

Juvenal addresses the poem to Corvinus and begins by telling him how happy and thankful he is that his friend Catullus has escaped alive from a shipwreck. This whole section is an elaboration of the commonplace theme that ships and sailing are evil, a motif that goes back at least as far as the Greek poet Hesiod. But Juvenal adds a twist of his own: the real reason why men take to the sea is, of course, to make money, and no one should put his life in peril for this reason. As if to underline this point, Juvenal himself appears in a rural atmosphere offering pious service to the gods. This is about as far as one can get away from seafaring.

In thanksgiving for Catullus' preservation from shipwreck, the satirist celebrates a holiday and makes special sacrifice to each of the three Capitoline deities, Jupiter, Juno, and Minerva. As in the eleventh satire, the poet disclaims wealth and says he would like to have put on a more expensive party for Catullus, but this is the best he can do. Friendship should carry no price tag anyhow.

Juvenal now proceeds to narrate the story of the storm in temporal sequence. First, the captain begins to jettison cargo in a vain attempt to save the ship. Catullus' goods, which are mainly art objects, go overboard with the rest, and the satirist seems to enjoy himself as he provides a comic catalogue in which the value of the property is facetiously exaggerated.

Eventually, the mast is pulled down in a final attempt to save human life at the cost of the ship. Juvenal remarks ironically that Catullus should always have an axe on shipboard in the future for just such occasions, if he is still determined to jeopardize his life in this way. As Catullus makes his choice for life rather than wealth, the Fates change their minds and let the storm abate. The wind drops, the sun begins to shine, and the ship, after a welcome view of Alba Longa in the distance, at last limps into safe harbor at Ostia.

It has already been pointed out that Juvenal develops a second commonplace theme in the latter half of the poem when he turns his attention to greedy legacy hunters. He begins by returning to the preparations he is making for celebrating Catullus' safe return. Then he turns to Corvinus with an apology, telling him that he should not suppose Juvenal is after Catullus' money. No, Catullus has three heirs of his own, and, besides, the poet is truly a rare friend, one who does something for nothing. But he is an exception, for under normal circumstances, if an heirless rich man should get the slightest touch of fever, all the legacy hunters would be out to get into his good graces by praying for his health. The poem concludes with an ironic praise of the legacy hunter, Pacuvius, who wins through and gets into a will.

Thus the satire achieves its unity in two handlings of the theme of greed. Catullus is saved from this vice just as much as he is saved from death by drowning, and so there is a double reason for Juvenal's celebration. Catullus also serves as a neat contrast with Pacuvius who is successful in his greedy ways. Or has he really been successful? The last two lines put the whole matter in the proper perspective (129-30): "May he possess as much as Nero stole and pile his gold mountain-high. As well, may he love no one and be loved by no one." This poem which began as a statement of thanks to the gods has ended with a curse!

Book Five (Satires 13-16)

The publication of this book of Juvenal's *Satires* may be placed with some confidence in or shortly after A.D. 127, since two satires contain clear reference to that year. In Satire 13 the poet mentions that the addressee, Calvinus, was born in the consulship of Fonteius—that is, in A.D. 67—and that he is now sixty years old (16-17), while in Satire 15 there is a reference to "the recent consul, Juncus" (27), who held office in A.D. 127.

The poems in this book suggest an intensification of the literary program of tranquility announced in Satire 10. Juvenal seems to be using the addressee of the thirteenth satire, Calvinus, as an allegory of his own poetic development from the impotent rage expressed in his early satires to the philosophical aloofness of his latest ones. Certainly the one emotion that Juvenal consistently condemns in this last book is anger.

Satire 13 centers around an injustice done Calvinus, who has recently been cheated of money deposited with a supposed friend. This other person, whose name is never mentioned, took a special oath to return the deposit, but later reneged and kept it for himself. Thus Calvinus laments in particular the theft of his money and in general the evils of the times (1-37).

Although the poem is composed in the rhetorical form of a consolation in which Juvenal is supposed to be sympathizing with his friend over his loss, it would more correctly be described as a "false consolation." Calvinus is an old man living through his second childhood, and Juvenal is really criticizing his foolishness:

> Don't you know what a laugh your stupidity provokes
> from mankind when you ask of anyone that he not
> take a false oath and think there is some divine presence
> in any temple or in any altar blushing with shame?
> (34-37)

What Calvinus desires in his childlike way is a return to the innocence and simple morality of the Golden Age. But, as Juvenal explains, his old friend should wake up to the hard facts: this is Rome, now, in the evil world of the present. In fact, the times are so bad that they outdo even the Iron Age in wickedness:

> We live in the Ninth Age, an era more evil than that
> of iron. Nature herself has found no name for its
> wickedness, no metal base enough to distinguish it.
> (28-30)

Juvenal's exaggerated emphasis on the unmitigated evils of contemporary life merely complements his refusal to allow Calvinus even wishful fantasies about a better time. Virtue is impossible in this worst of all worlds, and "wisdom" is a cynical thing that means Calvinus should expect to be cheated, even by friends.

Juvenal intensifies the atmosphere of cynicism by introducing a catalogue of sacrilegious oath-takers (71-142). At the same time, he tries to ridicule Calvinus' moral outrage by arguing that what he lost was only money, and a trivial amount at that (143-73). Since the injustice done him was slight compared with the troubles most people have to endure, there must be some hidden reason for all of this emotional reaction and moral posturing. It is plain, unadulterated greed that has caused Calvinus to go into mourning for his inconsequential loss and to carry on as if a beloved relative has passed away.

The remainder of the satire (174-249) contains Juvenal's reply to Calvinus' desire for revenge. "Will there be no punishment for perjury and sacrilegious theft?" Calvinus asks. Juvenal points out that even if Calvinus has his enemy within his grasp and can punish him at will, he will still lose his money. Then he goes on to insist that vengeance is a damaging pleasure; it reduces a man to the pettiness and impotence of a woman.

Soon, however, the satirist changes his tack and suggests how punishment may come to the guilty. In the opening lines of the satire he had already insisted that the only true vengeance is that which the criminal brings upon himself. Certainly no guilty man can escape his own conscience, since the fullest guilt for any misdeed lies in the mere desire to do it, and the minds of criminals are tormented by their own evil designs. Moreover, if the guilty man actually does go on to commit the crime, he will atone for the act with very concrete, physical punishments of the psychosomatic sort: his diet will go sour on him and he will be unable to eat; he will have troubled dreams, or he will think that thunder and lightning are actually sent by the gods to punish him. In this way, the man will bring about punishment for himself, even though no human agent is present to prosecute the cause of the gods.

Thus the relationship between the two arguments of the satire becomes clear. Crime indeed is now rampant because there is no divine providence or supernatural agency to prosecute the criminal. Calvinus' desire to retaliate is mistaken because he wants a justice that the present woeful state of affairs cannot give him. Paradoxically, the only way Calvinus can successfully avenge himself is by letting nature run its course. That is, by allowing the intrinsic corruption of the guilty party to lead him to his own doom.

Satire 14, addressed to Fuscinus, is another bipartite poem, dealing on the one hand with evil examples set by parents (1-106) and on the other with avarice, the primary vice taught by parents (107-331). The two ideas are part of the related themes that run through all of Juvenal's satires: the loss of the old virtues and traditions and the presence of greed, the worst of all Roman vices.

The topic of the first part is summarized in the opening lines of the satire:

> There are many things, Fuscinus, worthy of ill repute which fix a permanent stain on the fairest of reputations—things which parents show to their children and pass on. (1-3)

Instead of teaching their children virtues, as parents did in the good old days of the Republic, they now inculcate vices like gluttony, gambling, adultery, and murder. The moral order has been so subverted that even obedient children turn into perverted adults *because* they virtuously heed the corrupt example set by their parents. In Juvenal's eyes, vice is naturally more attractive than virtue anyway, and parents should therefore all the more refrain from wrongdoing.

The second half of the satire is intended as an elaboration of Juvenal's previous argument, since avarice is a unique, if not paradoxical, vice. The word "avarice" (*avaritia*) carries two meanings here, a passive one of "miserliness" and an active one of "greed." The two aspects of the word are, of course, complementary.

By now Juvenal has laid the groundwork for a discourse on the dangers inherent in amassing wealth. Fuscinus should look upon it as a game and regard himself literally as a spectator, maintaining tranquility while he watches others destroy themselves. Juvenal insists this is a better game than the one of sea-trading that Fuscinus has been playing all his life.

The poem concludes on a sardonic note as Juvenal seems to defend the virtues of satiety and moderation which both nature and wisdom dictate. But then he asks an imaginary interlocutor how much money would satisfy him. The answer he receives is an impossible amount: as much as Croesus and the Persian kings and the freedman Narcissus had, and more. Punning on the name of the goddess, Fortuna, which means both "good luck" and "wealth," Juvenal ends his satire with the observation that avarice has become a religion at Rome and is no longer a vice (315-16): "You would have no divinity, if we had wisdom. We make you a goddess, Fortune; we do it."

The fifteenth satire, a rather unusual piece on cannibalistic Egyptians, is addressed to Volusius Bithynicus, another unknown friend of the satirist. It remains a rather unpopular work, and has been studied mainly for the possible light it sheds on Juvenal's alleged exile. In the introduction (1-32), the poet recounts how the Egyptians in their religious madness will worship any animal and spare its life, though they have no qualms about feasting on human flesh. He then proceeds to elaborate a recent example of such cannibalism.

The background was a bitter rivalry between the two Egyptian towns of Ombi and Tentyra which apparently arose out of conflicting religious beliefs. It is interesting to note in passing that recent archaeological discoveries have demonstrated the historicity of these two cities and their perpetual feuding. An observation of Juvenal suggests that he may have been personally acquainted with the situation:

> To be sure, Egypt is a crude place, but in self-indul-
> gence, as I myself have observed, its barbarian throng
> does not take second place to ill-famed Canopus. (44-46)

Ombi decides to attack Tentyra when the latter is holding its religious festival, since at this particular time its population will be vulnerable because of excessive drink and merrymaking. The men of both sides are more like animals than human beings in their hatred of one another, so that when they close for battle, they tear at each other with tooth and nail in the manner of beasts. The Ombians are described as "starved with hatred," and the climax comes when they take advantage of an opportunity to satisfy their hunger. Worsted in the fight, the men of Tentyra take to their heels, but one of their number unfortunately slips and falls. The Ombians who catch him proceed to rip him limb from limb and devour him on the spot, while those who have been too slow to get any of the meat scrape the ground with their fingers for the last drops of blood.

Instead of moralizing at this point, Juvenal chooses to conclude the story humorously with what has to be one of his most shocking changes in direction. He ironically praises the cannibals for eating the man raw, because this way at least they did not pollute fire, which Prometheus had long ago given to mankind as a civilizing force.

In the second half of the satire, Juvenal portrays other instances of cannibalism. His purpose is to show that upon closer inspection there are extenuating circumstances for all of them. And so the malignant passions of the Egyptians are thrown into more glaring relief.

By way of complementing his argument, Juvenal turns to the theme of pity, a thoroughly human emotion, which contrasts vividly with the bestial Egyptian hatred. Examples are provided of all the things men should weep at, for it is tears which distinguish men from animals. This kind of concern is evidence of a feeling of fellowship which, working positively, has motivated human beings to get together, build homes and cities, and help one another in time of peace and war. Juvenal's description of human harmony in these lines is exactly contrary to his earlier depiction of the mutual hatred of the two Egyptian towns.

But at this point Juvenal once again makes a surprising change of direction. Throughout the satire he has used the animals as an example of bestial qualities which men should transcend. Now, however, he says the lesson of his tale about cannibalism is that animals show more fellow feeling than human beings do. Man remains a wolf to man, but, according to Juvenal, wolves, as well as lions, tigers, and bears, for all their ferocity toward their prey, do not attack their own kind.

The satire playfully closes with an allusion to Pythagoras, whose brotherhood abstained from animal flesh and even beans. How would this saintly man have reacted to the thought of eating human flesh? Could we expect disbelief, speechlessness, and flight? Perhaps the only solution is an escape from the bestiality of man into the humanity of animals.

The last satire, the sixteenth, is clearly incomplete. Only sixty lines have been preserved, and the poem breaks off abruptly at the end. What remains suggests that this was an ironic statement of the advantages of contemporary military life which Juvenal feels are largely based on persecution of and discrimination against civilians. The Roman love of war has led directly to a military tyranny, and the civilian has absolutely no redress, since all the laws favor soldiers if a suit arises. If he does want to go to court, he has to wait forever until his case reaches the docket. A soldier, on the other hand, can get justice immediately. Even in the matter of wills and inheritances, soldiers do not have to obey the customary laws, for all the rules have been changed to serve their interests.

And so the *Satires* end on a note that has been repeated often. Here is another time-honored Roman institution that has become so perverted that its performance is just the opposite of what it should be. The Roman army has adopted Rome and the Romans as its enemy.

Characteristics of the Satires

A comparison between the satires of Horace and Juvenal shows that the poets do not stand in quite the same relationship to their poetry. While Juvenal is present in all of his poems, autobiographical details such as Horace injects into his *Satires* are almost completely lacking. He prefers instead to be explicit only about his attitudes to life. In the early satires (1-6) he leaves the impression of being deeply involved in whatever moral problem is under consideration, and out of this personal concern come his feelings of indignation at wrongdoing.

In the later poems (7-16), on the other hand, because he views the world as so corrupt that no one can do anything about the problem of evil anyway, he remains serene and philosophical, aloof and transcendent. Here the moral problem is not his, but most often his addressee's. In the early poems the person addressed appears as an *alter ego* for Juvenal himself, but in the later satires he is very obviously someone with whom the satirist cannot identify, if not an outright adversary.

And so there are certain contradictions in the *Satires*. Juvenal pretends to be a plain, simple, and honest man who tells the blunt truth, yet the artistry of his rhetoric is noticeable at once. He purports to describe the world as it really is, but at the same time feels free to indulge in exaggeration and sensationalism as it suits his purpose. Actually, his so-called objectivity involves a rhetorical artificiality which distorts reality in the worst way.

To any reader who looks beyond sheer surface meaning there are always clues to indicate that Juvenal's solutions to moral problems are really superficial, conventional, and simplistic. The personality of the satirist offers a prejudiced moral outlook that the reader dare not take at face value, despite his enjoyment of the poet's dissection and destruction of his foes. Juvenal thrives on rhetorical exaggeration, overstatement, and distortion of the truth, and his bias for epideictic or demonstrative forms of rhetoric is patent. He produces example upon example of corruption and wrongdoing and concentrates on apotropaic rhetoric. Even in those satires which employ some elements of protreptic argumentation, there remains an underlying irony, inasmuch as Juvenal is satisfied with emphasizing the negative examples and playing down or even undermining the positive.

Since Juvenal is so effective a rhetorician, one natural consequence for his *Satires* and one major source of their popularity is the frequent use of epigrammatic phrases. Lengthy passages of argumentation and catalogues of examples are often made lucid by one clever and pointed remark, memorable for both its sound and sentiment. For example, in his tenth satire, where sententious wit is an obvious characteristic, the satirist delivers a series of rhetorical questions, asking what caused the downfall of mighty Sejanus. What was the charge against him? Did some informer come forth with witnesses? Who testified against him? Where was the trial? No, Juvenal replies ever so tersely after all the questions, it was none of these; it was just the word of Emperor Tiberius (71-72): "A wordy and inflated letter came from Capri."

Of course, Juvenal was writing in an era when the entire system of education beyond the beginning level was a training in rhetoric, and all of the significant aspects of imperial Roman society—politics, law, literature, and philosophy—were influenced, if not dominated, by it. It is more surprising than not that he, like the historian Tacitus, controlled rhetoric and developed a unique literary style. He was one of a very few authors who managed to use it for his own purposes rather than be used by it.

At this point it is perhaps worthwhile to emphasize once again Juvenal's success as a poet. His *Satires* should not be viewed simply as versified moral philosophy. He knows, for example, how to use verbal foreshadowing to prepare for an idea in advance. In the third satire, for example, every theme of Umbricius' criticism of the city of Rome has been hinted at in the opening remarks.

Again, he knows how to exploit almost every kind of language for the proper effect. This is especially true in the eleventh satire, where he uses extensive diminutives while dealing with the scale of things. In almost every satire Juvenal plays with imagistic language: "ambition" in the tenth, "religion" in the thirteenth, "beasts" in the fifteenth. In every sense he is the equal of the Golden Age authors in poetic craftsmanship, and a knowledge of the traditions of Latin literature is a prerequisite to understanding his literary parodies and mythological burlesques. Vergil and Ovid, especially, seem to have been favorite authors of his.

Perhaps topicality was not Juvenal's greatest strength. Domitian and the more important of his cronies were long dead by the time the fourth satire appeared. Similarly, there was a bare handful of the old nobility left to be criticized when Juvenal wrote the eighth. In almost every instance, the proper names which appear refer to persons long deceased or to universal character types. It would therefore be an error to view the *Satires* as lampoons or pamphlets. The world that Juvenal satirizes is the one that he lived through in the first half of his life, before he produced any poems. Echoes of his friend and older contemporary, the epigrammatist Martial, reverberate even in the latest of Juvenal's works because it is imperial society at the end of the first century that Juvenal is satirizing. Even his moral philosophy is based upon the more popular of the younger Seneca's works, the *Dialogues* and *Moral Epistles,* for example. This stance would have been acknowledged even in Seneca's time as thoroughly conventional, if not just another form of literary allusion.

Although Juvenal's works are primarily concerned with events and people from the past, his lively imagination, his talent for rhetorical vividness, his ability to take a poetic commonplace and make it something new help to create the impression that he is writing about *right now.* The people and events he is describing seem to pass before his very eyes. And so Juvenal displays his fascination with his own society and remains a social and moral critic, not an antiquarian or an archaizer. That he did reflect on the past and on tradition was only natural in a Roman author, since the Romans as a whole thought of themselves as conservative and traditional. It is also worth remembering that it was by now a convention of verse satire to choose examples from the past.

Unlike Horace with his self-styled pedestrian verses, Juvenal thought of himself as the tragedian and epic poet among satirists. He showed, especially in his sixth satire, that this kind of poetry need not be minor or non-serious, but that it could compete even with the loftier forms of poetry without abandoning any of its generic characteristics like personality, variety, criticism, and humor. Juvenal is helped in this by the "grand style" of his rhetoric. He himself says that his poetry is meant to supplant epic and tragedy, so it is no wonder that his verses take on qualities of grandeur and sublimity, in spite of the parody or self-parody that is often involved. Juvenal proved that satire need not take second place in the hierarchy of literary forms.

And so it is not as a great moralist of his times that Juvenal should be remembered. Indeed, an indication of this is the fact that he seems to have been thoroughly neglected by his own contemporaries and remained so for two centuries after his death. It is because he was able to set himself a poetic program in each book and follow it to a successful conclusion that later eras claimed him as *the* satirist of Rome.

Juvenal remained practically unknown for two and one half centuries after his death until late in the fourth century, when he started to become a widely read and acclaimed author. It is significant that the beginnings of the manuscript tradition, the comments of the earliest scholiasts, and the first of the manuscript *Lives* of Juvenal all date from these years.

EPILOGUE

Greek and Roman Satire After Juvenal

Already by the first century after Christ the doctrine of kinds, that is, the literary requirement that a specified content must have a set form, was beginning to fade. Juvenal, for instance, was the last verse satirist of the classical world to follow the Lucilian mold, and well before him Petronius was changing the shape of Menippean satire. But the spirit of the classical satirist, the modal satirist, lived on in the attitude and stance of subsequent writers. In some cases literary artists such as Julian turned to the past for models and revived the older forms, but for the most part what Quintilian would have recognized as verse or Menippean satire was never seen again. Accordingly, in the writers that fill this epilogue, it is more a spirit and adaptation—perhaps it should be called a transformation—of the classical genres than any lineal extension of earlier satire that marks their poetry and prose.

About A.D. 123, shortly before Juvenal finished writing, Apuleius was born to a Greek family living in the North African city of Madaurus. He was the first of several African writers who markedly influenced Roman culture and Latin literature. A number of his works have survived. Among them are selections of his rhetorical writings, several philosophical tracts including a piece on the "divine voice" of Socrates, and an interesting literary version of his court-room defense against charges that he had won his rich wife by witchcraft. He is best known for his *Metamorphoses of Lucius* or *The Golden Ass,* which was written sometime around 160. This prose

170

narrative in eleven books is purportedly a mélange of Milesian tales in which the narrator tells the story of a man named Lucius, who as a part of his adventures becomes involved with a slave girl named Fotis. Through his connection with the girl and his base curiosity he is transformed by mistake into an ass. The rest of the story involves his misadventures as an ass and his attempts to find the roses which he has been told will transform him back into human form. After a year has passed he does come upon them in a procession of Isis, and, after eating them and regaining his original appearance, he devotes himself to the goddess.

The artistic center of the book and its best known episode is the folktale of Cupid and Psyche which is related as a story for the entertainment of a young girl. While this is not an integral part of the narrative, it is important, inasmuch as it contains the themes of curiosity, magic, and love that play a significant role in the adventures of Lucius.

Many of the individual elements of classical verse and Menippean satire are present in *The Golden Ass.* The whole story, for example, is related in the first person as part of the life experience of the writer. There is a characteristic variety as well, for Apuleius has taken the story of Lucius' quest and mixed in a broad spectrum of adventures, many of them sexual. Finally, a critical and protreptic element may be seen in Lucius' progress from a position of ignorance and pride to one of knowledge and humility. And yet, in spite of the fact that such satiric ingredients are present, many of the classic elements are missing. Neither is *The Golden Ass* written in dactylic hexameters nor is it a medley of verse and prose. What is more, it lacks the topicality and urgency that has been noted as a characteristic of earlier satire. It does not, then, fit the formal definition for either verse or Menippean satire, although it has many of the characteristics of both.

Apuleius' creation, like Petronius' *Satyricon* earlier, represents a major step in the development of Western European narrative prose. But in neither case is it clear to what technically defined literary form the work belongs. The *Satyricon* has already been characterized as a mutant or hybrid, and Apuleius' *Golden Ass* is just as difficult to deal with. It has been called, among other things, a wonder romance, a comic romance, a serious novel, and a satirical composition. All of these assessments are based on one of two premises—either the work is a morally serious effort or it is not. Those who find it to be non-serious regard it as an entertainment

with insertions—Lucius' conversion in book eleven, for example—to
satisfy the Roman demand that a work edify as well as delight. On
the other hand, to view it as having a serious intent involves consider-
ing the light-hearted section as relief to keep the attention of the
reader. Perhaps it is best to view *The Golden Ass* as basically a
serious treatment of the Isiac conversion of Lucius containing several
books of entertainment. Generally speaking, then, it would fall into
the category of romance.

Apuleius' style deserves special attention, since it represents an
extraordinary step—some might wish to call it an aberration—in the
development of Latin prose. While his other works are written in a
language that comes close to fitting the Ciceronian mold, for the
story of Lucius he uses the so-called New Style which is first found
in Fronto, another African some twenty-five years Apuleius' senior.
Fronto, as part of a reaction against neo-Ciceronianism and the style
of Tacitus, combines a tendency to use the archaic language of
writers such as Ennius, Lucretius, and the Gracchi with a fondness for
the colloquial. Apuleius continued in this direction and added
neologisms in his own version of the New Style. What results,
strangely enough, is a brand of prose that is very close to poetry,
for the balanced sentences are characterized by a syntax that could
hardly be called classical and by clear patterns of rhyme, alliteration, and assonance. Actually, Apuleius' style in *The Golden Ass*
represents the extreme to which this style could be carried and
shows the profound influence that non-Roman provincials were
exerting on Roman thought and literature.

Lucian of Samosata in Syria, a contemporary of Apuleius, was
also active as a writer during the second half of the second century
after Christ. As a rhetorician he was typical of the Second Sophistic
and appears to have traveled widely, eventually winning an official
post in Roman Egypt. Lucian wrote in Greek and, although he
probably knew Latin, he never gives any indication of it. Nor is there
anything in his literary allusions to suggest that he had read widely
in Latin literature.

Most of Lucian's writings fall into three general categories:
rhetorical pieces, epistles, and satirical writings. The latter include
such works as his dialogues, the *True History,* the *Peregrinus,* and the
Lucius or the Ass, a short composition apparently based on the same
literary model as *The Golden Ass* of Apuleius. Perhaps the most
important of these are his satirical dialogues in some of which he

himself appears thinly disguised under the name Lycinus, while at other times he has Menippus take the part of principal interlocutor.

Lucian likes to play the exposer of sham and hypocrisy, and so it perhaps comes as no surprise to find that the pretensions of many of the philosophical schools, especially the Cynics and the Stoics, are prime objects of his scorn and ridicule. The reader is reminded of earlier satire by some of the devices and subjects which appear—mock trials, assemblies of the gods, absurd religious practices, and the hypocritical nature of many worshippers. The satirist also approaches literary-critical questions.

As in Varro's Menippeans, fantasy has a large part to play in Lucian's satires. Charon comes up to earth to see what it is men regret leaving behind, men go to the moon, prostitutes get lessons on how to handle customers, and the dead come to life. In almost all of his criticism, however, Lucian appears to be acting a part rather than playing himself. Because of this and because his topics and interests are drawn from the stock of school topics and from the past, his criticism lacks the dynamism of a man aiming to point out or heal the troubles of society.

The major literary influences that appear in his satires seem to come from the direction of Old Comedy, the Platonic dialogues, and the writings of Menippus of Gadara. Aspects of Old Comedy stand out in Lucian's insistence on freedom of speech and veracity. The Platonic dialogue is a tool he uses, perhaps most successfully in the *Hermotimus,* to probe in Socratic fashion the thinking of others. The extent of Menippus' influence is difficult to establish, though Lucian himself claims he found the philosopher's writings in some old papyrus rolls and followed them as models. This may or may not be true. But there can be no doubt that he is following in the Menippean tradition as he develops his serio-comic approach, makes occasional use of verse, and adopts themes that are also found in Varro. Furthermore, at one point Lucian calls his dialogues "hippocentaurs" (*Double Indictment* 34), by which he means to indicate that they are Platonic dialogues combined with the mixture of verse and prose that is characteristic of Menippean satire. In spite of this, however, his formal contribution to the genre was really quite limited, and it was in theme rather than in form that he exerted an influence on subsequent satirists.

Another African-born writer of the second century after Christ, the church father Tertullian (c. 160-c.225 A.D.), put his rhetorical training and considerable talent to work for the most part in Christian apologetic literature. But one of his works, *On the Pallium,* falls into the category of Menippean satire, and, in fact, some have even thought that it is based on one of Varro's creations. In this satire Tertullian offers justification for his laying aside the Roman toga and putting on the Greek mantle, a symbol here for Christianity. To some extent, the work has to be taken as self-justification, but there is no need to press this as its main purpose. It is more likely that the *On the Pallium* was simply an entertaining exercise. But no matter what Tertullian's reasons may have been for putting the treatise together, the piece is interesting as a thoroughly traditional literary form of the classical world that is now being used for Christian purposes.

In the fourth century Julian the Apostate (A.D. 332-363), who was noted for his zeal for the classics and the old pagan gods, produced the last classical Menippean satire in Greek. He titled it *The Caesars,* and wrote it after he became emperor in 360. Here Julian follows in the tradition of Seneca with a political spoof in which he ridicules some earlier emperors and shows that he himself is the true continuator of the Roman heritage. The setting is thoroughly Menippean, inasmuch as it involves a banquet and a gathering of the gods. The gods, deified emperors, and Alexander the Great assemble, and as part of the festivities the emperors are called upon to justify their actions and explain their philosophies of ruling. As the satire develops it gradually becomes clear that, while it is a medley of verse and prose fitting the classic standards for Menippean satire, it lacks the élan, the successful flights of fantasy, and the effectively biting humor that were hallmarks of the earlier writings in this genre.

It should also be mentioned in passing that Julian takes a satiric stance in another work, *The Beard-Hater,* though in form this is not a true satire. With an irony and self-satire based on the appearance of his beard, the emperor lashes out at the people of Antioch, who resisted his pagan restoration.

For all intents and purposes, what might be termed Roman satire comes to an end with three personalities of the fifth and sixth centuries. Claudius Claudianus, an Alexandrian-born writer whose early works were in Greek, was active in Italy between 395 and 404. The most noteworthy of his Latin writings are his inverted panegyrics which are actually invectives against the opponents of the imperial court. While these poems are quite restrained and even dignified, they are clearly part of the spiritual tradition of satire.

Nearly contemporary with Claudian is Martianus Capella from North Africa. Sometime in the first half of the fifth century, probably between A.D. 410 and 429, he made use of the Menippean form to describe Philology's ascent to heaven and her subsequent marriage to Mercury. The major part of this work, entitled *The Marriage of Mercury and Philology,* is devoted to a didactic treatment of the seven liberal arts.

About a hundred years after Martianus, Boethius (c. 480-524), a Roman aristocrat whose intellectual aim had been to reconcile the philosophic positions of Plato and Aristotle, was imprisoned on charges of treason. During his detention which ended with his execution, he wrote his *On the Consolation of Philosophy,* a mixture of verse and prose in which the author discusses with personified Philosophy the mistake he made in trusting Fortune.

Both *The Marriage of Mercury and Philology* and *On the Consolation of Philosophy* are commonly regarded to be Menippean in form but not in subject, which is about the same as saying that they are not really satires in the technical sense. This position can, however, be legitimately challenged, for it appears from the remains of Varro that aspects of education and the choice of life standards are in fact topics that were originally part of Menippean satire. The quality of the literary treatment may have changed, and the total length of the works may have increased markedly (Varro's longest satire covered two books while Martianus has nine and Boethius five), but the Menippean spirit, purpose, and form are still present to a greater or lesser degree.

And so the breakdown of the doctrine of kinds makes the identification of satire as a literary genre increasingly more difficult in the later empire. In the medieval period the levelling process becomes almost complete, so that instead of tracing the history of satire, it is more a matter of tracing the satiric spirit. Theodulf of Orléans, Hugh Primas of Orléans, and Walter of Châtillon are names that come to mind when satirical writing of this later period is being discussed. Each of these writers is concerned with ethical behavior and views himself, at least to some extent, as a healer of society. The personal element is present in their writings, though it does not always predominate. There is also a variety of format, subject, tone, language, and even meter. The critical element and the motivation of the satirist vary from writer to writer just as they do among the classical writers of verse satire. Most important of all, these authors appear to know the Roman verse satirists and seem to be making a conscious effort to put themselves in the same tradition. As an accommodation to changing reality, however, they have adapted and to some degree transformed the outer shape of the genre. From now on it is not any satiric form but a critical spirit that predominates and binds satiric literature together.

Renaissance and Modern Satire

It would be impossible to trace in any exhaustive way the influence that Roman satire has had on the western satiric tradition. But a brief glance at the history of English satire with a few excursions into the French will give at least some indication of how subsequent writers have viewed and used their classical predecessors.

The beginnings of English verse satire are closely connected with the Medieval religious tradition of allegory and sermon. William Langland's *Piers Plowman* (1362) is an early example coming from this background. From a later time there is Alexander Barclay's *Ship of Fools* (1509) which is actually a translation of Sebastian Brandt's *Narrenschiff.* Parable and beast fable are also early elements which remain influential.

But as early as the Tudor period the Roman satirists were finding favor with the English verse satirists. Juvenal, for example, served as a model for John Skelton as he experimented extravagantly with both meter and language in his versified invectives, while Horace was the poetic exemplar for Thomas Wyatt, who a little later introduced the Italian *terza rima* verse form into English literature as a satiric meter. From now on these two Roman satirists come more and more to represent two types of satirical poetry—Juvenal the "biting" or tragic satire, and Horace the "toothless" or comic satire. Persius tends to be included with Juvenal as an angry satirist. At the same time, the strictly philological confusion between "satire" and "satyr" also had an important influence on the development of this poetry because it was generally assumed that satire like the satyr was supposed to be rough, crude, unpleasant, and "shaggy."

In the English literary tradition verse satire remained an object of poetic experimentation almost until the seventeenth century, and some of the most famous names in English letters contributed to its growth and progress as a poetic form. An early work which might be singled out is Edmund Spenser's *Mother Hubberds Tale* (1591), a satire which is now interesting primarily because in it the author introduced the ten-syllable rhymed or "heroic" couplet as a vehicle for formal satire. From about the same time come John Donne's *Satires,* which are important for their free manipulation of the heroic couplet, and John Milton's satirical sonnets, some of which are based on Italian models.

Special mention should be made of the experiment conducted on the Elizabethan and Jacobean stage with the melancholy and angry satirist as a dramatic type. In the dramas of Ben Jonson (who also, incidentally, tried to make use of a Horatian type of critic), John Marston, and Joseph Hall, the indignant, vengeful satirist of Juvenalian cast becomes both a convention and mannerism of the theatre of the times. Modern audiences are more likely to be acquainted with Shakespearian examples like Thersites in *Troilus and Cressida* (1601-2) and Timon in *Timon of Athens* (1607-8). Fairly early in the seventeenth century, however, this particular dramatic experiment with satire was abandoned as unsuccessful, for when the rancorous personality of the satirist was no longer enclosed within the narrow limits of the first person address and his complete character was exposed on the stage, there was a tendency for the audience to feel a natural revulsion and become alienated.

Throughout the seventeenth century the heroic couplet becomes increasingly more popular as *the* satiric meter, and, while it was used for all sorts of poetry, even epic, it is important to notice that its major authors from the Elizabethan period to the Romantics are the satirists. The heroic couplet in many ways became the English equivalent of the Latin dactylic hexameter.

Andrew Marvell and Samuel Butler should be mentioned as two key personalities toward the end of the experimental phase of satiric writing in the second half of the seventeenth century. Butler is especially important because of his *Hudibras* (1663-78) in which he experimented with an eight-syllable couplet and a grotesque double-rhyme.

Yet the greatest and most influential of all the Restoration satirists is John Dryden whose writings may be said to usher in the great era of Neoclassicism in English literature. Dryden himself favored the Juvenalian mode of personality satire, as he indicates in his poem, *The Medall* (1682). In his famous treatise, *A Discourse concerning the Original and Progress of Satire* (1693), however, he is careful to give Horace and Persius their due, at least in theoretical terms. This essay turned out to be of almost overwhelming importance above and beyond the scholarly reconstruction of the history of the Roman genre which it contained, inasmuch as the author makes a convincing case for the serious moral function of satire. The translation (by several authors) of Juvenal and Persius to which the discourse was a preface is another indication that satire had now reached its acme of importance and popularity.

Other works of Dryden that should be mentioned are *Absalom and Achitophel* (1681), a narrative poem which brilliantly combines epic and satire, besides achieving a new artistic end by using an Old Testament theme as a vehicle for satiric verse, and *MacFlecknoe* (1682), a short, mock-heroic poem in the grand style which had a predecessor in the work of the contemporary French Neoclassical satirist, Nicholas Boileau. Throughout both of these satires Dryden demonstrated himself a master of the heroic couplet and gave it that rhymed, antithetical, syntactically and logically closed, two-line form which is now associated with Neoclassical satire in general. But by any estimate, the quality and character of Dryden's works form a line of demarcation in the history of English literature, and with him the period of poetic experimentation may be said to have ended.

An even more prolific verse satirist was Dryden's younger contemporary, Alexander Pope, who for the most part styled himself a Horatian critic, especially in the second half of his career. His main contribution to the genre was a versification that pushed the couplet to the point of being epigram. He also perfected the mock-epic in English literature, and *The Rape of the Lock* (1714) and *The Dunciad* (1743) have remained perennial favorites. But in *The Dunciad* Pope brings to perfection another element of the satiric tradition, one that had been implicit in the literature from its inception. Here he uses satire as a form of literary and aesthetic criticism.

Even among the Roman authors this genre had exhibited an aura of self-consciousness, and the satirists were continually offering critical pronouncements about the quality and character of the literary process. Pope preferred to use the Horatian form for this kind of critical comment, especially the versified literary epistle, which even among the Romans had some relationship to verse satire, ambiguous and vague though it was. This absolute identification of the perfected verse form with both moral didacticism and aesthetic.

criticism achieved by Pope and carried on by his successors through-out the eighteenth century has come to be recognized as the "Augustan" mode of literature, and as Pope was its most representa-tive author so satire was its most representative genre.

Throughout Augustan satire of the eighteenth century, above and beyond the various didacticisms which are obviously present, there is clear indication that the satirists took delight in applying the methods and subject matter of their Roman originals to contem-porary persons and events. Perhaps the two best known and most successful poems of this kind are Samuel Johnson's *London* (1738) and *The Vanity of Human Wishes* (1749), which are modelled on Juvenal's third and tenth satires respectively. In a sense, it was as much a devotion to literary erudition as it was any serious commit-ment to moral and satiric purposes that produced these satires. With these poems English verse satire reaches its apogee as a major poetic form.

The Romantic period, of course, followed closely upon Johnson's work, but even during the latter half of the eighteenth century attempts were made to escape the constricting formalism of Neo-classicism. The heroic couplet was modified radically or simply abandoned altogether, and there were experiments with other types of satire. Robert Burns and others of the Second Scottish School, for example, returned to the medieval traditions of writing in vernacular diction.

All in all, it must be said that Lord Byron's *Don Juan* (1819-24) is the last great work of formal verse satire in English. Among the Romantics satire was regarded at best as a trivial, second-rate poetry; at worst, as in the case of William Wordsworth, it was viewed with complete hostility as both aesthetically unpleasant and morally harmful. And this restatement of the quasi-magical, dangerous "power" of satire has remained in vogue well into the present century. The Romantics, then, performed a complete about-face on their Augustan predecessors in disrupting the perfection of their versification as well as insisting that the most moral of all genres, satire, was really immoral.

Certainly formal verse satire has not recovered its former reputa-tion and status in the hierarchy of literary genres, and more recent authors like Roy Campbell and Hugh McDiarmid must be judged minor poets. This should not necessarily be ascribed to the quality of the verse. Contemporary literature since Joyce and Eliot has so emphasized ironic and indirect modes of expression while avoiding overt didacticism that verse satirists have encountered a contradiction in meeting the demands of this irony while attempting to provide the directness and immediacy which had always been associated with earlier satire.

Another major reason for the general lack of verse satire in modern literature is the dominance of prose forms. Over the last seventy years or so the novel has tended to swallow up all other types of literature. Satire, being what it is, has been especially vulnerable. And so literary continuity might be expected in certain contemporary satiric productions in prose, ones which might be designated "personality" satire, where the voice of the satirist is heard loudly and clearly as he conflicts with or criticizes a wide range of human moral actions and character types. A satirist-critic like Philip Wylie, especially in his master work, *Generation of Vipers* (1942), would fit this description perfectly. This is critical, "personality" satire that is prose, but it is not in the least novelistic or narrative in form, so that despite the fact that is it prose, it is really closer to the traditions of formal verse satire.

By now the point has been made often enough that the continuity of the satiric tradition is not to be sought primarily in matters of form. This also holds true as far as the influences of ancient Roman Menippean on English satire are concerned. For here the continuity is visible first and above all in terms of the satirists' "cynical" outlook on life. What this really amounts to is a sort of anti-philosophy which rejects everything that could be called excessively abstract, absolutist, artificial, theoretical, or formulaic in favor of an emphasis on individual people, concrete actions, and real objects. The Menippean satirist, then, attacks extreme systematization wherever he finds it and always defends common sense and practical utility.

Examples abound and range all the way from Swift's ridicule of the sham, artificial politics and customs of the Lilliputians in the first book of *Gulliver's Travels* (1726), through Rabelais' castigation of outrageously pedantic theologians or Voltaire's exceptions to Leibnitz' rationalism, to anti-utopian satire of the present era that is found in works like Aldous Huxley's *Ape and Essence* (1948) and Mary McCarthy's *The Oasis* (1949). In fact, wherever a system of words and ideas has become sterilely complex and artificial, there we might expect to find a writer like Voltaire trying to jolt us back to simple, natural truths about ourselves. Sometimes the whole of human activity seems to be completely on the wrong track, and then the satirists can caricature all of human history and culture as a silly, grandiose pageant which traduces the simpler, even naive, side of human nature, as Anatole France does in his *Penguin Island* (1908).

It is easy to catalogue the people these Menippean satirists dislike: politicians, theologians, soldiers, scholars, doctors, lawyers, and philosophers—in fact, any types who get too far away from the concrete realities of everyday living and whose regimented existence (like soldiers and Catholic priests) prevents them from leading less than fully human, natural lives. And yet these satirists can also praise the healthy aspects of life, and close friends and good eating remain as important a part of Menippean satire as they were for the ancients. Sometimes the simple enjoyment of wine is part of it, too, as in Rabelais' *Gargantua* and *Pantagruel* (1552), where the natural pleasures of food and drink symbolically represent the common humanity of all of us. Natural functions are the great equalizers among men, and even in this cynical philosophy they signify that which is worth doing because it belongs to all people by nature.

There is also a second source of continuity for the satiric tradition in items of style. The first of these is the extravagant use of erudition for ironic effect. In Erasmus' *The Praise of Folly* (1509) or Robert Burton's *The Anatomy of Melancholy* (1621), for example, the satirist shows he can outdo the scholars and pedants at their own game of learning. This characteristic is clearly present in Renaissance writings and extends all the way to fairly recent works like Henry Miller's *Tropic of Cancer* (1934). Throughout this literature much of the wit depends on extensive catalogues, lists, and learned digressions, which are almost bookish in the extreme. The description of Gulliver's voyage, ship, and storm in the opening of the trip to Brobdingnag in *Gulliver's Travels, Part II*, or the excruciatingly detailed account of an operation entitled "Esther gets a nose job" in Thomas Pynchon's *V.* (1963) stands out.

An overemphasis on language for its own sake is another clue to the presence of a Menippean satirist. From the racy styles and unique dictions of Petronius and Apuleius to the neologisms, punning, and etymologies of James Joyce and the lyrical obscenities of Henry Miller, there is a whole line of satirists constructing wild, verbal universes, verging sometimes, as in Joyce's *Finnegan's Wake* (1939), on obscure "speaking in tongues" rather than on communication with readers. Lewis Carroll, too, belongs to this group, and the mad worlds he depicts are based on the highly specialized languages of mathematics and symbolic logic, or even, as in *Through the Looking-Glass* (1872), on chess, a rigorously mathematical game.

Other items of stylistic continuity may be mentioned briefly. Mock-epic descriptions are always popular, as in Swift's *The Battle of the Books* (1697). In Rabelais' *Gargantua,* there is the war over food between the giant and the Lerné bakers. There are also numerous literary allusions and parodies, so that Nathanael West in *A Cool Million* (1934) can do a literary imitation of the Horatio Alger stories with just one major twist—his young hero, instead of living out the American success story, "from rags to riches," is progressively crippled and dismembered in his confrontation with American society.

Actually, satirists of this group are so skilled at literary imitation that the reader who is not on his guard can easily miss the irony underlying the parody. Here Thomas More's *Utopia* (1516) with its difficult ambiguities for later readers comes to mind, and so do the mock-romances of the nineteenth century writer, Thomas Love Peacock, who is consistently misread because his works are judged to be novels rather than brilliant parodies of novels. And, in fact, the entire tradition of pamphleteering from Elizabethan times on belongs here as a particularly subtle variation on the Menippean tradition in English literature and one which has often resulted in tremendous hoaxes because men of normal intellectual gifts have often overlooked the heavy-handed ironies involved.

Finally, because of their innate cynicism, these authors have a predilection for offering violent changes in perspective so that the reader can see himself for what he really is from strange new angles of vision. One device that moderns employ is giganticism—Rabelais with his giants and their tremendously comical appetites, for example, and Swift with his Brobdingnagians and their loathesome giant rats and lice. Here again, however, Lucian in his *True History* provided a model.

The travelogue and journey offer still more opportunities for shifts in perspective, in Voltaire's *Candide* (1759) no less than in Samuel Butler's *Erewhon* (1872). The latter provides a reversal of the European moral vision, too, in having the hero visit a land where sickness is judged a crime and crime is treated like a disease.

Another variation is the extra-terrestrial journey, as in the satiric fantasies of Cyrano de Bergerac or Voltaire's *Micromégas* (1752).

ABBREVIATIONS

A:	*Arion*
AJP:	*American Journal of Philology*
BT:	*Bibliotheca Teubneriana*
CP:	*Classical Philology*
CQ:	*Classical Quarterly*
CR:	*Classical Review*
CW:	*Classical World*
GR:	*Greece and Rome*
H:	*Hermes*
L:	*Lustrum*
LCL:	*Loeb Classical Library*
Mn:	*Mnemosyne*
NJA:	*Neue Jahrbücher für das klassische Altertum*
OCT:	*Oxford Classical Text*
Ph:	*Philologus*
Phoen:	*Phoenix*
PW:	Pauly-Wissowa, *Real-Encyclopädie der classischen Altertumswissenschaft*
REA:	*Revue des études anciennes*
RM:	*Rheinisches Museum*
RS:	*Römische Satire = Wissenschaftliche Zeitschrift der Universität Rostock* 15 (1966)
TAPA:	*Transactions of the American Philological Association*
UCP:	*University of California Publications in Classical Philology*
WS:	*Wiener Studien*
YCS:	*Yale Classical Studies*

This was not really a new conception, since, as we have
Lucian and other ancient writers had their heroes travel to va
parts of the heavens. Swift had also taken Gulliver to Lillipu
Brobdingnag. In all of these cases, no land or planet is ever ;
geographical place; it is there to represent a pure system of idea
to shock the protagonist into a knowledge of what the real, cor
world is like. Perhaps, too, the idea-orientation of this type of
is what causes most of its heroes to appear as comical antil
and the majority of its minor characters to seem like lc
caricatures.

Although the ancient genre of Menippean is not the
as its more modern counterparts, a contemporary critic like 1
rop Frye can assess all of this satire from a modern persp
and rename the entire tradition—including both ancient and
ern examples—"Anatomy" to replace the more restrictive
"Menippean." Indeed, it is easy to proceed from here to
even wider influences of the genre in modern literature based
this anatomical habit of detailed classification, explication, digr
discussion, and dissection. Its presence is felt continuously fr(
Picaresque novel and Cervantes' *Don Quixote* (1615), to the
of Fielding and Sterne, to the "Tall Tales" of Ambrose Bier
the short stories of Mark Twain, and, finally, to contemporar)
humor and satirical science fiction.

SELECT BIBLIOGRAPHY

[For a complete list of recent books and articles see
W. S. Anderson, "Recent Work in Roman Satire (1937-
55)," *CW* 50 (1956), 33-40; (1955-62), *CW* 57 (1964),
293-301 and 343-48; (1962-68), *CW* 63 (1970), 181-99
and 217-22.]

Histories of Latin Literature

1. H. E. Butler, *Post-Augustan Poetry From Seneca to Juvenal* (Oxford:
    1909).
2. J. W. Duff, rev. A. M. Duff, *A Literary History of Rome From the Origins
    to the Close of the Golden Age*[3] (London: 1953).
3. ___, *A Literary History of Rome in the Silver Age*[3] (London: 1964).
4. F. Leo, *Geschichte der römischen Literatur. I. Die archaische Literatur*
    (Berlin: 1913) [all published].
5. H. J. Rose, *A Handbook of Latin Literature*[3] (London: 1966).
6. M. Schanz, rev. C. Hosius, *Geschichte der römischen Literatur* (Munich:
    vol. 1 1927, vol. 2 1935) [*Handbuch der Altertumswissenschaft*,
    Abt. 8, Teil 1 and 2].

General Works on Roman Satire

7. J. W. Duff, *Roman Satire: Its Outlook on Social Life* (Berkeley: 1936)
    [*Sather Classical Lectures* 12].
8. U. Knoche, *Die römische Satire*[3] (Göttingen: 1971).
9. N. Terzaghi, *Per la storia della satira* (Messina: 1944).
10. C. Van Rooy, *Studies in Classical Satire and Related Literary Theory*
    (Leiden: 1966).
11. O. Weinreich, *Römische Satiren* (Zürich: 1949).
12. E. C. Witke, *Latin Satire: The Structure of Persuasion* (Leiden: 1970).

CHAPTER I. ENNIUS AND THE ORIGINS OF ROMAN SATIRE

ENNIUS
PW 10.2589-2628; Duff (2), 100-13; Leo (4), 150-211;
Rose (5), 33-40; Schanz-Hosius (6), vol. 1, 86-100.

Texts, Translations, and Commentaries

L. Müller, *Q. Enni carminum reliquiae* (St. Petersburg: 1884).
J. Vahlen, *Ennianae poesis reliquiae*[3] (Leipzig: 1928).
E. H. Warmington, *Remains of Old Latin* (London: 1935), vol. 1, 382-95
[*LCL*] .

The Satires

> Duff (7), 38-42; Knoche (8), 11-20, 112f.; Van Rooy
> (10), 31-49; Weinreich (11), XXIV-XXX, 3-10.

M. Coffey, "Die 'Saturae' des Ennius," *RS* 417f.
L. Deubner, "Die Saturae des Ennius und die Jamben des Kallimachos,"
RM 96(1953), 289-92.
E. M. Pease, "The Satirical Element in Ennius," *TAPA* 27(1896), xlviii-l.
N. Rudd, "Horace on the Origins of *Satura*," *Phoen* 14(1960), 36-44.

ORIGINS

Greek Influences

> Duff (7), 23-38; Knoche (8), 4; Terzaghi (9), 7-98;
> Van Rooy (10), 90-116; Witke (12), 21-48.

J. Geffcken, "Studien zur griechischen Satire," *NJA* 27(1911), 393-411, 469-93.
G. L. Hendrickson, "*Satura tota nostra est*," *CP* 22(1927), 46-60.
C. W. Mendell, "Satire as Popular Philosophy," *CP* 15(1920), 138-57.
E. G. Schmidt, "Diatribe und Satire," *RS* 507-15.
C. Van Rooy, "Quintilian X 1, 93 Once More," *Mn* 4 ser. 8(1955), 305-10.

Satura

> *PW,* 2 Reihe, 3.192-200; Duff (7), 13-22; Knoche (8),
> 5-11, 111f.; Van Rooy (10), 1-29; Weinreich (11),
> VII-XXIII; Witke (12), 1-20.

F. Altheim, *Geschichte der lateinischen Sprache* (Frankfurt a.M.: 1951), 346-65.

E. Burck, "Nachwort und bibliographische Nachträge," in A. Kiessling and R. Heinze, *Q. Horatius Flaccus, Satiren*⁷ (Berlin: 1959), 367-81.

G. Gerhard, "Satura und Satyroi," *Ph* 75(1919), 247-73.

G. L. Hendrickson, "Satura—the Genesis of a Literary Form," *CP* 6(1911), 129-43.

J. Jolliffe, "Satyre: Satura: ΣΑΤΥΡΟΣ, a Study in Confusion," *Bibliothèque d'Humanisme et Renaissance* 18(1956), 84-95.

K. Kerényi, "Satire und Satura," *Studi e materiali di storia delle religioni* 9(1933), 129-56.

P. Meriggi, "Osservazioni sull'etrusco," *Studi Etruschi* 11(1937), 129-201.

F. Muller Izn, "Zur Geschichte der römischen Satire," *Ph* 78(1923), 230-80.

H. Nettleship, *The Roman Satura: Its Original Form in Connection with its Literary Development* (Oxford: 1878).

B. Snell, "Etrusco-latina," *Studi Italiani di filologia classica* 17(1940), 215f.

B. L. Ullman, "Dramatic 'Satura'," *CP* 9(1914), 1-23.

____, "The Present Status of the *Satura* Question," *Studies in Philology* 17(1920), 379-401.

R. Webb, "On the Origin of Roman Satire," *CP* 7(1912), 177-89.

O. Weinreich, "Zur römischen Satire," *H* 51(1916), 386-414.

A. L. Wheeler, "*Satura* as a Generic Term," *CP* 7(1912), 457-77.

CHAPTER II. LUCILIUS, THE DISCOVERER OF THE GENRE

PW 26.1617-37; Duff (2), 171-78; Leo (4), 406-29;
Rose (5), 82-86; Schanz-Hosius (6), vol. 1, 150-60.

Texts, Translations, and Commentaries

E. Bolisani, *Lucilio e i suoi frammenti* (Padua: 1932).

F. Marx, *C. Lucilii carminum reliquiae* (Leipzig: vol. 1 1904, vol. 2 1905).

L. Müller, *C. Lucili saturarum reliquiae* (Leipzig: 1872).

N. Terzaghi, *C. Lucilii saturarum reliquiae* (Florence: 1934).

____, *Lucilio* (Turin: 1934).

E. H. Warmington, *Remains of Old Latin* (London: 1938 [repr. 1961]), vol. 3, vii-xxvi, 1-423 [*LCL*].

The Satires

Duff (7), 43-63; Knoche (8), 20-34, 113f.; Van Rooy
(10), 51-55; Weinreich (11), XXX-XXXVI, 11-34.

R. Argenio, "I grecismi in Lucilio," *Rivista di studi classici* 11(1963), 5-17.

C. Cichorius, *Untersuchungen zu Lucilius* (Berlin: 1908).

G. Coppola, *Gaio Lucilio cavaliere e poeta* (Bologna: 1941).

G. C. Fiske, *Lucilius and Horace* (Madison: 1920) [*University of Wisconsin Studies in Language and Literature* 7].

J. Heurgon, *Lucilius* (Paris: 1959).

W. Krenkel, "Zur literarischen Kritik bei Lucilius" *Wiss. Zschr. der Univ. Rostock* 7(1957-58), 249-84.

I. Mariotti, *Studi Luciliani* (Florence: 1960).

L. Müller, *Leben und Werke des Gaius Lucilius* (Leipzig: 1876).

M. Puelma Piwonka, *Lucilius und Kallimachos* (Frankfurt a.M.: 1949).

A. Ronconi, "Lucilio critico letterario," *Maia* 15(1963), 515-25.

CHAPTER III. VARRO AND MENIPPEAN SATIRE

PW sup. 6.1172-1277; Duff (2), 241-53; Rose (5), 220-29; Schanz-Hosius (6), vol. 1, 555-78.

Texts, Translations, and Commentaries

F. Buecheler, rev. W. Heraeus, *Varronis menippearum reliquiae,* appended to F. Buecheler, *Petronii saturae*[6] (Berlin: 1922) [8 ed. 1963].

J.-P. Cèbe, *Varro: Satires ménipées* (Paris: 1972) [*Collection de l'ecole francaise de Rome* 9].

F. Della Corte, *Menippearum fragmenta* (Turin: 1953).

C. Lee, *Varro's Menippean Satires* (Univ. of Pittsburgh: 1937) [unpubl. diss.].

The Satires

Duff (7), 84-91; Knoche (8), 34-45, 114; Terzaghi (9), 71-86; Van Rooy (10), 55-57; Weinreich (11), XXXVII-XLVI, 35-50.

L. Alfonsi, "Intorno alle Menippee di Varrone," *Rivista di filologia e d'istruzione classica* 30 (1952), 1-37.

E. Bignone, "Le satire Menippee di Varrone," *Studi Mondolfo* (Bari: 1950), 321-44.

E. Bolisani, *Varrone Menippeo* (Padua: 1936).

J. Bompaire, *Lucien écrivain: imitation et création* (Paris: 1958).

P. Boyancé, "Les 'Endymions' de Varron," *REA* 41(1939), 319-24.

F. Buecheler, "Bemerkungen über die Varronischen Satiren," *Kleine Schriften* I (Leipzig: 1915), 169-98.

C. Cichorius, *Römische Studien* (Leipzig: 1922), 207-26.

H. Dahlmann and R. Heisterhagen, "Varronische Studien I. Zu den Logistorici," *Akad. der Wissensch. und Lit. in Mainz, Abhandl. der geistes- und sozial-wissensch. Klasse,* 1957, 123-74.

B. Marti, "The Prototypes of Seneca's Tragedies," *CP* 42(1947), 1-16.

A. Marzullo, *Le satire Menippee di M. Terenzio Varrone, la commedia arcaica e i sermones* (Modena: 1958).

B. P. McCarthy, "The Form of Varro's Menippean Satires," *University of Missouri Studies* 11, No. 3(1936), 95-107.

_____, "Lucian and Menippus," *YCS* 4(1934), 3-55.

B. Mosca, "Satira filosofica e politica nelle Menippee di Varrone," *Annali della scuola normale superiore di Pisa, classe di lettere, storia, e filosofia* 6(1937), 41-77.

K. Mras, "Varros menippeische Satiren und die Philosophie," *NJA* 33(1914), 390-420.

E. Woytek, *Sprachliche Studien zur Satura menippea Varros* (Vienna: 1970).

CHAPTER IV. THE DISCIPLINED SATIRE OF HORACE

PW 16.2336-99; Duff (2), 363-98; Rose (5), 265-82; Schanz-Hosius (6), vol. 2, 113-55.

Texts, Translations, and Commentaries

P. Bovie, *The Satires and Epistles of Horace* (Chicago: 1959).

H. Fairclough, *Horace: Satires, Epistles, and Ars Poetica* (London: 1926) [*LCL*].

A. Kiessling and R. Heinze, *Q. Horatius Flaccus, Satiren*[7] (Berlin: 1959).

F. Klingner, *Q. Horati Flacci Opera*[3] (Leipzig: 1959) [*BT*].

F. E. Plessis and P. LeJay, *Oeuvres d'Horace: Satires* (Paris: 1911).

E. Wickham, *Q. Horati Flacci Opera,*[2] rev. H. Garrod (Oxford: 1901) [*OCT*].

The Satires

Duff (7), 64-83; Knoche (8), 46-62, 114ff.; Van Rooy (10), 60-71; Weinreich (11), XLVI-LIII, 53-165; Witke (12), 49-78.

W. S. Anderson, "Imagery in the Satires of Horace and Juvenal," *AJP* 81(1960), 225-60.

_____, "The Roman Socrates: Horace and his Satires," in J. P. Sullivan, *Critical Essays on Roman Literature: Satire* (London: 1963), 1-37.

C. Brink, *Horace on Poetry* (Cambridge: 1963).

____, "On Reading a Horatian Satire: an Interpretation of Sermones II 6," *The Sixth Todd Memorial Lecture* (Sydney University: 1965).

G. C. Fiske, *Lucilius and Horace* (Madison: 1920) [*University of Wisconsin Studies in Language and Literature* 7].

E. Fraenkel, *Horace* (Oxford: 1957).

W. Krenkel, "Römische Satire und römische Gesellschaft," *RS* 471-77.

W. Ludwig, "Die Komposition der beiden Satirenbücher des Horaz," *Poetica* 2(1968), 304-25.

M. McGann, *Studies in Horace's First Book of Epistles* (Brussels: 1969) [*Collection Latomus* 100].

C. W. Mendell, "Satire as Popular Philosophy," *CP* 15(1920), 138-57.

A. L. Motto, "Stoic Elements in the *Satires* of Horace," *Classical, Medieval and Renaissance Studies in Honor of B. L. Ullman* (Rome: 1964), 133-41.

J. K. Newman, *Augustus and the New Poetry* (Brussels: 1967) [*Collection Latomus* 88].

J. Perret, *Horace,* trans. B. Humez (New York: 1964).

K. Reckford, *Horace* (New York: 1969).

N. Rudd, *The Satires of Horace* (Cambridge: 1966).

E. Schmidt, "Diatribe und Satire," *RS* 507-15.

C. Van Rooy, "Arrangement and Structure of Satires in Horace, *Sermones,* Book I," *Acta Classica* 11(1968), 38-72.

W. Wili, *Horaz und die augusteische Kultur* (Basel: 1948).

W. Wimmel, *Zur Form der horazischen Diatribensatire* (Frankfurt a.M.: 1962).

K. Zarzycka, "Literarische Problematik in den Satiren von Horaz," *RS* 547ff.

CHAPTER V. SENECA AND PETRONIUS: MENIPPEAN SATIRE UNDER NERO

SENECA

PW 2.2240-48; Butler (1), 31-74; Duff (3), 159-223; Rose (5), 359-76; Schanz-Hosius (6), vol. 2, 456-75; Duff (7), 91-96; Knoche (8), 62-68, 116f.; Weinreich (11), LXV-LXXIV, 285-304; Witke (12), 156ff.

A. P. Ball, *The Satire of Seneca* (New York: 1902).

M. Coffey, "Seneca, *Apocolocyntosis* 1922-1958," *L* 6(1961), 239-71.

R. Graves, "The Pumpkinification of Claudius, a Satire in Prose and Verse by Lucius Annaeus Seneca," in *Claudius the God* (New York: 1935), 566-82.

J. M. K. Martin, "Seneca the Satirist," *GR* 14(1945), 64-71.

O. Rossbach, *L. Annaei Senecae Divi Claudii apotheosis per saturam quae Apocolocyntosis vulgo dicitur*[2] (Berlin: 1967).

J. P. Sullivan, "Seneca: the Deification of Claudius the Clod," *A* 5(1966), 378-99.

R. Waltz, *Vie de Seneque* (Paris: 1909).

O. Weinreich, *Senecas Apocolocyntosis* (Berlin: 1923).

PETRONIUS
PW 37.1201-14; Butler (1), 125-39; Duff (3), 138-58;
Rose (5), 377ff.; Schanz-Hosius (6), vol. 2, 509-20.

Texts, Text History, Translations, and Commentaries

W. Arrowsmith, *Petronius, The Satyricon* (Ann Arbor: 1959).

F. Baldwin, *The Bellum Civile of Petronius* (New York: 1911).

F. Buecheler, rev. W. Heraeus, *Petronii saturae*[6] (Berlin: 1922) [8 ed. 1963] .

L. Friedlaender, *Petronii cena Trimalchionis*[2] (Leipzig: 1906).

S. Gaselee, "The Bibliography of Petronius," *Transactions of the Bibliographical Society* 10(1909), 141-233.

M. Heseltine, *Petronius, with an English Translation*[2] (London: 1969) [*LCL*] .

K. Müller, *Petronii Arbitri Satyricon* (Munich: 1961).

E. T. Sage and B. Gilleland, *Petronius: The Satiricon*[2] (New York: 1969).

G. Schmeling, "Petronian Scholarship Since 1957," *CW* 62(1969), 157-64.

H. C. Schnur, "Recent Petronian Scholarship," *CW* 50(1957), 133-36, 141ff.

W. B. Sedgwick, *The Cena Trimalchionis of Petronius together with Seneca's Apocolocyntosis and a Selection of Pompeian Inscriptions*[2] (Oxford: 1950).

J. P. Sullivan, *Petronius: The Satyricon and the Fragments* (Harmondsworth: 1969).

Life and Dates

G. Bagnani, *Arbiter of Elegance: A Study of the Life and Works of C. Petronius* (Toronto: 1954) [*Phoen* sup. 2] .

K. F. C. Rose, *The Date and Author of the Satyricon* (Leiden: 1971) [*Mn* sup. 16] .

The Satyricon

Duff (7), 96-105; Knoche (8), 68-79, 117f.; Terzaghi
(9), 155-216; Weinreich (11), LXXIV-IXC, 305-416;
Witke (12), 152-56.

E. Auerbach, *Mimesis: The Representation of Reality in Western Literature,* trans. W. Trask (Garden City, N.Y.: 1957), 20-43.

E. Courtney, "Parody and Literary Allusion in Menippean Satire," *Ph* 106(1962), 86-100.

H. D. Rankin, *Petronius the Artist: Essays on the Satyricon and its Author* (The Hague: 1971).

G. Sandy, "Satire in the *Satyricon*," *AJP* 90(1969), 293-303.

J. P. Sullivan, *The Satyricon of Petronius: A Literary Study* (Bloomington, Ind.: 1968).

H. van Thiel, *Petron: Überlieferung und Rekonstruktion* (Leiden: 1971) [*Mn* sup. 20].

P. G. Walsh, *The Roman Novel: The "Satyricon" of Petronius and the "Metamorphoses" of Apuleius* (Cambridge: 1970).

F. I. Zeitlin, "Petronius as Paradox: Anarchy and Artistic Integrity," *TAPA* 102(1971), 631-84.

CHAPTER VI. PERSIUS, THE PHILOSOPHER-SATIRIST

> *PW* sup. 7.972-79; Butler (1), 79-96; Duff (3), 224-36;
> Rose (5), 377; Schanz-Hosius (6), vol. 2, 477-84.

Texts, Translations, and Commentaries

W. Clausen, *A. Persi Flacci et D. Iuni Iuvenalis saturae* (Oxford: 1959) [*OCT*].

J. Conington, *The Satires of A. Persius Flaccus,*[3] ed. H. Nettleship (Oxford: 1893).

O. Jahn, *Auli Persii Flacci satirarum liber* (Leipzig: 1843).

W. S. Merwin, *The Satires of Persius* (Bloomington, Ind.: 1961).

G. Ramsay, *Juvenal and Persius* (London: 1918) [*LCL*].

J. van Wageningen, *Auli Persi Flacci saturae* (Groningen: 1911).

The Satires

> Duff (7), 114-25; Knoche (8), 79-87, 119f.; Terzaghi
> (9), 267-75; Van Rooy (10), 72-75; Weinreich (11),
> LIV-LVIII, 166-200; Witke (12), 79-112.

General Studies

C. Dessen, *Iunctura callidus acri: A Study of Persius' Satires* (Urbana: 1968) [*Illinois Studies in Language and Literature* 59].

E. Marmorale, *Persio*[2] (Florence: 1956).

B. Martha, *Les moralistes sous l'empire romain,*[7] (Paris: 1900), 101-54.

J. M. K. Martin, "Persius—Poet of the Stoics," *GR* 8(1939), 172-82.

Scritti per il XIX centenario dalla nascita di Persio (Volterra: 1936).

F. Villeneuve, *Essai sur Perse* (Paris: 1918).

Philosophy and Poetry

W. S. Anderson, "Persius and the Rejection of Society," *RS* 409-16.

H. Beikircher, *Kommentar zur VI. Satire des A. Persius Flaccus* (Vienna: 1969) [*WS* sup. 1].

G. d'Anna, "Persio *semipaganus*," Rivista di cultura classica e medioevale 6(1964), 181-85.

G. C. Fiske, "Lucilius and Persius," *TAPA* 40(1909), 121-50.

____, "Lucilius, the Ars Poetica of Horace, and Persius," *Harvard Studies in Classical Philology* 24(1913), 1-36.

G. Gerhard, "Der Prolog des Persius," *Ph* 72(1913), 484-91.

G. L. Hendrickson, "The First Satire of Persius," *CP* 23(1928), 97-112.

____, "The Third Satire of Persius," *CP* 23(1928), 332-42.

D. Henss, "Die Imitationstechnik des Persius," *Ph* 99(1955), 277-94.

L. Herrmann, "La préface de Perse," *REA* 34(1932), 259-64.

K. J. Reckford, "Studies in Persius," *H* 90(1962), 476-504.

J. Waszink, "Das Einleitungsgedicht des Persius," *WS* 76(1963), 79-91.

CHAPTER VII. JUVENAL: A RETURN TO INVECTIVE

PW 19.1041-50; Butler (1), 287-320; Duff (3), 477-98; Rose (5), 405-09; Schanz-Hosius (6), vol. 2, 565-79.

Texts, Translations, and Commentaries

W. Clausen, *A. Persi Flacci et D. Iuni Iuvenalis saturae* (Oxford: 1959) [*OCT*].

J. D. Duff, *D. Iunii Iuvenalis saturae XIV* (Cambridge: 1898) [rev. 1970].

L. Friedlaender, *D. Junii Juvenalis saturarum libri V* (Leipzig: 1895).

P. Green, *Juvenal: The Sixteen Satires* (Harmondsworth: 1967).

A. E. Housman, *D. Iunii Iuvenalis saturae*[2] (Cambridge: 1931).

R. Humphries, *The Satires of Juvenal* (Bloomington, Ind.: 1958).

U. Knoche, *D. Iunius Juvenalis: Saturae* (Munich: 1950).

J. R. C. Martyn, *Friedländer's Essays on Juvenal* (Amsterdam: 1969).

J. E. B. Mayor, *Thirteen Satires of Juvenal*[2] (London: vol. 1 1872, vol. 2 1878).

P. Wessner, *Scholia in Iuvenalem vetustiora* (Leipzig: 1931) [*BT*].

The Satires

Duff (7), 147-66; Knoche (8), 88-97, 120ff.; Van Rooy (10), 75-78; Weinreich (11), LVIII-LXV, 201-82; Witke (12), 113-51.

W. S. Anderson, "Juvenal 6: A Problem in Structure," *CP* 51(1956), 73-94.

____, "Studies in Book I of Juvenal," *YCS* 15(1957), 31-90.

____, "Juvenal and Quintilian," *YCS* 17(1961), 3-93.

____, "The Programs of Juvenal's Later Books," *CP* 57(1962), 145-60.

____, "*Lascivia* vs. *Ira*: Martial and Juvenal," *California Studies in Classical Antiquity* 3(1970), 1-34.

____, "Anger in Juvenal and Seneca," *UCP* 19(1964), 127-96.

G. Brugnoli, "Vita Iuvenalis," *Studi Urbinati* 37(1963), 5-14.

M. Coffey, "Juvenal Report for the Years 1941-1961," *L* 8(1963), 161-215.

L. Edmunds, "Juvenal's Thirteenth Satire," *RM* 115(1972), 59-73.

S. C. Fredericks, "Calvinus in Juvenal's Thirteenth Satire," *Arethusa* 4(1971), 219-31.

____, Rhetoric and Morality in Juvenal's 8th Satire," *TAPA* 102(1971), 111-32.

____, "The Function of the Prologue (1-20) in the Organization of Juvenal's Third Satire," *Phoen* 27(1973), 62-67.

J. G. Griffith, "The Survival of the Longer of the so-called 'Oxford' Fragments of Juvenal's Sixth Satire," *H* 91(1963), 104-14.

W. Heilmann, "Zur Komposition der vierten Satire und des ersten Satirenbuches Juvenals," *RM* 110(1967), 358-70.

W. C. Helmbold, "The Structure of Juvenal I," *UCP* 14(1951), 47-60.

W. C. Helmbold and E. N. O'Neil, "The Structure of Juvenal IV," *AJP* 77(1956), 68-73.

____, "The Form and Purpose of Juvenal's Seventh *Satire, CP* 54(1959), 100-08.

G. Highet, *Juvenal the Satirist* (Oxford: 1954).

E. J. Kenney, "The First Satire of Juvenal," *Proceedings of the Cambridge Philological Society* n.s. 8(1962), 29-40.

____, "Juvenal: Satirist or Rhetorician?" *Latomus* 22(1963), 704-20.

C. Lutz, "Democritus and Heraclitus," *Classical Journal* 49(1953-54), 309-14.

R. Marache, "Rhétorique et humour chez Juvénal," in *Hommages à Jean Bayet* (Brussels: 1964), 474-78 [*Collection Latomus* 70].

H. A. Mason, "Is Juvenal a Classic?" in J. P. Sullivan, *Critical Essays on Roman Literature: Satire* (London: 1963), 93-176. [Reprinted from *A* 1.1(1962), 8-44; 1.2(1962), 39-79].

A. S. McDevitt, "The Structure of Juvenal's Eleventh *Satire,*" *GR* 2 ser. 15(1968), 173-79.

A. L. Motto and J. R. Clark, "*Per iter tenebricosum:* The Mythos of Juvenal 3," *TAPA* 96(1965), 267-76.

E. N. O'Neil, "Juvenal 10.358," *CP* 47(1952), 233f.

____, "The Structure of Juvenal's Fourteenth *Satire,*" *CP* 55(1960), 251ff.

I. G. Scott, *The Grand Style in the Satires of Juvenal* (Northampton, Mass.: 1927) [*Smith College Classical Studies* 8].

J. P. Stein, "The Unity and Scope of Juvenal's Fourteenth Satire," *CP* 65(1970), 34ff.

EPILOGUE

Greek and Roman Satire After Juvenal
Witke(12), 159-266.

W. Adlington, rev. S. Gaselee, *Apuleius, the Golden Ass* (London: 1915) [*LCL*].

T. Barnes, *Tertullian. A Historical and Literary Study* (Oxford: 1971).

H. Barrett, *Boethius: Some Aspects of His Times and Work* (Cambridge: 1940).

H. Betz, *Lukian von Samosata und das Neue Testament* (Berlin: 1961).

L. Bieler, *Anicii Manlii Severini Boethii philosophiae consolatio* (Brepols: 1957) [*Corpus Christianorum, series Latina* 94].

J. Bompaire, *Lucien écrivain: imitation et création* (Paris: 1958).

G W. Bowersock, *Greek Sophists in the Roman Empire* (Oxford: 1969).

P. Courcelle, *La consolation de philosophie dans la tradition littéraire* (Paris: 1967).

A. Dick, *Martianus Capella* (Leipzig: 1925) [*BT*].

E. Gibbon, ed. J. B. Bury, *The History of the Decline and Fall of the Roman Empire,* 7 vols. (London: 1896-1900), 245-87; 396-530 [Julian].

R. Graves, *The Transformations of Lucius* (New York: 1951).

A. Harmon *et al., Lucian,* 8 vols. (1913-1967) [*LCL*].

W. Kaegi, *Research on Julian The Apostate, 1945-1964, CW* 58(1965), 229-38.

C. Lacombrade, *L'empereur Julien: oeuvres complètes. II.2. Discours de Julien empereur* (Paris: 1964) [*Budé*].

M. D. Macleod, *Luciani opera,* vol. 1 (Oxford: 1972) [*OCT*] [all published].

R. Pack, "Notes on the *Caesars* of Julian," *TAPA* 77(1946), 151-57.

H. Patch, *The Tradition of Boethius* (New York: 1935).

B. E. Perry, *The Ancient Romances* (Berkeley: 1967) [*Sather Classical Lectures* 37].

F. Raby, *A History of Secular Latin Poetry,*[2] 2 vols. (Oxford: 1957).

D. S. Robertson ed., P. Vallette trans., *Apulée: les Métamorphoses,*[2] 3 vols. (Paris: 1956) [*Budé*].

C. Schlam, "The Scholarship on Apuleius since 1938," *CW* 64(1971), 285-309.

A. Scobie, *Aspects of the Ancient Romance and its Heritage: Essays on Apuleius, Petronius, and the Greek Romances* (Meisenheim am Glan: 1969).

W. Stahl, R. Johnson, E. Burge, *Martianus Capella and the Seven Liberal Arts,* vol. 1 (New York: 1971) [all published].

H. F. Stewart and E. K. Rand, *Boethius: The Theological Tractates; The Consolation of Philosophy* (London: 1918), 128-411 [*LCL*].

Tertullian, *De pallio* in *The Ante-Nicene Fathers: Translations of the Writings of the Fathers Down to A.D. 325,* ed. A. Roberts and J. Donaldson, rev. A. Coxe, 7 vols. (Grand Rapids: 1950), 4, cols. 4-13 [American reprint of the Edinburgh edition].

P. G. Walsh, *The Roman Novel: The "Satyricon" of Petronius and the "Metamorphoses" of Apuleius* (Cambridge: 1970).

A. Weston, *Latin Satirical Writing Subsequent to Juvenal* (Lancaster, Pa.: 1915).

W. Wright, *The Works of the Emperor Julian,* vol. 2 (London: 1913) [*LCL*].

Renaissance and Modern Satire

R. C. Elliott, *The Power of Satire* (Princeton: 1960).

L. Feinberg, *The Satirist* (Ames, Ia.: 1963).

N. Frye, *Anatomy of Criticism* (Princeton: 1957).

J. Heath-Stubbs, *The Verse Satire* (London: 1969).

G. Highet, *The Anatomy of Satire* (Princeton: 1962).

A. Kernan, *The Cankered Muse: Satire of the English Renaissance* (New Haven: 1959) [*Yale Studies in English* 142].

____, *Modern Satire* (New York: 1962).

____, *The Plot of Satire* (New Haven: 1965).

G. D. Kiremidjian, "The Aesthetics of Parody," *Journal of Aesthetics and Art Criticism* 28(1969), 231-42.

E. D. Leyburn, *Satiric Allegory: Mirror of Man* (New Haven: 1956) [*Yale Studies in English* 130].

M. Mack, "The Muse of Satire," *Yale Review* 41(1951), 80-92.

R. Paulson, *The Fictions of Satire* (Baltimore: 1967).

M. C. Randolph, "The Structural Design of the Formal Verse Satire," *Philological Quarterly* 21(1942), 368-84.

J. Sutherland, *English Satire* (Cambridge: 1958).

H. Walker, *English Satire and Satirists* (London: 1925).

J. S. Williams, *Towards a Definition of Menippean Satire* (Vanderbilt Univ.: 1966) [unpubl. diss.].

D. Worcester, *The Art of Satire* (Cambridge, Mass.: 1940).

GENERAL INDEX

S.C.F.